Functional and Territorial Interest Representation in the EU

Despite a substantial legacy of literature on EU interest representation, there is no systematic analysis available on whether a European model of interest representation in EU governance is detectable across functional, and territorial, categories of actors. 'Functional' actors include associations for business interests, the professions, and trade unions, as well as 'NGOs' and social movements; territorial based entities include public actors (such as regional and local government), as well as actors primarily organised at territorial level. What are the similarities and differences between territorial, and functional, based entities, and are the similarities greater than the differences? Are the differences sufficient to justify the use of different analytical tools? Are the differences within these categories more significant than those across them? Is there a 'professionalised European lobbying class' across all actor types? Does national embeddedness make a difference? Which factors explain the success of actors to participate in European governance?

This book was originally published as a special issue of *Journal of European Integration*.

Michèle Knodt is Jean Monnet Professor for European Integration and Comparative Politics at the Technical University Darmstadt, Germany.

Christine Quittkat is a Researcher at the Centre for European Social Research (MZES)/ University of Mannheim, Germany.

Justin Greenwood is Professor of European Public Policy at the Robert Gordon University, Aberdeen, UK, and a Visiting Professor at the College of Europe.

Functional and Territorial Interest Representation in the EU

Edited by
Michèle Knodt, Christine Quittkat
and Justin Greenwood

LONDON AND NEW YORK

First published 2012
by Routledge
2 Park Square, Milton Park, Abingdon, Oxon, OX14 4RN

Simultaneously published in the USA and Canada
by Routledge
711 Third Avenue, New York, NY 10017

First issued in paperback 2017

Routledge is an imprint of the Taylor & Francis Group, an informa business

© 2012 Taylor & Francis

This book is a reproduction of the *Journal of European Integration*, vol. 33, issue 4. The Publisher requests to those authors who may be citing this book to state, also, the bibliographical details of the special issue on which the book was based.

All rights reserved. No part of this book may be reprinted or reproduced or utilised in any form or by any electronic, mechanical, or other means, now known or hereafter invented, including photocopying and recording, or in any information storage or retrieval system, without permission in writing from the publishers.

Trademark notice: Product or corporate names may be trademarks or registered trademarks, and are used only for identification and explanation without intent to infringe.

British Library Cataloguing in Publication Data
A catalogue record for this book is available from the British Library

Typeset in Times New Roman
by Taylor & Francis Books

Publisher's Note
The publisher would like to make readers aware that the chapters in this book are referred to as articles as they had been in the special issue. The publisher accepts responsibility for any inconsistencies that may have arisen in the course of preparing this volume for print.

ISBN 13: 978-1-138-10763-2 (pbk)
ISBN 13: 978-0-415-80992-4 (hbk)

Contents

1. Introduction: Territorial and Functional Interest Representation in EU Governance
   Michèle Knodt, Justin Greenwood & Christine Quittkat 1

2. The Problematic Coexistence of Functional and Territorial Representation in the EU
   Simona Piattoni 21

3. Collaboration and Consultation: Functional Representation in EU Stakeholder Dialogues
   Holly Jarman 37

4. Lobbying via Consultation – Territorial and Functional Interests in the Commission's Consultation Regime
   Christine Quittkat & Peter Kotzian 53

5. Strategies of Territorial and Functional Interests: Towards a Model of European Interest Intermediation?
   Michèle Knodt 71

6. Actors of the Common Interest? The Brussels Offices of the Regions
   Justin Greenwood 89

7. Social Movements and the European Interest Intermediation of Public Interest Groups
   Carlo Ruzza 105

8. Interests, Influence and Information: Comparing the Influence of Interest Groups in the European Union
   Adam William Chalmers 123

9. The Impact of National Business Cultures on Large Firm Lobbying in the European Union: Evidence from a Large-Scale Survey of Government Affairs Managers
   Andrew Barron 139

10. Weakness as Precondition of Smooth Integration? Representation Strategies of Functional Interest Groups from New Member States at the EU Level
    Heiko Pleines 159

Index 175

INTRODUCTION

Territorial and Functional Interest Representation in EU Governance

MICHÈLE KNODT*, JUSTIN GREENWOOD** & CHRISTINE QUITTKAT***

*Technical University Darmstadt, Institut für Politikwissenschaft, Darmstadt, Germany; **Robert Gordon University, Aberdeen, UK; ***Mannheim Centre for European Social Research (MZES), University of Mannheim, Mannheim, Germany

ABSTRACT This special issue starts from the assumption that, in contrast to the mainstream view, a convergence can be detected in strategies of interest representation across different actor types of functional and territorial interests, despite differences which remain. The question is posed here as to whether a European model of interest representation in European governance is detectable across categories of actors? It is assumed that the convergence over actor characteristics is due to the main characteristics of the European Union as an interactive and communicative system of multi-level governance which provides a special political opportunity structure to the different actors. The contributions of the issue compare territorial and functional interest representation regarding actor types, national embeddedness, policy field, and resources (financial and human resources, competences, capacity to act, learn and interact) with respect to the emergence of a highly complex European model of interest representation with cross-sectoral, intersectoral, and some intrasectoral, characteristics.

Research on interest representation in EU governance has addressed different kinds of actors, different policies and focused on different levels, drawing upon a variety of conceptual approaches. Interest representation of business interests at the European level has accompanied the EU ever since the creation of the EEC and it has been at the focus of research ever since, although with varying perspectives and intensity. The years after the

Single European Act were characterised by a significant increase of business interest groups, reflected in the studies of the EU (see, for instance, Mazey and Richardson 1993; Van Schendelen 1993; Greenwood 1997). Various 'state of the art' comprehensive reviews substantiate this concentration on functional interest representation (Woll 2006; Coen 2007; Dür and De Bièvre 2007; Beyers, Eising, and Mahoney 2008). These present in comprehensive detail various compilations of the different approaches and research questions in the analysis of EU functional interest intermediation. While drawing attention to business interest groups as well as social movements and NGOs, these issues did not set out to address the comparison of territorial and functional interest intermediation. The literature on territorial interest intermediation, with roots in the discourse on the 'Europe of the Regions' in the mid 1980s was a lead factor which triggered EU mobilisation by sub-national territorial units, analysed by some large scale research projects on regional interest representation.[1] A new 'political opportunity structure' for organised territorial actors, alongside traditional outlets of business organisations and organised civil society, has emerged. These arose from EU funding related opportunities, the search in the 2001 White Paper on Governance for a 'participatory democracy' outlet of democratic legitimacy, and the intensified assertion of territorial interests viz. member states since the 1990s. Also in this strand of literature there are volumes which mostly compare different regional interest representation within the EU (see for instance Knodt and Conzelmann 2002).

However, up to now a strict division between two communities can be detected, and in particular the territorial versus functional interest representation divide. Even though similar questions are addressed and the research focus has similar insights, the divide has continued with relatively little cross-reference. Even in those contributions where both functional and territorial interest intermediation is addressed (Balme and Chabanet 2008), the question of a systematical comparison of their interest intermediation strategies is not posed.

In addition, this divide is nourished by the treaty of the EU itself. The political opportunity structures of both functional and territorial interest representation at EU level belong to the 'participatory' democracy strand of Article 11 of the Lisbon Treaty, devoted to the democratic life of the Union. There is an absence of mechanisms linking both functional and territorial interest representation to the Treaty strand of Representative democracy (Balme and Chabanet 2008). In the case of functional interest representation, this is because of poor structural links to electoral mechanisms (Beyers, Eising, and Maloney 2008), while in the case of territorial interest representation there is a lack of formal devices connecting sub-national authorities with the Committee of the Regions (see Piattoni, Greenwood, and Knodt, this issue). However, despite a common paradigm of operating within the realm of EU participatory democracy, and the potential to share other unifying paradigms (such as the act of representation; Pitkin 1967), a highly bifurcated tradition of research between functional, and territorial, representation can be detected. Thus again, even though similar questions are addressed and the research focus has similar insights, the divide has continued with relatively little cross-reference.

It seems to be that this divide is caused by the hidden assumption of a cleavage between territorial, political representation and functional, societal representation. Because these modes of representation are seen as taking place in separated arenas, corresponding actors are treated as different types with different strategies. As will be shown in this issue, this is a misjudgement in reducing the scope for differences as well as convergence. The acknowledgement of the two sided character of territorial interests, articulated in the contribution by Simona Piattoni in this issue, is a first step in overcoming the territorial–functional cleavage of the common literature. Thus, the issue as a whole seeks to identify where we can find differences among actor categories, and where we can find convergence. Research which differentiates analytically between different types of interest groups, i.e. which systematically tests convergence and divergence of EU interest intermediation by different types of interest groups is still extremely rare, notwithstanding one example offered by Beyers and Kerremans (2007).

From the literature of the different actor categories — business interests, civil society and regional and local interest — we know that institutional embeddedness has a serious impact on the way actors represent their interests at the European level. This main idea of the shaping power of institutions was taken up in different approaches and thus labelled in different ways. Broscheid and Coen (2003), for instance, show in their study the impact of the incentives provided by the European Commission for business lobbying strategies. Another way of dealing with this idea is the distinction between the 'logic of influence' and 'the logic of membership' introduced by Schmitter and Streeck (1999), applied to the European Union by Quittkat (2006). There are a variety of studies of civil society involvement that point to the shaping power of the Commission's different consultation strategies (Knodt and Finke 2005; Knodt 2005; Steffek and Nanz 2008; Friedrich 2011). They discuss interest representation within the framework of the Commission's attempt to legitimise its work through civil society involvement. The literature on social movements has also worked on opportunities of institutional arrangements under the label of 'political opportunity structures' (see Imig and Tarrow 2001). Princen and Kerremans (2008) developed this by pointing to the interactive character of the relation between institutions and actors, as in their approach institutional arrangements are not just a given exogenous variable but there is an interaction with actors in the ways in which political opportunity structures are interpreted and constructed, whether strategically or otherwise. The literature of territorial — especially regional — interest intermediation within the EU was the starting point of discussing the impact of specific institutional governance arrangements within the European multi-level system. There is a broad literature on regional interest intermediation within the EU multi-level system developed in the 1990s which fed into the wider literature on Europeanization (see Heinelt and Smith 1996; Kohler-Koch *et al.* 1998; Knodt 1998; Börzel 1999), and which was used in the territorial as well as in the functional literature (see Beyers 2002; Saurugger 2003; Quittkat 2006).

Our assumptions within the special issue are the following:[2] First, we assume that, in contradiction to the common view of the representation cleavage between functional and territorial representation, we can find quite some convergence of functional and territorial interest representation besides still existing differences. Thus, 'public' territorial actors can resemble traditional organized civil society actors when faced with the ways in which regulation distributes costs and benefits. Where the interests of such actors are less at stake, so their role as public authorities make it possible for them to perceive, and act upon, civil society wide interests, and to mediate between a range of civil society interests in the positions they take up. The recent 'European Transparency Register' reflects this ambiguity, in that the original (2008) scheme excused public authorities from the requirement to register, but the scheme upgrade of 2011 requires their EU representative offices to do so (see Greenwood, and Quittkat and Kotzian, this issue). Where exactly are the similarities, and are the differences sufficient conceptually to treat such actors with different analytic tools in the study of EU interest representation? Whilst the remainder of the literature on interest representation is approaching saturation, this is one pocket which at yet remains unfulfilled in the literature. In shedding some light on these assumptions we will try to identify some principal characteristics of common strategies across different actor types of functional and territorial interest representation which possibly allow us to speak of an 'EU model of interest intermediation'. Thus, the central rationale for this special issue is the extent to which a European model of interest representation in European governance is detectable across categories of actors.

Second, we assume that the convergence can be explained by the impact of the specific character of the EU as an interactive and communicative multi-level system, or to put it in another way, the impact of the European political opportunity structure.

Third, we emphasise that policy often matters, too. The question here will be: How does the policy field, the competences of the EU, the way of decision-making, and the competing models of interest representation surrounding different institutions, influence interest representation?

The final dimension which is considered in the contributions is the impact of different kind of resources on European interest intermediation. Which are the relevant variables explaining the 'success' of some actors to participate in European governance — or the 'failure' of others, including financial resources, competences, capacity to act and interact, and entrepreneurship?

As the special issue does not represent the outcome of a common research project there is no attempt to develop common hypotheses and generalised assumptions. Also the 'too many variables, too few cases' catch would trap us here. Rather the aim of the effort is to generate concepts which help to illuminate the similarities and differences between the interest representation of different actors, their convergence and the degree of a common model of European interest representation in a comparative field which has not yet been subjected to sustained examination.

Across the contributions of this issue we look at these variables to explain differences within interest representation, as well as similarities. In seeking to establish whether the type of actor makes any kind of difference for the way of representing interests, we distinguish between *actor types*: Business interest associations, social movements/non-governmental organizations, and territorial entities (regional or local actors). Actor categories can appear at each level of the multi-level system, thus also different actor categories within several member states are analysed because it can be hypothesized that national embeddedness still makes a difference, even though some convergence may occur (Woll 2006). Further, the analysis concentrates on the question as to whether significant differences exist between the various types of actors (business, civil society, regions and cities) at the EU level (Dür 2008). Or, to put it differently, do we witness the emergence of a 'professional European lobbying class' across actor types? If a European model of interest representation in European governance has emerged we should rather find differences *within* each actor group between successful and less successful actors and not necessarily across actor types? Such intra-group differences are underlined by a number of recent contributions assessing the 'professionalisation' of organised civil society in EU interest intermediation (Quittkat 2005; Saurugger 2006; Kohler-Koch and Buth 2011).

The European Union as an Interactive and Communicative System of Multi-Level Governance

As regards the various special issues and edited volumes, a consensus on several findings can be detected. Coen and Richardson (2009), capturing 20 years of change in the way interest groups organize to address and influence the individual EU institutions across different policy fields, conclude that despite the uniqueness of the EU policy-making system the EU lobby system is basically no different to most national lobby systems (Coen and Richardson 2009, 341). Indeed, the move away from considering EU lobbying as a *sui generis* phenomenon is well established. This has resulted in a call for more comparative research (Woll 2006) but so far only a few scholars have engaged in comparing EU lobbying with, for example, lobbying in the US (Mahoney and Baumgartner 2008; Woll 2006). On the other side, while it is well accepted in research that associations need to adapt to institutional structures and prevailing processes within a relevant political arena (i.e., the so called 'logic of influence'; Schmitter and Streeck 1999), if they want to represent their members' interests successfully (Traxler 1995), many studies on EU interest intermediation have not responded to the model of multi-level governance. Most try to draw on concepts developed in comparative politics and shift them to the European level, disregarding the complexity and deviation of the European, compared to a nation state, political system (see Eising 2009 for a similar critique). Beyers, Eising and Maloney summarise these differences succinctly:

> Multi-level systems allow for greater interregional differences in interest group organisation than unitary states; cultural, social and economic differences are more pronounced in multi-level systems than in unitary states, leading to a greater variety of interest organisations; in unitary states, interest groups have greater incentives to concentrate on central level representation, whereas the dispersion of political authority in multi-level systems makes for greater differentiation within the associational landscape. (Beyers, Eising, and Maloney 2008, 1114)

Taking this, and the restraint from Coen and Richardson (2009), seriously, we take a short look at the specific characteristic of the EU as an interactive and communicative system of multi-level governance. Indeed, the European integration process has expanded the political space beyond national borders. This development did not leave the political system untouched. Common policy-making within the *Staatenverbund* of the European Union did not only concern the governments of the member states, but the process of Europeanisation had 'enlarged the scope of the relevant unit of policy-making' (Kohler-Koch 2000, 22). There is a strong tendency of blurring boundaries and of transnationalisation. The nature of international negotiations today means that significant territorial boundaries between national, European and international politics cannot any longer be maintained. The space for governments to act and the scope of unsolved problems are increasingly diverging. From this follows that the division between inside and outside is vanishing while, at the same time, the functional capacity of the nation state is put under pressure. As a result, for interest intermediation we can state that interaction beyond the national borders together with the functional differentiation of society is leading to a functionally (instead of a territorially) defined construction of the political space, and to the drawing of new functional boundaries (see Kohler-Koch *et al.* 1998). Following this logic, the core characteristics of a European system of governance could be described as a polycentric system where various centres of decision-making exist that are formally independent of each other (Ostrom, Tiebout, and Warren 1961; Ostrom 1999). The hierarchical centre of the system is replaced by functional networks, and a split into multiple, overlapping arenas characterised by loose coupling (Benz 2000, 152; Frey and Eichenberger 1999; Hooghe and G. Marks. 2001). These interlocked arenas include different actors, whose interests diverge. Thus, individual interests serve as the constitutive logic of the polity which has consequences for the type of involvement of interests and the strategies applied by the different actors. Further, research on European regional policy has demonstrated that a variety of sub-national, national, and European actors — both public and private — are involved in European governance (Heinelt 1996; Kohler-Koch *et al.* 1998; Knodt 1998). The very nature of the European multilevel system — comprising both supra-national institutions and member states acting together — paves the way to a different kind of governance. It includes the transformation of political institutions, processes and policies at and beneath the European level (Jachtenfuchs and Kohler-Koch 1996). Behind this background, the main assumption is that the transformation of governance causes changes in the basic functions of statehood. As regards the European system of interest intermediation this involves two types of adjustments. On the one hand, states and their territorial sub-entities (regions, departements, cities, etc) are forced to act across borders in order to regain the capacity to govern society. On the other hand, innovative forms of societal involvement in politics have to be designed and developed. And indeed, European Commission in particular has developed a new consultation regime (Kohler-Koch and Finke 2007), which is not only marked by a wide spectrum of consultation mechanisms (Knodt, this issue; Jarman, this issue), but also by its aim to integrate as many different stakeholders as possible into the policy-making process (European Commission. 2009), including both, functional as well as territorial interest representatives.

The emergence of an interactive and communicative system of multi-level governance impacts on the strategies of all interest representatives. The contributions to this issue analyse the different modes of interest intermediation provided or shaped by EU institutions, especially the European Commission, and take a close look at the ways different actors represent their interests within the European multi-level system, considering both learning processes as well as actor capacities.

Different Modes of Interest Representation in the European Multi-Level System

As a first step, the different forms of territorial and functional representation in a political system are analyzed in this issue. Simona Piattoni addresses this question from the view of political theory on representation. Her starting point is the problematic coexistence of functional and territorial representation in the EU in respect to the question of democratic legitimacy. Her contribution raises the fundamental questions of the types of representation in European governance and the debate on replacing territorial, political representation with functional, societal representation in order to overcome the democratic deficit of the European Union. Piattoni is very clear in her view that such a replacement is no solution of the problem. Her argument starts with the construction of two ways of representation. First, interests can be represented in a lumpy, collective form with roots in generated collective identities. Second, there is a way of representation of divisible individual interests, which in a careful operation of composition can be aggregated into larger interests. Both territorial and functional interests can be represented in a lumpy and divisible way. At the national level there are two main systems to relate territorial and functional interests and lumpy and divisible ways of representation. Simplifying, Piattoni assumes that federal systems treat territorial claims as lumpy and functional claims as divisible, whereas corporatist systems treat territorial claims as divisible and functional claims as lumpy: The former are willing to bargain on functional claims, while the latter are willing to bargain on territorial claims. The

European Union on the one hand does not fit easily into this classification, and on the other hand is characterised by its multi-level logic which enhances the complexity of interest representation modes. However, Piattoni assumes that the EU at the European level tries to involve sub-national territorial and functional interests as divisible interests on which bargaining and compromise are possible, whereas it delegates the representation of lumpy territorial interests to the national level. Piattoni discusses two alternative modes to mix lumpy and divisible ways to represent territorial and functional interests: Democratic experimentalism and multi-level governance. Both modes are described and judged in their democratic temper for lumpy and divisible ways of representing territorial and functional interests. Thus, the democratic temper of democratic experimentalism lies in its offering of new arenas for divisible representation, with a comprehensive inclusion of functional and territorial interests. Territorial representative chambers should secure the simultaneous representation of both types of claims in the model. The democratic temper of the multi-level governance mode lies in recognizing the existence of lumpy claims and giving territorial interests, in particular, the possibility to switch from a lumpy to a divisible way of representing their interests. This also emerges in the contribution by Knodt in this issue. In the same direction, three other contributions of this issue analyse the possible different modes of involving interests within European governance. The European Union, and especially the European Commission, has tried in recent years to develop strategies for the involvement of civil society actors (in a broad sense) that would increase the legitimacy of, and provide expertise to, the European Union. The contributions of Holly Jarman, Michèle Knodt and of Christine Quittkat and Peter Kotzian in this issue address the question of different modes of involvement by the Commission. While Knodt introduces two models of involvement — 'consultation' and 'deliberative communication' — in order to link different strategies of interest intermediation with the way of involving interests into European governance, Jarman analyses two types of involvement of functional interests and hints as to why there exist different types of relationship between the European Commission and functional interests. Even if labelled differently, the two ways of modelling types of involvement are very similar in their core ideas. Jarman examines attempts by the European Commission to shape its relationship with civil society groups (in a broad sense) in two different ways: Collaborative or consultative. She looks at two cases, the DG Trade Civil Society Dialogue and the DG SANCO Platform on Diet, Physical Activity and Health. She establishes that DG Trade, as a strong and relatively autonomous DG, has developed a consultative model of engagement, while DG SANCO, working in areas where EU competencies are relatively weak, carries out a collaborative model in which it can set the agenda and structure debates, but which fundamentally depends on industry association partners, rather than its own legal powers, to achieve its goals. Thus, the Commission's gateway of interest representation differs according to the policy field.

As Jarman points out, each of these ideal types has certain benefits for Commission officials. The consultation mechanism is seen as a means of holding Commission officials to account and as such a step towards more legitimate policy and a more legitimate institution. Knodt in her contribution sees things differently. She states that the consultation type of involvement can in no way enhance the legitimacy of the Commission and the EU as such, because of a lack of even the minimum standards of any kind of deliberative democracy. For Jarman the collaboration mechanisms offer officials with weak authority the opportunity not only to act in a controversial area, but to pass some of the responsibility for policy outcomes and the risks of failure onto outside actors, which is somewhat removed from a mechanism for increasing legitimacy. At the end of her contribution Jarman sets up fruitful hypotheses upon the relationship of the two types of involvement and the different interest groups. Quittkat and Kotzian take a different approach by focusing on participation in consultation instruments rather than on the question of legitimacy. But from their results it is quite clear that European policy-making via civil society involvement is not enhanced if measured on the basis of functional and territorial representation. To be sure, online consultations reach out to a large group of more remote interests like sub-national and local actors, which also fits with Piattoni's conception of divisible interests. But more exclusive consultation instruments, for example workshops and forums, show a rather biased participation structure in favour of EU level functional interests and national level public actors. While in an integrated and hierarchical (federal) interest representation system like the EU the domination of consultations through such actors might not be a problem, the unbalanced representation of different functional interests (society, business and labour) and of territories (old versus new member states), as revealed by the quantitative analysis, certainly is.

As these contributions show, involving interests within European interactive governance should not only be analysed by focussing on the role of the Commission, but also by evaluating the role of other actors. This is particularly evident in the contribution by Heiko Pleines, who in his empirical study of business groups, trade unions and value-based NGOs from new EU member states argues that interest groups from the new Central and East European member states could smoothly be integrated into the EU system of interest representation with the help of European umbrella organisations. He points out that European umbrella organisations offer immediate access to the EU level, provide a role model of engagement at the EU level and also increase information flows from the EU level to national interest groups and with that into national debates and national policy-making processes.

Paths and Strategies of Interest Representation within the European Multi-Level System

Interests can be represented by different paths in an interactive and multi-level European governance system; they can either exclusively address the European level or they are represented by a complementary strategy, i.e., they can be represented directly as well as indirectly through other associations/organizations and levels. The degree of network building within the European multi-level system can vary to a great respect. Interests can address different institutions. They can make use of professional help (consultants, etc) or use public discourses as an instrument of interest representation in the sense that some actors might act as norm entrepreneurs to secure their interests. Our aim is to get to know about different kinds of actors (territorial and functional) and their strategies within the European multi-level system, and to detect similarities and differences. Does, for instance, the EU's multi-level character require strategic resource mobilization at different levels and at the same time, or are resources of little relevance when the agendas of interest organisations coincide with those of the Commission?

In her contribution Michèle Knodt shows that throughout the actor categories of functional and regional as well as local actors, actor strategies of interest intermediation have converged. Both actor categories have adapted their internal organisations or institutions to the European action sphere and different measures to improve processing of European information have been installed. Both actor categories make use of the possibilities to be represented via their respective European representation bodies. The construction of transnational communication areas is also a strategy in a different kind of arrangement, which both actor categories have deployed from the beginning and extended considerably throughout the last years. Territorial as well as functional actors also make intensive use of the possibilities of direct presence on the European level for their interest representation. For some types of territorial actors the strategy of secondment depicts a customary, whereas for functional actors it is a new strategy. Overall, both actor categories deploy all strategies and channels at the same time and thus use a complementary strategy. Obviously, comparing functional as well as territorial interest intermediation strategies, we can deduce that in the EU interactive multi-level system operating at only one level or relying only on one strategy is not considered to lead to the intended effect.

Carlo Ruzza shows how social movements have found a niche which fulfils a variety of functions they need to meet. They become norm entrepreneurs at EU level, bringing ideas into the EU environment, sometimes putting forward an often utopian vision of desirable policy change that other more moderate organizations can utilise as a negotiating standard. Characterising a type of organisation which lies somewhere between traditional social movements, and institutionalised actors in the political system, he moves beyond traditional caricatures of once independently minded organisations whose destiny is to become progressively institutionalised and removed from their grass roots origins. He identifies a set of intermediate organizational forms that retain some of the features of social movements but have also acquired some of those distinctive of NGOs, including a degree of professionalisation, service delivery roles, and better legal skills. Direct representation arises through organisations which are part of the social movement 'family', such as Greenpeace and Friends of the Earth, but who can also play the 'institutional politics' game, apparently without too much compromise or tension. Beyond the environmental movement, Ruzza notes the recent arrival on the Brussels scene of the anti-globalisation movement with capacities to act as institutional players, and which are highly embedded within complex networks of social movements, and through which policy focused alliances arise. They are linked to the institutionalised world of EU interest representation through organisations (such as Greenpeace and Friends of the Earth) capable of 'bridging' the two worlds (Hadden 2009), and by building up structures developed to address the EU level specifically. Thus, the anti-globalisation Corporate Europe Observatory (CEO) built a coalition (ALTER–EU) built upon established Brussels NGOs coalescing around a specific issue with broad appeal, but later broadened the agenda into a common EU critical alliance, bringing a different edge to the positions of established Brussels NGOs in both positions and tactics. CEO has recently taken up presence among environmental NGOs in a purpose adapted 'eco-building' in Brussels (Ruzza, this issue). This puts a different perspective to the caricature of an anti-globalisation movement ill at ease with the prospects of institutionalised politics in a system underpinned by the lack of public space and an ethos of liberalisation in which electoral levers are relatively few (Balme and Chabanet 2008). To the contrary, the EU may be a favourable arena for strategic 'venue shopping' (Princen and Kerremans 2008) by taking issues to venues where business interests cannot dominate decision-making due, inter alia, to its fragmented nature and generally welcoming environment for contributory voices to the public arena. In transmitting norms to the arenas in which they participate at EU level, they also contribute to otherwise limited understanding of social and territorial issues, and provide a voice for otherwise marginalised parts of civil society as well as a check and balance upon producer orientated lobbies. Prince and Kerremans review work which describes how framing can become a strategic exercise, because the way in which an issue is framed affects where the venue will be dealt with (Princen and Kerremans 2008). In this way, framing can become a determinant of opportunity structures, rather than the opportunity structures being a given to which interests adapt to.

The findings of Chalmers also challenge perspectives that NGOs are somehow systematically excluded from the policy process. In his analysis, the role of information is central to the ability of an interest group to efficiently process information, i.e., the more efficient interest groups are at information processing, the more frequently they will interact with EU decision-makers. This provides the basis for an empirical examination of how interest groups gather, filter, generate and transmit information to decision-makers, drawing upon literature which sees information as subsidising the work of the converted, rather than changing the mind of opponents. One notable feature of his results is that most types of interest groups in the EU have similar information processing capabilities and thus, that influence in the EU appears to be, on balance, fair and impartial. Public authorities display results as relatively efficient information processors, operating in ways similar to those of traditional interest groups.

The extent to which information — as asymmetries in principal/agent exchanges — plays a role also informs the analysis by Greenwood of whether territorial offices in Brussels act like interest groups or as extensions of bureaucratic politics. The bifurcation he finds between quasi autonomous offices able to set their own agendas, and delegates working to specific briefs set by of regional administrations, highlights the importance of differences within, as well as across, interest capacities. Those with a relatively high degree of autonomy tend to develop agendas which are civil society orientated, rather than acting as an agent of particularistic interests. The former type displays a high degree of embeddedness in NGO oriented networks, whereas the latter have little scope to expand their brief. Here, the degree of purpose in establishing the office is the key issue. Some authorities established an office with a very clear purpose in mind, such as the continuation of centre–regional power struggles in domestic politics through to another venue. Typically, these are regional governments in federal type states, where these principals determine and monitor the work of their seconded delegates in outreach offices in Brussels. On the other hand, authorities from countries with a 'medium' degree of devolved regional authority had much less clear purpose in establishing a presence in Brussels, and often employing those from the Brussels circuit to run their offices who could find ways of interpreting their general duties which was interesting for them, and for which a case could be made to their employers of the value their work created at local and regional levels. Typically, this has involved citizen orientated agendas, such as public health, participating in and often creating Brussels networks. Some such offices are capable of perceiving and representing 'the common interest', true to type of regional and local authorities which, after all, have broadly based public remits. This brings an interesting twist to public choice grounded caricatures of 'professionalisation' as problematic, in which autonomy is seen as leading to self-serving behaviour likely to run counter to the public interest, and for which the solution is to equip principals with better tools to make their agents accountable. In similar adaptation, Saurugger casts a sceptical eye towards the movement towards professionalisation of Brussels based interest groups, in which 'Brussels talks to Brussels', with organisational representatives drawn from the circuit of Brussels elites trained on EU studies courses, and removed from the grassroots constituent interest (Saurugger 2006). In Greenwood's contribution here, however, the professionals which run such offices are seen in a less hostile way, characterised more as the 'new class' members cast by Gouldner, as enlightened figures capable of perceiving, and representing, the common interest (Gouldner 1979). Connections are also drawn here to the work of Pitkin, the inevitable disjuncture between 'represented' and 'representative', and the role of office heads as 'trustees' (Pitkin 1967), able to continue with their work provided they file regular reports in which, provided nothing seems out of line, then they remain free to carry on with their work. Andrew Barron looks at another group of actors, focusing at the lobbying strategies of government affairs managers in large firms from the perspective of strategic management. His contribution investigates cross-national differences on the basis of original data collected through an online survey in 2010. His findings indicate significant relationships between respondents' culturally-grounded attitudes towards time (short-term versus long-term strategies) and their level of engagement with policy-makers as well as between their culturally-conditioned attitudes towards power and hierarchy and their choice of political tactics when seeking to promote their political interests. Further, Barron's findings also support the idea of a special elite in Brussels. Barron's results underline the specific function of government affairs managers located in Brussels, in that they appear to consider it their raison d'être to pursue individual political action as a supplement to their employers' need to also follow collective political action. To do so, government affairs managers will usually be oriented towards long-term, issue-spanning relationships with policy-makers, with trustworthiness often obtained through many years of professional relations as one of the prime prerequisites of successful lobbying.

Convergence through Learning Processes

Some of our contributions have shown that within the EU interactive multi-level governance system of interest representation actors learn from each other. These learning processes take place across actors' categories as well as within the same actor category and across different levels.

Thus, Michèle Knodt's contribution shows that through the strategy of direct interest representation and secondment, the different actor categories (territorial and functional) learn from each other. Other contributions also demonstrate that, over time, interest intermediation across actor categories has converged to a great extent. Greenwood shows how certain types of territorial outlets in Brussels have developed agendas from the connections they have established with NGOs. Ruzza demonstrates the pivotal role in such a process of organisations such as Greenpeace, and Friends of the Earth, through their ability to perform Janus-like roles with links to both political institutions and social movements. Whilst hostile interpretation sees a process of professionalisation and institutionalisation involving such organisations, another perspective emphasises instead their extent of participation in (and their centrality to) social movement initiated campaigns, such as the European Transparency Register (Greenwood in press).

Thus, the learning processes could as well take place within the category of functional interests and over different levels, as evident from the contribution by Pleines. In the case of the bigger business associations from the new Central and East European member states the learning processes were initiated through bilateral 'twinning' partnerships with peer organisations from the old member states. However, learning can also be a bitter experience and result in rivalries, as Pleines points out with regard of the dominant role of the European Women's Lobby (EWL), where dissenting groups such as the Polish women NGO Karat Coalition find it difficult to gain access to the Commission. Themes of learning also emerge from some of the issues reviewed below.

Actor Capacities

The retracing and analysis of interest intermediation strategies in the EU clearly points out one specific aspect: Territorial and functional actors need to possess particular capacities in order to represent successfully their interests at EU level. Most obviously, *administrative and financial resources* would seem to make a difference in the capacity to undertake interest representation at the European level. Whilst business interests have a superior resource base viz. other types of interests, the extent of alternative sources of funding located by other organisations partly offsets this apparent advantage. Whilst EU institutions account for a significant degree of funding for EU level NGOs, less institutionalised actors who have recently begun to engage with the EU system have developed their own funding streams (Ruzza). Yet, as Barron demonstrates, resources provide only part of the picture. The history of business interest representation is littered with examples of clumsy interventions by multinational companies. Such large organisations can be incoherent 'public affairs' actors by virtue of their size and extent of decentralisation between the different components, to the point that they are hardly able to co-ordinate and reconcile sometimes competing positions between different product divisions. Barron draws upon literature from management science, and political economy, most notably the 'behavioural theory of the firm', to demonstrate how acting in the political arena is beyond the comfort zone for many firms, and how non-decision-making, and 'drift' characterises political (in)action by some interests. However, variability is the watchword, and this literature provides guidance as to the characteristics of sectors, and firms, which predict the ability to act effectively on the political stage. The multi-level governance nature of the EU, with its fragmented power structure add significantly to this environment, limiting the ability of any one actor to achieve and pursue their goals in isolation from other types of stakeholders, and here the traditional capacity of citizen orientated organisations to 'frame' issues and to build alliances are significant capacities (Ruzza). A key issue is not so much the extent of resource holding, but the ability to make messages resonate with those of EU institutions, and where these intents and messages converge, so an actor — irrespective of the type — can achieve a high degree of policy access. Conversely, actors with a frame which is entirely contradictory to those of EU institutions can be 'frozen out' until such time as they re-evaluate their own interest frame to be consistent with the direction of travel of EU institutions (Woll 2009). This resonates with the work of Baltz *et al.* (cited in Beyers, Eising, and Maloney 2008) where states drive through public policy initiatives, moderating pressures from special interest pressures by strategic use of joint decision traps (Grande 1996). Woll shows how business interests can be frozen out from EU decision-making if they operate within a frame (such as protectionism) which is entirely contrary to that of the

Commission, and, how such interests have to re-position themselves, if necessary doing a complete about-turn to project liberalisation as consistent with their own interest set (Woll 2009). Bouza finds something similar in the case of social NGOs which take a reality check first with the Commission to see the direction of travel before taking up detailed positions on issues (Bouza 2010). Issues of administrative and financial resources contribute to a high degree of variability in the presence of regional interests and, thereby, to a selective performance at the European level.

Beyond this, it emerged in the literature that the ability to interact strategically was most important for a successful regional presence. Baden-Württemberg, for instance, clearly had a greater potential to interact strategically than did Lower Saxony. Moreover, its regional network was tighter and the contacts with the European level denser. Lower Saxony, whose network configuration was less developed and consolidated, turned out to possess many difficulties with regional and European communication and interaction (Knodt 1998). The same holds true for functional actors, which we can see if we closely observe different functional actors, e.g., out of different national contexts. It has been shown that the national experience, and policy styles, of the functional actors out of different national states make a difference in the ability to interact strategically with the European institutions (Eising 2009; Quittkat 2009). But it is not interaction alone which makes a difference. Other factors are decisive for applying the 'right' lobbying strategy, including knowledge of the European logic of interest intermediation, the fit between national and European logic of interest intermediation (Schmidt 1999), and in its most basic form via membership in EU level associations, as Pleines shows in his contribution. Now, with the emergence of the Commission's new consultation regime, additional and new forms of policy-making involvement for interest representatives have opened up. As Quittkat and Kotzian show, knowledge of the interlocking of different consultation instruments offers a head start for lobbyists. Participation in online consultations, which consume scarce organisational resources and are open to hundreds of interest competitors, is a pre-requisite for becoming part of the more exclusive circle of conference speakers and forum participants. Nonetheless, the extent of engagement by NGOs organised at national level in Commission consultations is a striking finding in the contribution by Quittkat and Kotzian.

Conclusion: A European Model of Interest Representation in European Governance?

The comparison of interest representation roles and strategies for different functional and territorial actors in European policy-making opens up a whole range of new insights for future analysis. The most dominant picture presented here is one of convergence, although it is not surprising that the contributions to this issue should also reveal persistent differences. There is a trend of 'Europeanisation' which becomes visible in the increased presence of interests across different actor categories which were previously only indirectly and/or marginally represented. New territorial offices have opened up in Brussels (Greenwood), even the local level has become present at the European level (Knodt), the anti-globalisation movement has found institutionalised routes (Ruzza), and new Central and East European member states have become integrated into the EU system of interest representation with the help of European umbrella organisations (Pleines). Further, different actor categories perform similar roles, in that public actors, NGOs and business associations all gather, filter, generate and transmit information to decision-makers (Chalmers), and participate in the Commission's new consultation regime (Quittkat and Kotzian), fulfilling a transmission-belt function with regard to their 'constituencies', for which they create networks and professionalise.

The contributions show that the uniqueness of the EU as a multi-level system brings about several strategies that all actor categories apply, such as the use of complementary representation at the same time at different levels of the multi-level system. It emerges that territorial interests, particularly at the outset, had to learn how to perform as a functional interest group within a multi-level system in which they have very limited formal roles in political representation. As such, they learnt the need to compensate through direct interest representation. It seems to be that the special requirements of multi-level systems, rather than the *sui generic* character of the EU *per se*, creates these challenges for territorial interests. On the other side, functional interests also went through learning processes by making use of the longstanding experience of territorial interests with secondment strategies, which seems to have been uplifted by territorial actors from experience with federal systems.

The comparison also however brings to the open considerable differences between, within, and across, interest representative categories. These differences are related to the mission assigned to the interest representatives by both the addressee (i.e., EU institutions), as well as by those represented. The latter provide boundaries for the autonomy, and in consequence the scope of interest intermediation by the interest representatives, as the examples herein provided by territorial offices (Greenwood), company representations (Barron) and to some extent social movements (Ruzza), clearly shows. Principal agent models may neatly capture, and help explain, behaviour by business and union organisations, but need adaptation in the case of public authorities (Greenwood), and vary substantially in the extent of applicability to citizen orientated organisations, and in particular between associations of associations, and loose network organisations (Ruzza).

The addressee, such as the Commission, also impacts on the specific shape of interest representation by functional and territorial actors. As different contributions have shown, the mode of involving interests in the interactive European multi-level system of governance does make a difference in the way actors try to represent their interests. The impact depends on which mode of involvement (consultation, cooperation or communication) it allows for (Jarman, Knodt, Piattoni, Quittkat, and Kotzian), which in turn is often related to the issue at stake (Jarman, Quittkat, and Kotzian). As such, policy matters.

The differences found in this issue draw our attention also to the capacities of actors. But it is not the distinction of functional versus territorial interests as such which yields substantive difference in interest representation, but their ability to access administrative, financial and network resources, and that the differences across policy fields and sectors can be as substantive as within a policy field and a sector.

Indeed, from the analyses we learn that the European system of interest intermediation has widened and the spectrum of interests represented has broadened. We find all kinds of local actors, be they NGOs, social movements, single companies or cities, but on the other side we also detect continued preferential access for all those interest representatives who bundle large number of stakeholders (EU level associations and national public actors). We see that most interests apply a multi-level strategy of interest representation, thus are simultaneously active at different levels of the EU multi-level system. Similarly, the analyses show the use of many different access points to the European Commission across all types of actors. However, what is needed is a systematic comparison of EU interest intermediation by different actors and across EU institutions, preferably on the basis of datasets which include different actor categories. While the overall picture is clear and we find a basic European model of interest representation in European governance, we also see a highly complex model with cross-sectoral and intersectoral characteristics, without being fully informed about *systematic* variations. Does the organisational level, disregarding the interests represented, impact on strategies? For example does EU interest intermediation of sub-national actors show lopsidedness towards those EU institutions which are rooted more strongly in the member states, i.e., the European Parliament and the Council of Ministers? And how do different resources impact on EU interest intermediation strategies? Knowledge and information as well as financial and personnel resources are of high value in EU lobbying; yet to conceptualise these resources in a way that applies to all functional and territorial actor categories alike, and which allows for results which go beyond the banal statement that resources count, is one of the challenges to take up for future research.

Notes

1. For example the Mannheim project on 'Regional governance in the EU (REGE)'.
2. In a first attempt to address the research question, the authors organized a 'CONNEX' Workshop at the Mannheim Centre for European Social Research (MZES)/Mannheim University in 2008 to bring together experts from both territorial and functional interest representation. It was the starting point of continuous dialogue which is documented in this special issue.

References

Balme, R. and D. Chabanet. 2008. *European governance and democracy. Power and protest in the EU*. Plymouth: Rowman and Littlefield.
Benz, A. 2000. Entflechtung als Folge von Verflechtung: Theoretische Überlegungen zur Entwicklung des europäischen Mehrebenensystems. In *Wie problemlösungsfähig ist die EU? Regieren im europäischen Mehrebenensystem*, eds. E. Grande and M. Jachtenfuchs, 141–64. Baden-Baden: Nomos.
Beyers, J. 2002. Gaining and seeking access: the European adaptation of domestic interest associations. *European Journal of Political Research* 41, no. 5: 585–612.

Beyers, J., R. Eising, and W. Maloney. 2008. Researching interest group politics in Europe and elsewhere: much we study, little we know. *West European Politics* 31, no. 6: 1103–28.
Beyers, J., and B. Kerremans. 2007. Critical resource dependencies and Europeanization of domestic interest groups. *Journal of European Public Policy* 14, no. 3: 460–81.
Börzel, T. 1999. Towards convergence in Europe? Institutional adaption to Europeanisation in Germany and Spain. *Journal of Common Market Studies* 39, no. 4: 573–96.
Bouza Garcia, L. 2010. Civil society expectations on Article 11 TUE; more democracy or better access? Paper prepared for presentation at the UACES Annual Conference, Bruges, September 5–7.
Broscheid, A., and D. Coen. 2003. Insider and outsider lobbying in the European Commission. *European Union Politics* 4, no. 2: 165–89.
Coen, D. 2007. Empirical and theoretical studies in EU lobbying. *Journal of European Public Policy* 14, no. 3: 333–45.
Coen, D., and J. Richardson. 2009. *Lobbying the European Union: Institutions, Actors, and Issues* (Oxford/New York: Oxford University Press).
Dür, A. 2008. Interest groups in the European Union: how powerful are they? *West European Politics* 31, no. 6: 1212–30.
Dür, A., and D. DeBièvre. 2007. The question of interest group influence. *Journal of Public Policy* 27, no. 1: 1–12.
Eising, R. 2009. *The political economy of state-business relations in Europe. Interest mediation, capitalism, and EU policy-making*. London: Routledge.
European Commission. 2009. *Impact assessment guidelines*, SEC(2009) 92.
Frey, B., and R. Eichenberger. 1999. *The new democratic federalism for Europe. Functional, overlapping, and competing jurisdictions*. Cheltenham: Edward Elgar.
Friedrich, D. 2011. *Democratic participation and civil society in the European Union*. Manchester: Manchester University Press.
Gouldner, A. 1979. *The future of intellectuals and the rise of the new class*. London: Continuum.
Grande, E. 1996. The state and interest groups in a framework of multi-level decision making: the case of the European Union. *Journal of European Public Policy* 3, no. 3: 318–38.
Greenwood, J. 1997. *Representing interests in the European Union*. New York: St Martin's Press.
Greenwood, J. In press. The lobby regulation element of the European transparency initiative: between liberal and deliberative modes of democracy. *Comparative European Politics*.
Hadden, J. 2009. Two worlds of European collective action? Civil society spillover(s) in European climate change networks, paper prepared for the conference on Bringing Civil Society in the European Union and the Rise of Representative Democracy, European University Institute, Florence, March 14.
Heinelt, H. 1996. *Politiknetzwerke und europäische Strukturfondsförderung. Ein Vergleich zwischen EU-Mitgliedstaaten*. Opladen: Leske and Budrich.
Heinelt, H., and R. Smith. 1996. *Policy networks and European structural funds*. Aldershot: Avebury.
Hooghe, L., and G. Marks. 2001. Types of multi-level governance. *European Integration online Papers* 5, no. 11, http://eiop.or.at/eiop/texte/2001-011a.htm (accessed 31 August 2010).
Imig, D.R., and S.G. Tarrow. 2001. *Contentious Europeans: protest and politics in an emerging polity*. Lanham, MD: Rowman and Littlefield.
Jachtenfuchs, M., and B. Kohler-Koch. 1996. Einleitung: Regieren im dynamischen Mehrebenensystem. In *Europäische Integration*, eds. M. Jachtenfuchs and B. Kohler-Koch, 15–47. Opladen: Leske and Budrich.
Knodt, M. 1998. *Tiefenwirkung europäischer Politik. Eigensinn oder Anpassung regionalen Regierens?* Baden-Baden: Nomos.
Knodt, M. 2005. *Regieren im erweiterten europäischen Mehrebenensystem – die internationale Einbettung der EU*. Baden-Baden: Nomos.
Knodt, M., and T. Conzelmann. 2002. *Regionales Europa – Europäisierte Regionen*, Volume 6. Mannheimer Jahrbuch zur Europäischen Sozialforschung 2001/2002. Frankfurt/Main: Campus.
Knodt, M., and B. Finke. 2005. *Europäisierung der Zivilgesellschaft. Konzepte, Akteure, Strategien*. Wiesbaden: VS.
Kohler-Koch, B. 2000. Europäisierung: Plädoyer für eine Horizonterweiterung. In *Deutschland zwischen Europäisierung und Selbstbehauptung*, eds. M. Knodt and B. Kohler-Koch, Volume 5, 11–3. Frankfurt/Main: Campus.
Kohler-Koch, B., and B. Finke. 2007. The institutional shaping of EU–society relations: a contribution to democracy via participation? *Journal of Civil Society* 3, no. 3: 205–21.
Kohler-Koch, B., and V. Buth. 2011. Der Spagat der europäischen Zivilgesellschaft — zwischen Professionalität und Bürgernähe. In *Die Entzauberung partizipativer Demokratie. Zur Rolle der Zivilgesellschaft bei der Demokratisierung von EU-Governance*, eds. Kohler-Koch Beate and Quittkat Christine, 167–210. Frankfurt/Main: Campus.
Kohler-Koch, B. et al. 1998. *Interaktive Politik in Europa: Regionen im Netzwerk der Integration*. Opladen: Leske and Budrich.

Mahoney, C., and F.R. Baumgartner. 2008. Converging perspectives on interest group research in Europe and America. *West European Politics* 31, no. 6: 1253–73.
Mazey, S., and J. Richardson. 1993. *Lobbying in the European Community*. Oxford: Oxford University Press.
Ostrom, V. 1999. Polycentricity (Part I and II). In *Polycentricity and local public economies. Readings from the workshop in political theory and policy analysis*, ed. M. McGinnis, 52–74. Ann Arbor: University of Michigan Press.
Ostrom, V., C. Tiebout, and R. Warren. 1961. The organization of government in metropolitan areas: a theoretical inquiry. *American Political Science Reviews* 55, 831–42.
Pitkin, H. 1967. *The concept of representation*. Berkeley: The University of California Press.
Princen, S., and B. Kerremans. 2008. Opportunity structures in the EU multi-level system. *West European Politics* 31, no. 6: 1103–28.
Quittkat, C. 2005. Die Europäisierung nationaler Wirtschaftsverbände: Lehren für die Einbindung der organisierten Zivilgesellschaft in den europäischen Politikprozess. In *Europäische Zivilgesellschaft. Konzepte, Akteure, Strategien*, eds. M. Knodt and B. Finke, 365–88. Wiesbaden: Verlag Opladen.
Quittkat, C. 2006. *Europäisierung der Interessenvermittlung. Französische Wirtschaftsverbände zwischen Beständigkeit und Wandel*. Wiesbaden: VS-Verlag.
Quittkat, C. 2009. The Europeanization of professional interest intermediation: national trade associations in a French–German comparison. In *Interest groups and lobbying in Europe*, ed. C. McGrath, 125–59. Lewiston: Edwin Mellen Press.
Saurugger, S. 2003. *Européaniser les intérêts? Les groupes d'intérêt économiques et l'élargissement de L'Union européenne*. Paris: L'Harmattan.
Saurugger, S. 2006. The professionalisation of interest representation: a legitimacy problem for civil society in the EU? In *Civil society and legitimate European governance*, ed. S. Smismans, 260–76. Cheltenham: Edward Elgar.
Schmidt, V.A. 1999. National patterns of governance under siège: the impact of European integration. In *The transformation of governance in the European Union*, eds. B. Kohler-Koch and R. Eising, 155–72. London: Routledge.
Schmitter, P., and W. Streeck. 1999. The organization of business interests. *MPfG Discussion Paper* 99, no. 1: 1–95.
Steffek, J., and P. Nanz. 2008. Emergent patterns of civil society participation in global and european governance. In *Civil society participation in European and global governance: a cure for the democratic deficit?*, eds. J. Steffek, C. Kissling and P. Nanz, 1–29. Houndmills, Basingstoke: Palgrave Macmillan.
Traxler, F. 1995. Two logics of collective action in industrial relations? In *Organized industrial relations in Europe: what future?*, eds. C. Crouch and F. Traxler, 23–44. Aldershot: Avebury.
Van Schendelen, M.P.C.M. 1993. *National public and private EC lobbying*. Aldershot: Dartmouth.
Woll, C. 2006. Lobbying in the European Union: from Sui Generis to a comparative perspective. *Journal of European Public Policy* 13, no. 3: 456–69.
Woll, C. 2009. Trade policy lobbying in the European Union. In *Lobbying the European Union: institutions, actors and issues*, eds. D. Coen and J. Richardson, 277–97. Oxford: Oxford University Press.

The Problematic Coexistence of Functional and Territorial Representation in the EU

SIMONA PIATTONI

University of Innsbruck, Austria

ABSTRACT   The paper explores the difficult coexistence between territorial and functional representation in the European Union. It starts by presenting a rather general framework for the analysis of territorial and functional claims that distinguished between 'lumpy' claims — indivisible claims that can be made only by representatives of collective actors on the basis of shared identities and that cannot, therefore, be parceled out or compromised upon — and 'divisible' claims — claims forthcoming from individual actors that can be aggregated and presented as 'categorical', but whose aggregation does not give rise to any collective identity. After discussing (and discarding) the more radical views that consider territorial representation as wholly outdated and ineffective, it sketches two more nuanced solutions to the problematic coexistence of territorial and functional representation — democratic experimentalism and multi-level governance — that purport to describe the ways in which binding decisions are made in the EU. It concludes that the representational mixes embodied in these solutions are indeed viable, but that they both require the willingness on the part of territorial and functional representatives to shed their 'lumpy' claims and to be ready to compromise over 'divisible' claims.

Introduction

The European Union (EU) is particularly apt at raising questions that challenge conventional political science wisdom, forcing reconsideration of fairly old and apparently settled issues. The unusual institutional setup of the EU has been prompting questions regarding its 'nature' (theories of European integration), the way it is governed (the 'governance turn'), and its democratic legitimacy (the 'normative turn') — all while heated methodological debates have flared up and disciplinary divides have been crossed. Theoretical, empirical and normative questions are raised by the way in which the EU is structured (polity), the type of political mobilization that it stimulates or fails to stimulate (politics), and the legitimacy of the decisions that it produces (policy). Common to these debates is the contrast between an inter-governmental and a supra-national interpretation of the Union: Between a vision that assigns primacy to territorial loyalties and one that acknowledges the power of functional interests. In this paper I will explore the problematic coexistence of territorial and functional representation in the EU, an issue that raises both theoretical and normative concerns.

Ever since the rediscovery of corporatism — labeled 'new' or 'neo' corporatism for its bottom-up, societal nature in contrast to the top-down, statist nature of 'old' corporatism typical of fascist regimes (Schmitter 1981) — scholars have been debating the uneasy relationship between functional and territorial representation. The debate found a temporary equilibrium in the acknowledgment of the complementary relationship between the two (remember Stein Rokkan's dictum 'votes count but resources decide') and of the economic edge that it afforded those countries that had a well-functioning system of societal corporatism (e.g., Katzenstein 1985). The growing concern about the democratic temper of the European Union and, in particular, the release of the *White Paper on European governance (WPEG)* (CEC 2001) rehashed this debate which, however, took a new turn. While before no one had proposed to replace territorial with functional representation (as this smacked as a return to pre-democratic, 'old corporatist' regimes), more recently scholars have suggested that such a replacement is not only conceivable, but even desirable precisely as a way of overcoming the EU democratic deficit. While speculations about a post-parliamentary democracy are perhaps justifiable in the context of the European Union, the wider implications of these ideas must be carefully assessed for they easily impinge also upon democracy in the member-states and beyond the EU itself (Schmidt 2006).

The coexistence between territorial and functional representation is particularly problematic at EU level for three reasons. First, the manner in which territorial and functional, general and particular interests are represented in the EU does not quite fit our analytical and normative maps, which are normally drawn by reference to the nation state (Jachtenfuchs 1995; Leibfried and Zürn 2005). The political science community is looking for alternative conceptions of democracy: In this quest, many forms of 'representation' have been identified testifying to the difficulty of coming to grips with democratic representation in post-national polities (Pollak 2007). Second, the institutional actors that populate the EU scene themselves find problematic having to act in ways they are not used to and that they could not normatively justify and, conversely, find problematic not being able to act in ways they are used to and that they could easily normatively justify. Therefore, they experience a displacement of means to ends, of behaviours to roles. For example, members of the Committee of the Regions (CoR) think of themselves as representatives in a political institution, while they are considered by the Treaties as experts in a consultative committee (Piattoni in press). This dissonance between their self-perception and the letter of the Treaties has been the source of the CoR's effort to define its own contribution to Europe's multi-level governance in more political terms (CoR 2009). Third, EU citizens cannot quite come to grips with the institutional structure of the EU or understand the functioning of the many modes of governance through which decisions are made and, therefore, feel 'detached' if not 'alienated' from the Union (CEC 2001). The source of this alienation may well be cognitive, but it quickly becomes also normative. For all these reasons, revisiting the problematic coexistence of territorial and functional representation is important for the life of today's Union.

The paper proceeds as follows. The next section argues, in general and abstract terms, that democracy can function smoothly only if individual claims are represented in aggregate form as when individual claims are pressed as particular instances of more general claims. Conversely, democracy is jeopardized by the representation of lumpy (uncompromising) claims that do not allow for their disaggregation and re-aggregation into more encompassing categories. The following section explores the solutions — federalism and corporatism — that have been found at the national level to accommodate lumpy (territorial or functional) claims and discusses their applicability at the EU level. The fourth section discusses two extreme positions — *organic governance* and *functional governance* that favour the partial or total supersession of territorial representation in favour of exclusive functional representation — and proposes two more nuanced solutions to the problematic coexistence of territorial and functional representation in the EU — *democratic experimentalism and multi-level governance* that promise to overcome the pitfalls of the more radical solutions. The last section concludes by discussing the democratic temper of these solutions and the likelihood of their permanence and diffusion.

The Difficult Coexistence of Territorial and Functional Representation

Territory and function are among the most common and powerful principles around which interests can coalesce and identities get formed. Functional and territorial forms of representation have always been central in all democratic systems but have also always stood in an uneasy relationship to one another. The idea that individuals, rather than social groups, economic guilds, subnational communities or religious congregations should find representation in territorially apportioned districts made its way slowly into modern political thinking. Still in the late eighteenth century, the notion that citizens could be the carriers of individual interests that had to be aggregated (by some sort of algorithm) in order to be represented in the parliamentary assembly was inconceivable (Burke 1774, as quoted in Pitkin 1967, chapter 8).

The prevalent idea was that individuals were characterized by interests principally dictated by the function that they performed in society — be it economic, military, religious or otherwise — and that they could therefore be represented in a 'lumpy' form.[1] It is only in this perspective that one can make sense of Burke's idea that, insofar as the functional interests of a commercial city like Birmingham were promoted by the representatives of another commercial city like Bristol, then effective representation had been secured to the citizens of both commercial cities. Such a conception of representation (*virtual representation*) clearly reflects the situation of the time (before the French Revolution) in which Burke was writing, where only few economic and social groups had actual representation in parliament. The revolutionary idea that every person had the right to cast his/her vote and thus be individually represented was yet to be accepted. But also in more recent times we can find instances of lumpy representation of functional interests, such as that offered by those farmers' and workers' parties which infused in their members a sense of community and identity and catered for them 'from cradle to coffin' (as the programme of the German Social democratic Party stated; Michels 1949).

While functional representation has very old roots (in many ways stretching back to the *Ständestaat*; Poggi 1978), territory became an alternative focus for representation only with the introduction of universal suffrage. We know from Duverger (1951) that the first organised 'party' that got formed in the French representative assembly was the *Club Breton*, which grouped in the original 1798 Estates General convened in Versailles representatives from Brittany, who shared a common language and common territorial interests, and which later included also representatives from other areas of France eventually giving birth to the *Jacobins* faction (Mavrogordatos 1996). While in this case territory simply acted as a first aggregative focus, we know that territory can act as a focus of lumpy representation particularly for representatives elected from regions characterized by special cultural or economic features. Generally, however, territory is just the partition in which votes are counted and the electoral formula applied to translate votes into parliamentary seats; therefore, it is simply the basis for the aggregation of votes along ideological lines. It was further assumed that, in most countries, with the 'nationalization' of politics (Caramani 2004) lumpy territorial and functional claims would give way to divisible claims that could be then aggregated along ideological lines that encompassed both territorial and functional interests in a manageable form. Ideologies provided narratives that could bridge these sometimes convergent, sometimes contrasting focuses of representation, and sealed the unity of territory and function at the national level. The process of European integration calls this accommodation into question and allows for the re-emergence of potentially divisive lumpy claims.

Territory and function are still the two most powerful catalysts around which individual preferences coalesce and get represented, and they may come into conflict with one another. Both can generate collective identities that demand to be represented in a lumpy form, but they can also be the basis for the expression of divisible claims that can be then aggregated into larger interests through careful composition. The balancing of lumpy territorial and functional interests at the national level occurs mainly in two ways. *Federal systems* organize very carefully the territorial voice at two or more levels, attributing to each level exclusive or concurrent governmental competence and granting each level a constitutionally protected say on that very allocation (Burgess 2006; Elazar 1995, 2001). *Corporatist systems* strive to aggregate the functional voice into encompassing, hierarchically organized but democratically structured associations that can then interact authoritatively with the central government and agree to macroeconomic and social policies that affect the entire society (Lehmbruch and Schmitter 1979; Schmitter and Lehmbruch 1982; Schmitter 1981; Offe 1981).

Simplifying somewhat, we could say that federal systems treat territorial claims as lumpy and functional claims as divisible, whereas corporatist systems treat territorial claims as divisible and functional claims as lumpy. In the former, people are willing to bargain on functional claims; in the latter, they are willing to bargain on territorial claims. Both systems rely on a credible exchange — between the federal government and the federated units, in the case of federalism, and between the central government and the employers' and workers' associations, in the case of corporatism — of guarantees of reciprocal jurisdictional integrity and autonomy for the commitment to finding a working solution to joint-decision problems. In both cases, political parties may be instrumental in finding an accommodation between the sometimes concurrent and sometimes competing claims stemming from territory and function and in lending coherence and unity to political systems that could otherwise fall apart (Rokkan 1966).[2]

In the European Union, there is no party system (yet) that may bridge over and recompose territorial and functional claims (for a more optimistic view, see Hix 2008). The composition of territorial and functional claims must be sought by other means. The European Union strives to encourage the disaggregation of lumpy claims into divisible claims by ruling out as much as possible the use of veto power. As is known, member states have reluctantly given up unanimity rule in the Council (though they still retain it in certain matters). Veto power, after the Luxembourg compromise, 'must be justified in terms of a *substantive interest, not the defense of national sovereignty itself*' (Hooghe and Marks 2001, 19, emphasis added). Moreover, the EU avoids legislating on those issues that might elicit the emergence of lumpy functional claim-making: For example, the Union has so far avoided legislating in the social field and rather limited itself to registering, through the Social Dialogue and the OMC, the convergent will of national functional groups (Eberlein and Kerwer 2004). The Union has also chosen to grant only consultative powers to functional groups — employers, workers and civil society — represented in the Economic and Social Committee (ESC). Similarly, the Union avoids getting involved in the territorial organization of the individual member states so as not to upset entrenched national territorial traditions, limiting itself to requesting the creation of (at least) administrative regions in order to distribute the Structural Funds.[3] Rather, the Union involves subnational territorial representatives in decision-making through the Committee of the Regions (CoR) in a consultative capacity, as if they were the makers of divisible claims over which bargaining and compromises were possible (Piattoni in press).

Territorial Representation: Obstinate or Obsolete?

In the absence (so far) of a European Parliament fully capable of operating the disaggregation of lumpy claims into divisible ones to then re-aggregate them along programmatic lines, what other mechanisms are there to recompose potentially divergent territorial and functional claims?

Some scholars (Andersen and Burns 1996; Smismans 2004) argue that representative democracy, based as it is on divisible territorial representation, is outdated and incapable of yielding parliaments capable of tackling the problems of modern societies. Problems have become just too complicated for elected representatives to be able to muster the knowledge necessary to debate and legislate in an informed way on the possible alternatives. Even if parliaments (including the European Parliament) were to create, as they often do, special committees charged with collecting information and hearing the public before deliberating on specific issues, they would still under-perform with respect to specialized committees that are composed of experts and concerned actors. While Andersen and Burns' (1996) 'organic governance' assumes that such independent committees will form spontaneously to manage social problems, Smismans' (2004) 'functional governance' considers mostly committees that are specifically created and carefully crafted to help the Commission collect information, draft framework legislation, implement regulation, and monitor its implementation. Andersen and Burns foreshadow a world in which each problem elicits its own fully capable and representative committee, while Smismans' rejection of parliamentary democracy (and the associated myth of the 'hierarchical and neutral bureaucracy') is bred by scepticism about the capacity of parliaments to handle the technical complexity of much current regulation. Andersen and Burns would gladly do altogether away with electoral, territorial representation as redundant. Smismans assigns to it, at best, a secondary role since he questions the presence, in the EU, of the pre-conditions for representative democracy and the possibility that EU bureaucracy may be hierarchical and neutral as the 'transmission-belt model of public administration' (Smismans 2004, 7) requires. Therefore, he too discounts territorial representation.

The critique of territorial representation, and its de facto replacement with functional representation performed by these authors, cannot be accepted as such. It must be doubted that functional representation *alone* can convey the information necessary for effective rule and can command the legitimacy necessary for democratic rule. Faith in the existence of a 'continuous, unbroken link between the citizen, associated groups, the state and the international community' (Burgess 2006, 176) characteristic of the European, Althusian tradition of federalism, discounts the problem inherent in the jump from divisible to lumpy representation. As was recalled in the previous section, rather than privileging one principle of representation (territorial or functional) over the other, viable solutions imply their judicious combination. Yet, the potential tension between territorial and functional claims is not completely eliminated and stalemates can still arise. In what follows I will examine two ways in which this problematic coexistence can be handled.

The burgeoning literature on EU's democracy (see Abromeit 1998; Beetham and Lord 1998; Hix 2008; Kohler-Koch and Rittberger 2007; Scharpf 1999; Schmitter 2000) has produced insightful analyses of the problem and suggested that certain already detectable developments might eventually yield a durable solution. This is hardly surprising, as any future accommodation of very different principles and modes of representation will certainly take a long time to develop and stabilize. I will here dwell on two such analyses and their attendant promises for solution: Democratic experimentalism and multi-level governance.

Democratic Experimentalism

Democratic experimentalism (Cohen and Sabel 1997; Gerstenberg and Sabel 2002; Sabel and J. Zeitlin 2007, 2010) is probably the most sophisticated and visionary solution to the problem of the difficult coexistence of territorial and functional representation currently present in the EU literature. It systematizes and lends credibility to a series of more naive attempts to subsume territorial representation under functional representation (Smismans 2004) or to do away with the former altogether (Andersen and Burns 1996). Labelled from time to time in different but equivalent ways — such as directly deliberative polyarchy (Cohen and Sabel 1997; Gerstenbergen and Sabel 2002) and experimentalist governance (Sabel and Zeitlin 2007) — according to the features in turn emphasized, democratic experimentalism provides an articulated, though somewhat visionary, argument for the existence of a new balance between territorial and functional representation in the EU. As in a *Gestalt* exercise in which an obvious shape reveals an unexpected object or a concave form appears after a while as convex, democratic experimentalism shows order and wisdom in what may appear at first as disorderly and quixotic.[4]

Sabel and Zeitlin (2007, 6) argue that all too easily the 'underlying architecture of public rule making in the EU' is overlooked if attention is focussed solely on the conventional coupling of function to structure that we would expect from traditional systems of rule. Similarly, the democratic quality of this governance architecture is missed if we look for a conventional division of labour between different forms of representation as that which is 'normally' found in national states. It is worth quoting extensively from the authors to gain a sense for this 'democratically experimentalist' governance architecture.

> In this decision-making design, framework goals (such as full employment, social inclusion, 'good water status', a unified energy grid) and measures for gauging their achievement are established by joint action of the Member States and EU institutions. Lower-level units

(such as national ministries or regulatory authorities and the actors with whom they collaborate) are given the freedom to advance these ends as they see fit. Subsidiarity in this architecture implies that, in writing a framework rule, the lower-level units should be given sufficient autonomy in implementing the rules to be able to propose changes to them. But in return for this autonomy, they must report regularly on their performance, especially as measured by the agreed indicators, and participate in a peer review in which their results are compared with those pursued by other means. Finally, the framework goals, metrics, and procedures themselves are periodically revised by the actors who initially established them, augmented by such new participants whose views come to be seen as indispensable for full and fair deliberation. (Sabel and Zeitlin 2007, 6–7)

Clearly, also democratic experimentalism, like organic and functional governance, places faith in the capacity of ad hoc participatory structures (networks, committees, etc.) to produce inclusive and fair deliberation that reflects all concerned interests. It traces its origins back to 'associational democracy', which combines two types of democratic activity: Representation and participation. Representation is the way in which territorial claims are normally conveyed; participation is the way in which functional claims are conventionally expressed. The combination of these activities secures the representation of both territorial and functional claims by encouraging the activation of citizens in two different capacities: Indirectly, as principals of territorially elected agents and, directly, as functional agents.

Direct participation in secondary associations was seen by the New Left as a way of correcting the elitism inherent in electoral democracy (Cohen and Rogers 1978). According to the New Left, democracy entails not only equal participation of all citizens in self-government but also their empowerment to do so effectively. However, wary of the potential filters and distortions that may inhibit direct participation of all citizens through secondary associations, New Left thinkers set several conditions for genuinely democratic and open participation. First, they requested solid affirmative action on the part of the state to endow all citizens with the skills and the resources to participate. Second, they demanded that secondary associations themselves guarantee some of the basic principles of representation (for example, their leadership must be elected, regularly report to the membership, and be subjected to scrutiny and accountability). Third, they required that the contribution of secondary associations be not limited to putting pressure (through campaigns or electoral subsidies) on elected representatives so that they legislate in their favour, but requested a much more thorough and direct involvement of these associations in policy-making. Associations must propose ideas, debate issues, deliberate solutions, and help implement them — and take responsibility for the results. Fourth, secondary associations must be encompassing enough to make sure that they do not promote narrow (particular) interests, but, while necessarily balancing the interests of many members, they must articulate these interests as broad (potentially general) interests (Cohen and Rogers 1978).

Democratic experimentalism takes inspiration from associational democracy on a number of scores. It takes the same positive position about active citizen involvement in self-government bodies and shares the same positive appreciation of intermediate associations as means for active citizen participation and fulfilment of their civic potential. It also sets conditions on the format and operation of these secondary associations, requiring that they embody in their inner working those same democratic principles that should characterize the entire polity. Finally, its proponents are aware of the potential conflict between 'association and democracy' (Cohen and Rogers 1995, 69). Yet, in assessing the gravity of this problem, they also resolve to compare the potential pathologies of their associative scheme 'to alternative systems of governance as they are (among mass capitalist democracies) and not as an ideal that lies beyond the reach of human beings as they are and institutions as they can be' (ibid., 70).

Multi-Level Governance

Multi-level governance is the European answer to the risk of the EU being caught in 'joint-decision traps', a nifty term that exposes the problematic coexistence of territorial and functional representation while also projecting the typical stalemate that their coexistence creates in federal systems. The term was coined by Fritz Scharpf (1988) who, contrasting American and German federalism, likened the EU more to German cooperative federalism than to American competitive (or dual) federalism. The difference between the two lies in the degree of interdependency between the two levels of government, the federal and the state levels, which is much more pronounced in Germany than in the US. In order to decide and to implement legislation, the German federal government needs the assent and collaboration of the Länder to a much larger extent — this is Scharpf's (1988, 246) argument — than the US federal government does that of the states. Similarly, in the EU, supranational institutions — the Commission, the European Parliament, and the European Court of Justice — cannot rule alone, but need the assent and active collaboration of the member states in the Council and back at home. Indeed, the balance is so tipped in favour of the member states that it is they that decide how much room of manoeuvre supranational institutions have in deciding and enforcing EU legislation.

Moreover, in contrast to both US and German federalism, decisions in the Council are taken either by unanimity or by qualified majority voting, but even in this case consensus is normally striven for. This means that decisions in the EU are difficult to make and to unmake, so that the status quo is exceptionally sticky. Even if many member states were to conclude that a past policy decision has lost its *raison d'être* and should be changed, this would prove very hard indeed so that decisions, good and bad, tend to stay. Referring to German federalism, particularly after the 1969 Constitutional reform that accentuated its cooperative character (*Politikverflechtung*), Scharpf says that: 'In addition to being allegedly inefficient, inflexible and sometimes unnecessary, joint programmes are also often criticized for their undemocratic character, confronting parliaments with *faits accomplis* of bureaucratic negotiations between the two levels of government' (ibid., 249). This is the situation one would expect whenever two conditions apply: '(1) that central government decisions are directly dependent upon the agreement of the constituent governments, (2) that the agreement of the constituent governments must be unanimous or nearly unanimous' (ibid., 254). Under these circumstances, *'the territorial distribution of societal interests is emphasized at the expense of other dimensions of multi-dimensional interests'* (ibid., 254, my emphasis). Therefore, 'the policy output of joint decisions systems, when compared with unitary governments or the American model of federalism, will be less responsive to constituency interests and more oriented to the institutional self-interest of governments' (ibid., 254). What I take Scharpf to be saying is that, in joint-decision systems, the lumpy representation of territorial claims will have primacy over any other form of claim representation and, what's more, it is not even lumpy territorial claims that will be represented as the claims of *those institutions that were created to represent them*. In other words, it is the claims of the subnational *governments* (and of their institutional representatives) that get represented in the EU, and not so much those of their *constituencies*. Were this, in effect, the situation in the EU, it would lend credibility to the Commission's contention that it alone can represent the 'general will' of the EU citizenry.

In the American model of federalism, by contrast, the federal level and the states can independently make claims for their own constituencies and a compromise is normally found by reference to *the claims of the constituencies rather than at those of the institutional actors that represent them* (Fabbrini 2007). Moreover, in American federalism territorial and functional claims overlap to a much greater extent than they do in Europe, so that territorial-functional representational mixes are more easily attained (Sbragia 2007).

> I would argue that the conflict between territorial governments and functional politics lies at the heart of the politics of federalism in the United States. National institutions, Congress in particular, are organized by functional areas whereas the representation of subnational governments' interests involves the introduction of territorial criteria into that functionally dominated process... In the EU the functional takes a secondary role, when it comes to the importance of territorial governments. The dominance of executives allows territorially-based governments in Europe to represent their unitary interests as understood and defined by the executive. (Sbragia 2007, 12–13)

US Congress did not always work like that: Originally, Senators were elected by state legislatures, thus they were induced to represent the lumpy interests of the states rather than the divisible interests of their citizens. After a long period in which conflicts, stalemates and cases of bribery emerged in state legislatures, one state after another introduced the direct election of Senators. Finally, in 1912, the House proposed an amendment (the seventeenth) to the Constitution, which was approved and introduced in 1913, establishing that Senators would be directly elected by their state constituencies. The EU is not yet there: State representatives are members of state executives just as regional and local representatives are members of regional and local representatives, so they are obviously inclined to promote the lumpy interests (and institutional prerogatives) of their countries, regions and localities. If the EU is indeed becoming more similar to the US (Fabbrini 2007), then subnational authorities may well be fighting a rearguard battle against being demoted to the level of 'public' or 'governmental' interest group as happened in the US. But it is equally possible that the EU, perhaps because of its stronger statist tradition, may be preserving a particular role for territorial interests.

> As the influence of state and local leaders lessened, the influence of the federal government over state and local governments increasingly became treated as if they belonged to the private sector rather than to a privileged portion of the public sector. In fact, state and local officials are forced to lobby just as are other interests. Governments are represented by lobbyists rather than being integrated into national decision-making as they are in Brussels. State and local officials have organized what are known as governmental interest groups which represent governments rather than voters. These are known as 'public interest' lobbies and are viewed as being interested in who gets to implement federal policy to a greater extent than its outcomes. (Sbragia 2007, 14)

Yet, even in the absence in the EU of momentous institutional transformations such as those that took place in the US, already today pressure is exerted on state, regional and local representatives to represent the divisible claims of their constituencies rather than their lumpy claims. In fact, a less formalistic interpretation of multi-level governance (not surprisingly akin to democratic experimentalism) avoids the rigidity of joint-decision systems. In contrast to the 'tightly-coupled' nature of joint-decision systems, multi-level governance is 'loosely-coupled' (Benz 1998, 2000). 'We can expect European multi-level governance to evolve into a pattern consisting of separated, but loosely coupled, arenas. They are linked primarily by communication, and not by resource dependencies or control' (Benz and Eberlein 1999, 333). In a series of contributions, Arthur Benz argues that decisions in the EU are the outcome of 'an interlocking of European, national and subnational levels. Consequently, the transfer of powers to the EU should no longer be considered a zero-sum game' (Benz & Zimmer 2008, 17). This implies a new type of competence sharing among different levels and a new type of behaviour on the part of governmental actors.

> This approach on multi-level governance disaggregates states into actors involved in European politics... It sheds light on the dynamics of interdependent policy-making and the flexibility of structures in which supranational actors participate more as political entrepreneurs

than as holders of particular competences. In any case, the concept of multi-level governance challenges the assumption that any kind of vertical allocation of competences between levels can determine policy-making. (Benz and Zimmer 2008, 17)

This means that while the assent of all levels of governments is sought also in loosely-coupled multi-level systems in order to decide and implement policies, in these systems upper levels do not try to impose ready-made solutions onto the lower levels (which would trigger their reaction and their attempt to use their institutional powers in order to veto undesirable decisions), but only provide a legal framework and some resources that the lower levels can then ply to their particular needs. Lower levels of government will no longer threaten to veto decisions, but will use their power to better tailor the proposed legislation to the needs of their own constituency. In this way, *it is not the institutional interests of the representatives of the lower levels of government that are represented, but those of their constituencies*. Moreover, as also social partners and civil society organizations are necessarily invited to participate in decision-making — they, too, without veto power — and to implement policy decisions, both divisible and lumpy expressions of territorial and functional claims are represented within multi-level governance systems. Compromises may be fashioned by representatives of both territorial and functional claims because no one can derail the decision-making and implementation processes by withholding assent.

Conclusion: How Democratic are Representational Mixes?

We have seen that the coexistence of divisible and lumpy territorial and functional claims generates a series of questions. How can accommodation be found among lumpy claims? Does it matter if territorial and functional claims are represented, simultaneously, in a divisible and lumpy form? Which institutional arrangements can be devised to channel this variety of representational modes? And what types of political processes would ensue as a result? Finally, how democratic is the resulting representational mix? The democratic temper of the two 'solutions' outlined above to the problematic coexistence of territorial and functional representation is not easily assessed for two reasons.

First, neither mix fully meets the ideal standards of representation in liberal democracies nor does it correspond to whichever compromise is embodied in existing democracies (Lord 1998, 2001, 2004). Therefore, in comparison to both ideal standards and existing democracies, each representational mix is faulty. Second, when claims are represented as lumpy, *aggregation* becomes objectively more difficult. Many lumpy claims can perhaps reinforce each other in that they all get recognition of their lumpiness, but devising an institutional arrangement that satisfies them all is not simple. Therefore, lumpy claim-makers are presented with a choice: They may succeed in claiming veto power over decisions that infringe upon their lumpiness and accept the decision-making stalemate that will probably ensue or they accept that their functional and territorial claims be represented as divisible claims ready to be aggregated categorically and weighed against competing claims to yield effective solutions. The first type of option is linked to cooperative federal systems and has the tendency to produce joint-decision traps. The second type of option gives rise to multi-level governance arrangements that may work only insofar as representatives of lumpy claims — be they functional or territorial — engage mostly in lobbying and arguing, rather than in bargaining and vetoing. When interests are represented as divisible, aggregation and compromises become possible: The force of numbers becomes available, but the force of identity is lost. While this is not so problematic for functional interests in an age of declining class identities, it may still be a problem in an age of still lively territorial identities.

This is the predicament in which, it seems to me, territorial claims find themselves today in the European Union. While it would seem unlikely, at this point, for functional interests to propose a lumpy, neo-corporatist form of representation (Schmitter and Grote 1997), it appears still possible for territorial interests to do so. Both national and subnational territorial claims are today virtually or actually represented at EU level both in their lumpy and in their divisible forms. National interests are represented in a lumpy fashion in the Council of the European Union and in the European Council (and by the permanent representations that assist them). In the Council, national communities speak through their governmental representatives projecting first and foremost their national lumpy claims (but even more the claims of governmental representatives). In the European Parliament, territorial interests give increasingly way to partisan alignments so that, in that context, national territorial claims may be recombined in innovative ways by the powerful aggregative forces of parties and ideologies (Hix 2008).

Subnational territorial claims are in a different situation. Their institutional representation in the Committee of the Regions is a weird mix of both modes of representation. Because the members of the Committee are elected representatives of subnational territorial jurisdictions (or are politically responsible before elected assemblies), they are the expression of territorial aggregations of divisible claims at various levels. However, because CoR members represent subnational territorial jurisdictions in their entirety, and not just the voters who elected them, they may also represent their territories in a lumpy manner. CoR members are, therefore, caught in a contradictory role: They are both institutional representatives of territories, therefore tempted to supply a lumpy representation of territorial claims, and they are also political representatives of divisible claims, therefore capable of further aggregating these claims across territorial borders. Caught between a divisible and a lumpy mode of territorial representation, they are pressured into representing regional claims 'as if' they were categorical claims by the Commission that would be unable to deal with another set of lumpy claims (in addition to the national ones).

To conclude, the democratic temper of *democratic experimentalism* lies in its prompting 'new forms of dynamic accountability and peer review which discipline the state and protect the rights of the citizens without freezing the institutions of decision-making' (Sabel and Zeitlin 2007, 9). It is the combination of extremely open, transparent and receptive forms of functional representation, that go well beyond inclusion of the usual suspects (employers' and workers' associations, agricultural, industrial and commercial associations, individual corporations) to include sub-national authorities and civil society organizations and the periodic review of these deliberative exercises by territorially representative chambers that should secure the simultaneous representation of both types of claims. Territorially elected assemblies, in other words, function as judges and 'repositories' of good deliberative practices.

The democratic temper of *multi-level governance*, in turn, lies in recognizing the existence of lumpy claims and yet in channelling them in such a way that they cannot ensnare legislation in joint-decision traps but only contribute to making it more suitable for their own constituencies. This presupposes transforming lumpy claims into categorical — aggregations of divisible — claims and, therefore, imposing to the representatives of these claims a dual representative mode — a sort of hat-switching — that can at times be taxing and confusing: While at EU level they have to perform as any other categorical representative, back at home they are charged with responsibility for the effective representation of the lumpy claims of their territories. In exchange for recognition of subnational territorial claims subnational representatives give up lumpy representation: Their representation may occur categorically, as aggregation of divisible claims, and the balance between territorial and functional claims must be sought through deliberation.

Notes

1. I here use 'lumpy' to mean collective, indivisible claims that can be made only by collective actors on the basis of a shared identity and that cannot, therefore, be parcelled out and 'divisible' to mean claims that, although made by individual actors, can be aggregated and presented as 'categorical', but whose aggregation does not give rise to any collective identity.
2. For an opposite view based on an analysis of German federalism, see Scharpf (1988).
3. The Commission has requested the creation of (at least) administrative regions also in the recent enlargement countries, only to then retrench somewhat from fully involving them, given the difficulty of handing over to them the management of the Structural Funds (see Hughes, Sasse, and Gordon 2003).
4. This definition, taken from Wikipedia, summarizes effectively the essence of Gestalt theory: 'Gestalt psychology (German: *Gestalt* — 'essence or shape of an entity's complete form') of the Berlin School is a theory of mind and brain positing that the operational principle of the brain is holistic, parallel, and analog, with self-organizing tendencies. The Gestalt effect is the form-generating capability of our senses, particularly with respect to the visual recognition of figures and whole forms instead of just a collection of simple lines and curves... Gestalt psychologists find it is important to think of problems as a whole'. Source: http://en.wikipedia.org/wiki/Gestalt_psychology (accessed 17 March 2011).

References

Abromeit, H. 1998. *Democracy in Europe. Legitimising politics in a non-state polity*. New York: Berghahn Books.
Andersen, S.S., and T.R. Burns. 1996. The European Union and the erosion of parliamentary democracy: a study in post-parliamentary governance. In *The European Union: how democratic is it?*, eds. S.S. Andersen and K.A. Eliassen, 227–67. London: Sage.

Beetham, D., and C. Lord. 1998. *Legitimacy and the European Union*. London: Longman.
Benz, A. 1998. From cooperative federalism to multi-level governance: German and EU regional policy. *Regional and Federal Studies* 10, no. 3: 505–22.
Benz, A. 2000. Two types of multi-level governance: intergovernmental relations in German and EU regional policy. *Regional and Federal Studies* 10, no. 3: 21–44.
Benz, A., and B. Eberlein. 1999. The Europeanization of regional policies: patterns of multi-level governance. *Journal of European Public Policy* 6, no. 2: 329–48.
Benz, A., C. Harlow, and Y. Papadopoulos. 2007. *European Law Journal*, special issue, 13, no. 4.
Benz, A., and C. Zimmer. 2008. The EU's competences: the 'vertical' perspective on the multilayered system. *Living Review on European Governance* 3, no. 3, http://www.livingreviews.org/lreg-2008-3 (accessed 10 September 2010).
Burgess, M. 2006. *Comparative federalism: theory and practice*. New York: Routledge.
Caramani, D. 2004. *The nationalization of politics. The formation of national electorates and party systems in western Europe*. Cambridge: Cambridge University Press.
Cohen, J., and J. Rogers. 1995. *Associations and democracy*. London: Verso.
Cohen, J., and C. Sabel. 1997. Directly-deliberative polyarchy. *European Law Journal*. 3, no. 4: 313–342.
Commission of the European Communities (2001). European Governance. A White Paper. Brussels, COM(2001) 428 final. http://eur-lex.europa.eu/LexUriServ/site/en/com/2001/com2001_0428en01.pdf. (accessed 28 July 2011).
Committee of the Regions. 2009. *The Committee of the Regions' White Paper on multi-level governance*, CdR 89/2009 fin FR/EXT/RS/GW/ym/ms, http://www.cor.europa.eu/pages/EventTemplate.aspx. (accessed 10 September 2010).
Duverger, M. 1951. *Les partis politiques*. Paris: Colin.
Eberlein, B., and D. Kewrer. 2004. New governance in the European Union: a theoretical perspective. *Journal of Common Market Studies*. 42, no. 1: 121–42.
Elazar, D. 1995. From statism to federalism: a paradigm shift. *Publius: The Journal of Federalism*. 25, no. 2: 5–18.
Elazar, D. 2001. The United States and the European Union: models of their epochs. In *The federal vision. Legitimacy and levels of governance in the United States and the European Union*, eds. K. Nicolaidis and R. Howse, 1–53. Oxford: Oxford University Press.
EUSA Review Forum 2001. The Commission White Paper and European governance. *EUSA Review* 14, no. 4: 1–8.
Fabbrini, S. 2007. *Compound Democracies. Why the United States and Europe Are Becoming Similar*. Oxford: Oxford University Press.
Gerstenberg, O., and C.F. Sabel. 2002. Directly-deliberative polyarchy: an institutional ideal for Europe? In *Good governance in Europe's integrated market*, eds. C. Joerges and R. Dehousse, 289–341. Oxford: Oxford University Press.
Hix, S. 2008. *What's wrong with the European Union and how to fix it*. Cambridge: Polity Press.
Hooghe, L., and G. Marks. 2001. *Multi-level governance and European integration*. Lanham, MD: Rowman & Littlefield.
Hughes, J., G. Sasse, and C. Gordon. 2003. EU enlargement and power asymmetries: conditionality and the Commission's role in regionalization in Central and Eastern European. Working Paper 49/03, http://www.one-europe.ac.uk. (accessed 10 September 2010).
Jachtenfuchs, M. 1995. Theoretical perspectives on European governance. *European Law Review* 1, no. 2: 115–33.
Katzenstein, P. 1985. *Small states in world markets. Industrial policy in Europe*. Ithaca, NY: Cornell University Press.
Kohler-Koch, B., and B. Rittberger. 2007. *Debating the democratic legitimacy of the European Union*. Lanham, MD: Rowman and Littlefield.
Lehmbruch, G., and P. Schmitter. 1982. *Patterns of corporatist policymaking*. London: Sage.
Leibfried, S., and M. Zürn. 2005. *Transformations of the state?*. Cambridge: Cambridge University Press.
Lord, C. 1998. *Democracy in the European Union*. Sheffield: Sheffield University Press.
Lord, C. 2001. Assessing democracy in a contested polity. *Journal of Common Market Studies* 39, no. 4: 641–61.
Lord, C. 2004. *A democratic audit of the European Union*. London: Palgrave-Macmillan.

Lord, C., and J. Pollak. 2010. The EU's many representative modes: colliding? cohering? *Journal of European Public Policy* 17, no. 1: 117–36. Accessed 10 September 2010.

Mavrogordatos, G.T. 1996. Duverger and the Jacobins. *European Journal of Political Research* 30, no. 1: 1–17.

Michels, R. 1949. *Political parties. A sociological inquiry of the oligarchical tendencies of modern democracies*. Glencoe, IL: Free Press.

Offe, C. 1981. The attribution of public status to interest groups: observations on the West German case. In *Organizing interests in western Europe*, ed. S. Berger, 123–58. Cambridge: Cambridge University Press.

Piattoni, S. 2010. *The theory of multi-level governance: conceptual, empirical and normative challenges*. Oxford: Oxford University Press.

Piattoni, S. In press. The committee of the regions and the upgrading of subnational territorial representation. In *Democracy and representation in the EU*, ed. S. Kröger and D. Friedrich,. Houndmills, Basingstoke: Palgrave-Macmillan.

Pitkin, H. 1967. *The concept of representation*. Berkeley, CA: University of California Press.

Poggi, G. 1978. *The development of the modern state. A sociological introduction*. Stanford, CA: Stanford University Press.

Pollak, J. 2007. Contested meanings of representation. *Comparative European Politics* 5, 87–103.

Rokkan, S. 1966. Norway: numerical democracy and corporate pluralism. In *Political opposition in western democracies*, ed. R. Dahl. New Haven: Yale University Press. pp. 70–115.

Sabel, C., and J. Zeitlin. 2007. Learning from difference: the new architecture of experimentalist governance in the European Union. European Governance Papers (EUROGOV), No. C-07-02, http://www.connex-network.org/eurogov/pdf/egp-connex-C-07-02.pdf. (accessed 10 September 2010).

Sabel, C., and J. Zeitlin. 2010. *Experimentalist governance in the European Union. Towards a new architecture*. Oxford: Oxford University Press.

Sbragia, A. 2007. Intergovernmental relations or multi-level governance? Transatlantic comparisons and reflections, paper prepared for delivery at the EGPA's Annual Conference on Public Administration and the Management of Diversity, Madrid, Spain, September 19–22.

Scharpf, F. 1988. The joint-decision trap: lessons from German federalism and European integration. *Public Administration* 66, 239–8.

Scharpf, F.W. 1999. *Governing in Europe: effective and democratic?* Oxford: Oxford University Press.

Scharpf, F. 2009. Legitimacy in the multilevel European polity. *European Political Science Review*. 1, no. 2: 173–204.

Schmidt, V. 2006. *Democracy in Europe. The EU and national polities*. Cambridge: Cambridge University Press.

Schmitter, P. 1981. Interest intermediation and regime governability in contemporary Western Europe and North America. In *Organizing interests in Western Europe*, ed. S. Berger, 287–330. Cambridge: Cambridge University Press.

Schmitter, P. 2000. *How to democratize the European Union... and why bother*. Lanhman, MD: Rowman and Littlefield.

Schmitter, P., and G. Lehmbruch. 1979. *Trends toward corporatist intermediation*. London: Sage.

Schmitter, P., and J. Grote. 1997. *The corporatist Sisyphus: past, present and future*. EUI Working Papers SPS No. 97/4.

Smismans, S. 2004. *Law, legitimacy and European governance. Functional participation in social regulation*. Oxford: Oxford University Press.

Collaboration and Consultation: Functional Representation in EU Stakeholder Dialogues

HOLLY JARMAN

SUNY Albany, Rockefeller College of Public Affairs and Policy, Albany, USA

ABSTRACT   In the past decade, the EU has experimented with various types of consultation mechanisms intended to address perceived deficits in policy knowledge and decision-making legitimacy within the European system. I examine attempts by the European Commission to build up its decision-making legitimacy and inform policy via various formal mechanisms, focusing on the extent to which the relationship between the Commission and its civil society groups is collaborative or consultative. In particular, I examine two such experiments: The DG Trade Civil Society Dialogue (CSD) and the DG SANCO platform on Diet, Physical Activity and Health. DG Trade, a strong and relatively autonomous DG, developed a consultative model of engagement, gaining legitimation by consulting with advocacy groups. DG SANCO, working in areas where the EU competencies are weak, adopts a collaborative model in which it can set the agenda and structure debates but fundamentally depends on industry association partners, rather than its own legal powers, to achieve its goals.

The EU's democratic deficit and inter-agency power struggles have resulted in multiple attempts to legitimate policy through new modes of governance. This article examines two of these experiments within the European Commission: DG Trade's Civil Society Dialogue and DG SANCO's Platform on Diet, Physical Activity, and Health. Both attempt to bring disparate groups face-to-face to share potential solutions to common problems: To create functional representation mechanisms which incorporate many different types of interest group. There are broad membership criteria in each case. Both for-profit and non-profit groups can join and government representatives sit alongside advocacy groups and industry associations. Through these mechanisms and others, officials are creating a very different pattern of interest group activity in Europe, based on diverse functional representation and specialist knowledge (Sanchez-Salgado and Woll 2007; Kohler-Koch 2010).

I use these two case studies to develop some general hypotheses about the nature and effectiveness of these types of mechanisms. First, I suggest that these mechanisms are more likely to be created when authority over a policy area is contested and the lines between the Commission's and member states' mandates for action are blurred. In both trade policy and public health, the contemporary policy agenda causes problems for traditional policy-making as it is filled with problems that cut across issue boundaries and treaty bases, straddle the private and public spheres, and stray dangerously into member state territory. I relate the specific dialogues in this study to the Commission's governance agenda and the range of mechanisms created to navigate these authority contests.

Second, I explain how these mechanisms might be classified. I argue that the Commission has opted for formal mechanisms over informal mechanisms for two reasons: To legitimate policy decisions, and to inform policy. In doing so, I draw a distinction between two core concepts: Consultation and collaboration. Consultation is based upon the exchange of information, both facts and opinions. Interest groups are consulted for their views on a topic, seen as representing an important group of actors and/or possessing important specialist knowledge. What consultation does not imply, however, is any guarantee that these views or information will be acted upon. Collaboration denotes a slightly different policy process in which officials and interest groups share responsibility for policy outputs. Collaborative dialogues rely on actors outside the EU institutions to do some or much of the work. This classification could allow us to talk about a diverse variety of mechanisms without focussing on just those which are intergovernmental or in one particular policy area.

Third, I discuss the strategies adopted by different types of interest group across the two cases. In the case of the Civil Society Dialogue, which I class as consultative, I find that there are pressures for different types of interest groups to behave in a similar way. Both industry associations and advocacy groups adopt knowledge-based strategies: Providing high quality information is a valuable lobbying strategy in a mechanism where officials alone control policy outcomes. In contrast, the Platform, a collaborative mechanism, creates considerable inter-group pressure to improve policy outcomes. These findings suggest that the structure of a dialogue mechanism can have important effects on group strategies and illuminate a divide between group types which could form the basis for future research.

The data for this study is drawn from a series of interviews with interest groups and policy-makers at the European level, supplemented by EU policy documents and a literature review. The cases were chosen from among the many and varied governance mechanisms the EU employs because they both incorporate different types of interest group within a single mechanism. The number of active players is roughly the same in each case, a mixture of corporate and non-profit entities, and the relevant DGs finance participating interest groups at a similar level.

There are some important limitations to this study. First, it examines two formal, transparent mechanisms. Less formal dialogues have existed in Europe for a long time and will continue to exist. These include meetings between government ministers and between officials and lobbyists. Second, this study does not focus on intergovernmental interactions in the EU, but on the policies and politics surrounding the Commission. I am not claiming that what goes on in the Commission is somehow more important than member state politics, or that the Commission is the most powerful actor in either of these policy areas. Finally, the EU lobbying literature is notoriously fragmented and conceptually fuzzy (see Beyers, Eising, and Maloney 2008, and the rest of that issue, Dür 2008). There is little that can be done to fix that in a few thousand words, but this paper does offer a study of two of the newer forms of 'experimentalist' policy mechanisms (Sabel and Zeitlin 2010; Piattoni 2011, 369–84), and thus contributes to the ongoing debate on this question throughout this special issue.

In the following sections I place these types of dialogue mechanism within the context of the Commission's wider governance agenda and the relevant academic literature on new forms of governance, provide the details for the two case studies, and conclude with a discussion of my findings and avenues for future research.

Contesting Authority: Governance in Hard to Reach Places

Although trade policy has been a Commission competency since the Treaty of Rome, in practice, authority is divided between the Commission and the member states, with the details of this addressed extensively in the academic literature (for example Meunier and Nicolaidis 2000). While the Commission has considerable agenda setting power in well established areas such as trade in goods, and negotiates the EU's trade agreements within the WTO and with other trading partners, in newer areas such as trade in services and intellectual property, or cross-cutting issues such as trade and the environment or trade and social policy, the division of authority is not quite as clear. Formally, European Court of Justice (ECJ) jurisprudence has allowed member states to take a greater role in formulating policy in new areas (Eeckhout 2004), while informally, the economic interests of some of the largest member states at times provoke fierce debate over the Commission's role and threats by those states to derail negotiations. The Commission's actions are also limited by other WTO members, many of whom are highly suspicious of any efforts to focus on the social or environmental impacts of trade.

While the Commission's role in trade policy-making is substantial but contested, its role in health policy is weaker and even more controversial. There is no single treaty base which justifies health policy at the EU level. Although health policy coordination has taken place for many years between ministers in informal settings, and the EU has long made policies with public health effects, the creation of distinct 'health policy' is largely the result of a string of actions by the ECJ (Martinsen 2005; Greer 2006). In upholding the rights of individuals to consume services in EU member states other than their own, the ECJ created a huge push towards a common EU health market which left Commission officials scrambling to define a policy response. Overall, due to a lack of a clear basis in EU treaties, the series of ECJ cases, and the competing interpretations which have been placed upon them, EU health policy remains poorly defined (Mossialos et al. 2010; Lamping & Steffen 2009).

Legitimacy Through Transparency

Contested authority and questionable legitimacy arguably led to the proliferation of consultation forums such as the CSD and the Platform. In its 2001 White Paper on Governance, the Commission pledged to consult more extensively with other actors in return for 'more guarantees of the openness and representativity of the organisations consulted', and also to employ a wider range of policy tools, including 'co-regulatory mechanisms' which share responsibility for policy outputs with outside interest groups (European Commission 2001; Wincott 2002; Armstrong 2002). These two pledges, legitimation through transparency (informing a range of interest groups and the public about policy decisions) and gathering information from a range of groups to inform policy are central to the types of forum the Commission has decided to create.

The white paper and subsequent practice suggest that new governance does not just emerge as a way to bring the EU into new areas, but also exists as part of policy-making in established competencies. The first reason is that they increase transparency and therefore procedural legitimacy. There are many good reasons for making policy debates public and transparent, and many of them have a normative element: Transparent policy-making promotes accountability among policy-makers, for example (Coen 2007). The Commission was still emerging from a period of turmoil following allegations of fraud and poor accountability among officials that contributed to the resignation of the Santer Commission en masse (Greenwood 2007, 352). But the mechanisms since adopted by the Commission also have implications for interest groups. A public, formal mechanism shines a light on all of the parties involved, meaning that these mechanisms can be used by officials who want to bring pressure to bear on specific groups of lobbyists or member states, just as they can be used by outside groups to keep an eye on the Commission. A public record of consultations and the associated debates is a very helpful bargaining tool, whether the Commission's negotiating partners are member state officials, commercial interests, or other countries.

Second, formal mechanisms aggregate opinions while representing large parts of society. Creating a forum creates a focal point for interest groups to focus at least some of their lobbying efforts. This can help to create a critical mass of interested groups around a particular issue, something that may be very useful to officials who want to place an issue firmly on the EU's agenda, or raise its profile. The distinct element of the current mechanisms is their diverse membership. Rather than a corporatist style system where government representatives form close relationships with a specific kind of group, for example trade unions, membership criteria are left open, bringing a much wider range of interested parties into contact with officials — and each other. This multi-stakeholder approach can be important where policies affect a range of diverse sectors or interest groups: Participants can provide specialist knowledge over a wide range of issues and hopefully form a broad consensus for future policy action. It is to some extent a means for channelling and managing opposition to Commission positions.

Consultation and Collaboration: Comparing Interest Group Strategies

The relationship between the Commission and lobbyists is often described in the academic literature as a series of transactions between groups and policy-makers (Bouwen 2009, 22–3; Bouwen 2002; Broscheid and Coen 2003). Interest groups benefit from accessing decision-makers, while policy-makers gain legitimacy, and both groups exchange valuable information. But this exchange is not necessarily an equal transaction. Those in authority have the ability to alter their relationship with interest groups based upon their normative preferences (Knodt 2005). In this case, the Commission often has the ability to shape the terms of the deal — in other words, policy-makers can construct a forum which gives them what they want, by defining the terms of membership, determining the degree of transparency, or by funding certain types of groups to balance out the degree of access between corporations and NGOs. The degree of authority has an effect on the way in which policy-makers construct interest representation. Although the Commission almost always needs information and expert input to make policy, its need for legitimation is variable. The extent of its need for legitimation allows us to distinguish between the different kinds of mechanisms it creates in its forums.

Where Commission authority is strong, it does not require as much 'back up' from other actors.[1] We might expect the resulting mechanism to be more *consultative*, focussing on the exchange of useful information, with lobbyists competing to supply information to the powerful Commission. The term consultation implies this exchange of information. In practice, stakeholder consultation is often more about information exchange than legitimation because the Commission needs less legitimation from interest groups, but can use their information. Consulting a group does not necessarily mean that officials must pay attention to what it says and alter their decision-making accordingly. The CSD, I will argue, is a primarily a consultation mechanism.

Where policy-makers' authority is relatively weak, we might expect a more *collaborative* mechanism to result. In a collaboration, responsibility for policy outputs and outcomes is shared between officials and outside interest groups through a form of peer review. Collaboration develops when the Commission needs legitimation from outside groups as well as information in order to act. Perhaps the Commission is sharing its authority more extensively with member states, or perhaps the basis for supranational policy is not particularly clear. The Platform, I will argue, is a collaborative mechanism. The Commission is creating a 'supporting coalition' (Greer 2009a), agenda-setting to create a policy community in an area where it does not really have much power and cannot act legitimately alone. The public 'evidence base' that the Platform creates can be used to legitimate further Commission action. Although the platform contains elements of self-regulation by design, it is distinct in that compliance is assured through peer pressure and collective monitoring of progress towards goals — elements of policy which might seem more familiar from the Open Method of Coordination.

Conceptualizing forums in this manner speaks to, but does not sit neatly within, existing debates about the pluralist or corporatist nature of interest group politics in the EU (see Eising 2008, for a detailed discussion). The justifications given by the Commission for creating consultation mechanisms fit most closely with pluralist assumptions about the nature of interest group politics. Consultation mechanisms create avenues for lobbying activity and group competition, if only for those actors (such as umbrella organizations and member state governments) that already hold prominent positions within the EU political system (Quittkat and Kotzian 2011, 401–18). Nor is collaboration entirely synonymous with corporatist mechanisms in which public power to implement policy is delegated to private actors in a formal way — there is little power to entrust. But it does resemble corporatism in that it organizes private interests to work towards collectively-agreed goals which are purportedly in the public interest. In many ways, these mechanisms tell us more about the Commission, its governance agenda, and its power than they do about interest group influence.

Within the institutional frameworks that the Commission constructs based on its level of authority, interest groups adopt some combination of a 'representation' or 'information' strategy: Either aiming to represent the views and interests of a particular group, or providing evidence and expertise that can inform policy. We might expect that group strategies would vary strongly based on the type of group in question, i.e., that non-profit advocacy organisations would behave very differently to groups representing businesses. In the case of the CSD, the Commission's authority to set the trade policy agenda is relatively strong compared to the other issues Commissioners deal with. Interest groups that regarded themselves as successful lobbyists, regardless of type, reported using information-based strategies. In the Platform, the Commission's policy authority is much weaker, and so the forum is designed to give groups a much more active role. Here there is a much greater split between types of group: European level umbrella organisations representing large corporations focus on reporting their members' commitments. Public health advocacy groups in the platform, while also required to make commitments, focus on a watchdog role.

In light of these case studies, I suggest that the most important difference lies not in variations between groups *per se*, but in policy-makers' degree of authority. When officials have a lot of control over policy decisions, there are only so many strategies that make sense to interest groups wanting to seek access — there are only so many things that officials need groups to do. When officials have to rely on groups themselves to be responsible for policy outputs and outcomes, it seems reasonable that a wider range of plausible group strategies would exist.

The following sections compare and contrast the CSD and the Platform, before conclusions are drawn from this study about their effectiveness and future avenues for research.

The DG Trade Civil Society Dialogue (CSD)

The DG External Trade Civil Society Dialogue was launched in 1999. On paper, it aims to 'develop a confident working relationship between all interested stakeholders in the trade policy field and to ensure that all contributions to EU trade policy can be heard' (DG Trade 2005a) in the context of developing 'responsive policy' (DG Trade 2005b). In practice, the European Commission has two goals in maintaining the dialogue. Lacking an electoral mandate, the Commission aims to increase its legitimacy by involving outside groups in the decision-making process. Officials also hope to improve the quality of trade policy by making use of the expert knowledge that groups can provide (interview, Commission official, Brussels, 2006).

In terms of enhancing legitimacy through transparency, the definition of civil society within the CSD is certainly broad, including 'social, development and environmental non-governmental organisations (NGOs), research institutes, trade unions, chambers of commerce, business, consumer and professional associations', religious groups and community organisations. Neither are the criteria for participating particularly stringent. Participants are 'non-profit-making representative organisations' based in the EU or with an office in the EU (DG Trade 2005a), including commercial actors such as industry associations, but not single firms. At the end of 2009, there were 889 organisations registered in the CSD database, including business associations, development organisations, consumer and public health organisations, organisations promoting environmental protection, trade unions, representatives of local and regional governments, animal welfare groups, and women's organisations. However, the number of active participants in the CSD has been historically much smaller. The 2009 Annual Report singles out 38 organisations as participating actively in various dialogue activities, representing a cross-section of functional categories (DG Trade 2009a).

There have been successive attempts to make the Commission's actions within the dialogue more transparent: To clarify goals, provide more basic information online, and classify CSD members. The casual browser on DG Trade's web site can access a broad range of information: Minutes, a membership database, copies of ministers' statements, and statistics on attendance.

But trade is not a naturally transparent policy area, and despite increased procedural transparency, the details of negotiations are politically and economically sensitive and often remain secret. There has been some contention among CSD members over whether they have the right to access information on negotiations (with business associations in particular keen for clarification), as opposed to the privilege. In many cases, the formal and transparent nature of the CSD has served to illuminate the breadth of the trade policy debate and the diversity of opinions it contains, but it has not always illuminated Commission motivations or bargaining positions.

Nor is transparency necessarily strong on the interest group side. From October 2008, new organisations registering with the CSD were also required to participate in the European Transparency Initiative (ETI) register. By 3 March 2010, 263 organisations had included their ETI number in the CSD database (DG Trade 2010), a number far lower than the total number of organisations.

The quality of substantive debate in the CSD is also questioned by some participants, with groups asking for extended discussions after briefings, or more extensive treatment of feedback from groups (Knodt 2005; Slob and Smakman 2006). Of course, the trade-off in a more formal process is that greater transparency and public accountability for all parties increases bureaucratic requirements. Counting meetings, participants, grants, and so on does not really tell us much about the extent or quality of debate. There is a danger that the consultative process could be reduced to tick-box legitimacy: 'The ability of DG Trade to articulate that it has held how ever many meetings with how ever many stakeholders and that it paid for how ever many of them to travel from outside Brussels' (Fazi and Smith 2006, 69). In a two-day conference convened in part to discuss ways to improve the dialogue, some groups 'questioned the actual impact that civil society organisations had through their participation in the Dialogue, and, from this perspective, they identified a gap between trade associations and NGOs' (DG Trade 2009b). This is typical of the accountability and transparency debate that has characterised the dialogue in recent years. Those groups that are willing to trade on their expertise in specialist areas of trade policy have formed closer and more successful relationships with the Commission (Jarman 2008).

In terms of making better policy, there are certain areas in which the CSD seems likely to have had an effect. Pressure for EU action to increase the availability of generic medicines in developing countries to tackle diseases such as HIV/AIDS, referenced at the start of this section in the quote by Pascal Lamy, is often mentioned by participants as a success, as is the Everything But Arms policy that allows duty-free access to imports from least-developed countries and the introduction of Sustainability Impact Assessments (SIAs) as a tool to assess the environmental and social impacts of trade agreements. However, quantifying the degree to which these policies have been influenced by the dialogue more broadly, rather than its most mobilised members, is very difficult. The European Parliament also has a more important role to play in setting the agenda on these issues than it in other aspects of trade policy (see, for example, the European Parliament resolution on access to medicines, 2007).

But here, the CSD reaches its limits. One of the biggest challenges for the dialogue has been that some groups are much more used to criticising policies — holding officials to account — than they are at offering innovative solutions (Bizzarri and Iossa 2007, 3). Commission officials have noted in meetings that there are some elements of the CSD that advocacy groups pushed for where their participation has not lived up to expectations, taking part in the impact assessment of trade agreements, for example (DG Trade 2009b).

The broad membership of the CSD presents a perfect opportunity to test for the presence of a 'professional European lobbying class' (introduction, this issue). While we might reasonably assume that advocacy groups and industry associations would adopt very different strategies within the dialogue, this has not necessarily been the case. The groups interviewed that reported the most success in gaining access to DG trade officials and related privileged information were those who talked about their research and its utility as a lobbying tool. They talked about policy solutions as much or more than they talked about issue advocacy, valuing expertise in a particular subject area as a key part of their lobbying strategy. Surprisingly, this group of actors was not dominated by commercial interests and included a number of prominent advocacy organisations working on environment, development and public health issues related to trade (Jarman 2008).

This is the result of two problems at the core of the CSD. It attempts to address both representation and information goals simultaneously, and ultimate authority for policy lies solely with the Commission and the member states, not outside groups. The least influential groups may choose not to offer policy solutions either because they feel they will be ignored, or because a growing emphasis on bilateral and regional agreements rather than the multilateral Doha round means that the problems in trade policy are less clear and motivation to tackle them is lower. It is in these two regards that the CSD differs markedly from the Platform.

The DG SANCO Platform for Action on Diet, Physical Activity and Health

The first clue as to the purpose of the Platform for Action on Diet, Physical Activity and Health is in the name. A platform is stable by nature, a solid place to stand while building upwards towards loftier policy goals. In constructing a platform around various disparate interest groups (many of whom should by rights be bitter enemies) DG SANCO is building a coalition of support for future policies in an area in which its own authority is comparatively weak.

The Platform was established by DG SANCO's Director-General Robert Madelin soon after his arrival in 2004. At that time, Madelin had just moved from DG Trade, where he played an important role in shaping the CSD under Commissioner Pascal Lamy. The Platform is just one of a number of governance mechanisms that EU health officials use (see Mossialos et al. 2010; Steffen 2005; Lamping and Steffen 2009; Greer 2009b), including the High Level Group, Open Method of Coordination, European Reference Networks on Rare Diseases, the Public Health Programme, networks addressing the Blood Directive and cancer treatment, and the European Alcohol and Health Forum, a mechanism replicating the Platform's structure. It was intended from the outset as not just a venue for discussion, but also as a 'catalyst for action'. Its members would present 'plans to contribute concretely to the pursuit of healthy nutrition, physical activity and the fight against obesity', discuss those plans, and report on policy outcomes so that 'over time better evidence is assembled of what works, and Best Practice more clearly defined' (DG SANCO 2005).

The membership criteria for the Platform are wide, and members represent almost every group which has an interest in tackling obesity, including health departments, public health advocacy groups, the food industry and a several organisations with a focus on activity and exercise. This diverse membership is not typical among EU health governance mechanisms. The choice to become part of the Platform 'appears idiosyncratic, and is usually made by groups with no other involvement in [EU] health forums' (Greer, da Fonseca, and Adolph 2008). As in trade policy, the focus of the forum on a cross-cutting issue contributes to its diverse membership. Unlike the CSD, members are all organisations at the European level. National, regional and local groups can only be represented by umbrella organisations, a decision made to 'keep the Platform at a manageable size' (DG SANCO 2009).

As with the CSD, the number of active groups is lower than the total membership. As of 2009, there were 32 active members out of a total of 56. Unlike the CSD, however, inactive members can leave, or be removed. Some organisations have voluntarily withdrawn their membership, citing an inability to meet their commitments. If organisations make commitments that they consistently fail to fulfil, there is a chance that their membership will be suspended (EUFIC 2009; DG SANCO 2009).

The Platform includes representatives from other organisations with 'observer' status, for example from the World Health Organisation, the EU Presidency, Member States, European Food Safety Authority, and European Parliament. Member state involvement is uneven: The UK Food Standards Agency is active in the Platform and has made a number of commitments (DG SANCO 2010), agencies such as the Spanish Food Safety Agency and the French Ministry of Agriculture and Fishing have participated in meetings but not made commitments, and some member states are absent (DG SANCO 2007, 2008, 2009).

An important element of the Platform is that groups are held responsible for policy outcomes. Participants meet approximately four or five times per year to discuss their problems and proposed solutions. They are encouraged to make public 'commitments' to tackle obesity and improve diet or physical activity, to carry out those plans, and review their own performance. The Commission facilitates this process, but it does not drive it. The Commission engages outside contractors to produce regular monitoring reports which evaluate the quality of participants' monitoring. Here again, the interest groups are in the drivers: Participants are part of a formal mechanism which allows them 'to demonstrate their impact to others and learn from their own practices' (Hallsworth and Ling 2007).

At the time of writing, members had made approximately 200 commitments on a range of activities as diverse as improving food labelling, the reformulation of food products, modifying portion sizes, limiting food advertising to children, education on nutrition and physical activity, changing food consumption patterns, implementing lifestyle programmes in the workplace, promoting participation in sports and conducting research (see Hallsworth and Ling 2008). These commitments are not 'binding' in the strictest sense, but they are public, as are members' evaluations of their own progress and the secondary monitoring reports. Members cannot fail in the Platform by falling short of their stated goals, but can fail if they do not adequately report their progress (EUFIC 2009). Those participants who are found wanting are encouraged to seek 'mentoring' assistance from the Commission in improving their monitoring and achievement of commitments.

Another important feature of the Platform is the relationship between for-profit and non-profit groups. As in the CSD, these groups are still somewhat divided. European level umbrella organisations representing large corporations focus on reporting their members' commitments, treating the Platform largely as a forum for information exchange. Public health advocacy groups in the platform, while also required to make commitments, focus on a watchdog role.

Advocacy groups in the Platform have mobilised to keep pressure on its commercial members. Public health advocates come together to hold pre-meetings and share talking points which critique industry action and inaction[2]. The Platform is a friendly forum for public health groups that fulfils many of the same information functions that the CSD does for its respective advocacy groups. One piece of evidence for this watchdog strategy comes from an independent evaluation of the Platform's effectiveness in July 2010. The majority of commitments made by non-profit groups in the Platform to date are related to policy and advocacy, and extensions of, or public statements relating to, their existing core activities. Profit-making members, by contrast, make more commitments and more easily-measurable commitments (Evaluation Partnership 2010, 48–9).

For representatives of the food, retail, catering and advertising industries, participating in the Platform 'hedges their bets. It publicises and gains official standing for strategies they probably would have adopted anyway on grounds of corporate social responsibility and political self-defence' (Greer 2009b). Well-known companies that have made commitments to the Platform through their respective umbrella groups include PepsiCo, Kraft, Danone, Nestle, Mars, Cadbury, Unilever, Kellogg, and Carrefour (DG SANCO 2010; DG SANCO 2008), with the publicity that participation implies. But while the names of these individual companies that are present in press releases relating to Platform commitments and listed on the commitments database, representation at meetings is largely carried out by umbrella groups. Many of these groups find the Platform useful as an informational tool — giving them more information about the nature and scale of the public health problems covered by the Platform (Evaluation Partnership 2010, 67), as well as important information about policy-makers' ideas and goals.

While NGOs have adopted collective strategies within the Platform amongst themselves, there is little evidence that industry associations and

NGOs have worked together or improved their views of each other. In terms of building face-to-face working relationships between corporate and public health groups, the Platform does not live up to its potential. Although the industry associations that participate in the Platform do view it as a valuable way to build relationships with key policy-makers as well as an informational tool, this strategy is contingent upon the continued attendance of high level policy-makers.[3]

The Commission is using the Platform strategically, to form a public critique of the range of policy solutions offered under a system of pure self-regulation. In this sense, the Platform is a public evidence base that can form part of an argument for future action.[4] Central to this is a database of the commitments, published on the web, which contains details about each program in operation, the actor proposing it, and the series of annual progress monitoring statements they provide. The Platform becomes an alternative approach to self-regulation, effectively 'coordinated voluntarism', in the words of Robert Madelin (EUFIC 2009). Debates within the Platform's plenary meetings echo this perspective, 'that self-regulation is not sufficient alone and must be placed within a supporting legal framework' (DG SANCO 2008). As with many forms of self-regulation, the threat of government action is still implied: 'If the experiment does not work the Commission still has the traditional tools of public policy, such as regulation, at its disposal' (DG SANCO 2005).

Discussion and conclusions

The above cases demonstrate that these types of mechanisms are valuable to Commission policy-makers in areas where authority is still relatively contested. The two cases vary in some important ways, however, and exploring these differences further gives rise to some interesting hypotheses for future research. In particular, the dialogues differ in terms of the scope of their goals and the way in which responsibility for policy outputs and outcomes is divided among the participants. This is because the CSD is primarily still a mechanism for consultation, while the Platform focuses on collaboration between officials and groups.

The CSD has a very broad remit, as a focal point for the many and varied debates over the negative externalities of the EU's numerous trade policies, and is DG Trade's main contact point with advocacy groups dealing with non-economic issues. The Platform, on the other hand, is just one of many formal mechanisms employed by DG SANCO. As with most of DG SANCO's mechanisms, it has a much more focussed goal (tackling the causes of obesity) even though moving towards this goal still requires action across various policy areas. Evidence is gradually emerging that mechanisms of this type with tightly focussed, specific goals seem to be more effective in generating new policy solutions. This is worrying for those who argue that questions for debate should emerge from below rather than being imposed from above. In particular, greater use of mechanisms with narrow goals weakens the argument that consultation mechanisms can somehow be feasible substitutes for representative democracy. If there is indeed a trade off between effectiveness in building consensus around policy ideas and the breadth of a particular dialogue, which one of these features is more desirable? More practically, how should they be balanced within the Commission's overall strategy?

Second, allocation of responsibility for policy outputs and outcomes differs between the cases. In the Platform, the onus is on groups to come up with policy 'commitments', as well as public progress reports on how far they have moved towards achieving those goals. In the CSD, policy decisions are made by officials, who require only limited advice about policy from groups. Technical advice on specific economic trade topics is provided in other forums. Groups are asked to contribute expert advice in terms of the implications of trade for other related issues such as the environment, social, or development policy, and are given opportunities to extract information from officials in return. Thus the focus of the CSD is on information exchange, whereas the Platform emphasises participant action.

This distinction is reflected in the behaviour of interest groups within each forum. Within the CSD, groups that aimed to provide expertise to policy-makers, regardless of type, reported better access to policy-makers and greater satisfaction with the forum. Groups which only served a 'legitimation' function, offering broad opinions on policy direction, were much less likely to say they were satisfied. Within the Platform, the emphasis on industry self-reporting and behaviour modification has placed advocacy groups in the role of 'watchdogs', collaborating to put pressure on industry associations to meet their targets.

By using this finding to inform two 'ideal types', the distinction between these two cases can be helpful in thinking about the range of mechanisms that the Commission uses or may use in the future. Each of these ideal types, consultation and collaboration, has certain benefits for Commission officials. Formal consultation mechanisms are put forward as one method of holding Commission officials to account, a step towards making more legitimate policy and a more legitimate institution. Collaboration mechanisms, on the other hand, offer officials with weak authority the opportunity not only to act in a controversial area, but to pass some of the responsibility for policy outcomes and the risks of failure onto outside actors. Both types of mechanism, by means of making group deliberations public, contribute towards forming a supporting coalition for future action, although collaboration mechanisms arguably push this process further by encouraging participants to commit publicly to specific actions.

The point here is not to suggest that these elements are entirely separate, or that ideal types are the same as the mechanisms we find in reality, but rather to suggest that thinking in terms of ideal types can be fruitful for future research. We might hypothesise, for example, that certain groups would benefit from collaborative relationships: Those groups which claim a seat at the table based on 'representation', representing a particular constituency, might have a harder time getting their ideas heard compared to those groups who claim a seat at the table based upon 'expertise' in a particular topic. Perhaps, collaborative mechanisms could be said to be more valuable in inter-institutional bargaining, or vice versa. Most importantly, the overall effectiveness of different types of mechanisms in implementing new policy ideas (something unfortunately outside the scope of this paper) could be evaluated.

These questions will likely be pertinent for some time to come. In particular, at the time of writing, the role of the European Parliament under the new institutional settlement is still to be fully tested. Even though the EP remains relatively weak in terms of decision-making power when compared to the other institutions, the general upward trend towards MEPs becoming more influential in terms of circulating ideas, setting agendas, and formulating policy continues. This is recognised by Commission officials experimenting with new policy tools. The extent to which they emphasise collaborative or consultative mechanisms in the future will in part be a reflection of this new power structure.

Notes

1. This article refers to stakeholder consultation. As Quittkat and Kotzian in this volume explain (pp. 401–18), the Commission also frequently consults with scholarly subject experts and the public.
2. Personal communication, 20 November 2009.
3. Personal communication, 22 July 2010.
4. Personal communication, 14 September 2009.

References

Armstrong, K. 2002. Rediscovering civil society: the European Union and the White Paper on governance. *European Law Journal* 8, no. 1: 102–32.
Beyers, J., R. Eising, and W. Maloney. 2008. Researching interest group politics in Europe and elsewhere. Much we study, little we know? *West European Politics* 31, no. 6: 1103–28.
Bizzarri, K., and M. Iossa. 2007. From hearing to listening: improving the dialogue between DG trade and civil society, http://trade.ec.europa.eu/doclib/docs/2007/may/tradoc_134642.pdf (accessed 20 July 2007).
Bouwen, P. 2002. Corporate lobbying in the European Union: the logic of access. *Journal of European Public Policy* 9, no. 3: 365–90.
Bouwen, P. 2009. The European Commission. In *Lobbying the European Union: institutions, actors and issues*, eds. D. Coen and J. Richardson, 19–38. Oxford: Oxford University Press.
Broscheid, A., and D. Coen. 2003. Insider and outsider lobbying of the European Commission. *European Union Politics* 4, no. 2: 165–89.
Coen, D. 2007. *EU lobbying: empirical and theoretical studies*. Abingdon: Routledge.
Council of the European Union. 2008. Minutes, 18 February.
DG SANCO. 2005. EU Platform for Action on Diet, Physical Activity and Health: questions and answers, MEMO/05/91, 15 March.
DG SANCO. 2008. *EU platform annual report*. Brussels: European Union.
DG SANCO. 2009. Diet, physical activity and health: an EU platform for action. Minutes, 11th September.
DG SANCO. 2010. EU Platform for Diet, Physical Activity and Health, Platform database, http://ec.europa.eu/health/nutrition_physical_activity/platform/platform_db_en.htm (accessed 15 April 2010).
DG Trade. 2005a. Purpose of the civil society dialogue, http://ec.europa.eu/trade/issues/global/csd/dcs_proc.htm (accessed 2 October 2006).
DG Trade. 2005b. Responsive policy: dialogue with civil society, http://trade.ec.europa.eu/doclib/docs/2005/june/tradoc_113527.pdf (accessed 20 March 2007).
DG Trade. 2009a. *Civil society dialogue annual report*. Brussels: European Union.
DG Trade. 2009b. The EU and civil society, working together for fair and open trade: trade, sustainable development and the global economic crisis, Brussels, 26–27 May. http://trade.ec.europa.eu/civilsoc/meetdetails.cfm?meet=11296 (accessed 21 August 2009). Brussels: European Union.
DG Trade. 2010. Civil society dialogue statistics, http://trade.ec.europa.eu/civilsoc/statistics.cfm (accessed 5 April 2010).
Dür, A. 2008. Measuring interest group influence in the EU: a note on methodology. *European Union Politics* 9, no. 4: 559–76.

Eeckhout, P. 2004. *External relations of the European Union: legal and constitutional foundations.* Oxford: Oxford University Press.

Eising, R. 2008. 'Clientelism, committees, pluralism and protests in the European Union: matching patterns? *West European Politics* 31, no. 6: 1166–87.

EUFIC. 2007. Second anniversary of the EU Platform for Action on Diet, Physical Activity and Health, interview with Robert Madelin, http://www.eufic.org/page/en/show/eu-initiatives/fftid/2nd-Anniversary-of-the-EU-Platform/ (accessed 5 March 2009).

EUFIC. 2009. Fast tracking action: the EU Platform for Action on Diet, Physical Activity and Health celebrates its 4th anniversary, interview with Robert Madelin, http://www.eufic.org/page/en/show/eu-initiatives/fftid/Fast-tracking-action/ (accessed 7 January 2010).

EU Platform for Action on Diet, Physical Activity and Health. 2005. Mission statement, 15 March.

EU Platform on Diet, Physical Activity and Health. 2008. *Annual report.*

European Commission. 2001. European governance: a White Paper, COM(2001) 428.

European Parliament. 2007. The TRIPS agreement and access to medicines, P6_TA(2007)0353, adopted 12th July.

European Parliament. 2008. White Paper on nutrition, overweight and obesity-related health issues, P6_TA(2008)0461, adopted 25 September.

Evaluation Partnership, The. 2010. Evaluation of the European Platform for Action on Diet, Physical Activity and Health, final report, July.

Fazi, E., and J. Smith. 2006. Civil dialogue: making it work better. Civil Society Contact Group, http://act4europe.horus.be/code/en/default.asp (accessed 15 June 2007).

Greenwood, J. 2007. Organised civil society and democratic legitimacy in the European Union. *British Journal of Political Science* 37: 333–57.

Greer, S.L. 2006. Uninvited Europeanization: neofunctionalism and the EU in health policy. *Journal of European Public Policy* 13, no. 1: 134–52.

Greer, S.L. 2009a. Efflorescence and extinction in European Union health policies, paper delivered at University of Wisconsin-Madison, 9 October.

Greer, S.L. 2009b. *The politics of European Union health policies.* Buckingham: Open University Press.

Greer, S.L., E. Massard da Fonseca, and C. Adolph. 2008. Mobilizing bias in European Union health policy. *European Union Politics* 9, no. 3: 403–33.

Hallsworth, M., and T. Ling. 2007. The EU platform on diet, physical activity and health: Second monitoring progress report.

Hallsworth, M., and T. Ling. 2008. The EU platform on diet, physical activity and health: Third monitoring progress report. http://ec.europa.eu/health/ph_determinants/life_style/nutrition/platform/platform_en.htm. (accessed 25 February 2009). Cambridge: Rand Europe.

Jarman, H. 2008. 'The other side of the coin: NGO lobbying in EU trade policy'. *Politics* 28, no. 1: 26–32.

Knodt, M. 2005. *Regieren im erweiterten europäischen Mehrebenensystem – die internationale Einbettung der EU,* Nomos Verlagsgesellschaft.

Kohler-Koch, B. 2010. Civil society and EU democracy: 'astroturf' representation? *Journal of European Public Policy* 17, no. 1: 100–17.

Lamping, W., and M. Steffen. 2009. European union and health policy: the 'chaordic' dynamics of integration. *Social Science Quarterly* 90, no. 5: 1361–79.

Lamy, P. 2002. Opening statement, meeting with Civil Society, 4 July.

Martinsen, D.S. 2005. Towards an internal health market with the European Court. *West European Politics* 28, no. 5: 1035–56.

Meunier, S., and K. Nicolaïdis. 2000. EU trade policy: the 'exclusive' versus shared competence debate. In *The state of the European Union: risks, reform, resistance and revival,* eds. M. Cowles and M. Smith, 325–46. Oxford: Oxford University Press.

Mossialos, E., G. Permanand, R. Baeten, and T. Hervey. 2010. *Health systems governance in Europe: the role of EU law and policy.* Cambridge: Cambridge University Press.

Nicolaïdis, K., and S. Meunier. 2002. Institutional challenges in the European Union. In *Revisiting trade competence in the European Union: Amsterdam, Nice and beyond,* eds. M. Hosli, A. van Deemen, and M. Widgren, 173–201. London: Routledge.

Sabel, C.F., and J. Zeitlin, eds. 2010. *Experimentalist governance in the European union: towards a new architecture.* Oxford: Oxford University Press.

Sanchez-Salgado, R., and C. Woll. 2007. L'européanisation Et Les Acteurs Non Étatiques. In *L'europe En Action: L'européanisation Dans Une Perspective Comparée,* eds. B. Palier and Y. Surel, 145–92. Paris: L'Harmattan.

Slob, A., and F. Smakman. 2006. *Evaluation of the civil society dialogue at DG trade: assessment of relevance, effectiveness and efficiency of CSD policy and procedures.* Rotterdam: Ecorys.

Steffen, M. 2005. *Health governance in Europe: issues, challenges and theories.* London: Routledge.

Wincott, D. 2002. The governance White Paper, the Commission and the search for legitimacy. In *Accountability and legitimacy in the European Union,* eds. A. Arnull and D. Wincott, 379–98. Oxford: Oxford University Press.

Lobbying via Consultation — Territorial and Functional Interests in the Commission's Consultation Regime

CHRISTINE QUITTKAT & PETER KOTZIAN

Mannheim Centre for European Social Research (MZES), University of Mannheim, Mannheim, Germany

ABSTRACT Starting off with a short introduction to the current Commission's consultation regime the paper analyses participation of various actors in different consultation instruments of Directorate General Employment, Social Affairs and Equal Opportunities and Directorate General Health and Consumers based on quantitative data. Analyzing participation patterns of different groups of actors, we explain differences in participation patterns recurring to actor's resources and the properties of the instrument as a means to effectively advocate positions. In particular, we test whether the new consultation instruments, designed to counter-balance the dominance of specific groups and professional lobbyists, meet their intended purpose in that they effectively reach out and include new, additional sets of actors. Our results indicate a spill-over between consultation and lobbying and underline the different roles attributed to different actors such as functional and territorial interest representatives in the Commission's consultation regime.

Introduction

Over the past decade the European Commission has considerably changed its consultation regime, i.e., its formalized relationship with (organised) civil society. In line with the Commission's intention to tackle the perceived democratic and legitimation deficit, (Greenwood 2004), the shift — the 'participatory turn', to use Saurugger's (2008a) term — is especially oriented towards the inclusion of those groups which represent weak or difficult to organise interests, i.e., advocacy groups or non-governmental organisations (NGO) pursuing the public interest. The Commission's new consultation regime is marked by a wide spectrum of consultation mechanisms ranging from expert-oriented instruments reminiscent of 'traditional' expert groups, to stakeholder-oriented instruments like restricted-entry policy forums (Broscheid and Coen 2002), to citizen-oriented instruments as for example European Citizens' Conferences or online forums (Boussaguet and Dehousse 2008; Wright 2007) and finally to instruments open to the wider (interested) public, namely conferences and online consultations. While these instruments — from the Commission's perspective — are instruments of consultation, from the perspective of stakeholders these consultation instruments are (potential) lobbying instruments.

Indeed, it is this interrelation between consultation and lobbying, i.e., the process of interest intermediation, which is at the centre of our paper. In the existing research literature the two processes of consultation and lobbying are usually treated separately. Research on the Commission's consultation regime most often has a normative thrust, analyses the implementation of the Commission's consultation regime with reference to the Commission's self-implied criteria of openness, transparency, and inclusiveness or focussing on the more abstract term of accountability (Hüller 2008; Kohler-Koch and Quittkat 2011; Persson 2009; Steffek and Ferretti 2009). Lobbying and classical interest group research, on the other hand, focuses (inter alia) on the appearance of new types of actors in the lobby of EU institutions (Balme and Chabanet 2008; Greenwood 2007; Saurugger 2008b), on the impact of EU institutions on the dynamics and structure of interest representation at the different levels of the EU multi-level system (Eising 2009; Mahoney and Baumgartner 2008; Quittkat 2009), as well as on the impact of lobbying on EU policies, that is the influence of lobbyists (Bernhagen and Trani 2009; Dür and De Bièvre 2007).[1]

In our paper, we suggest to abandon this division and to look at the intersection of lobbying and consultation. The term consultation describes a process by which the Commission requests the public's input in order to improve transparency, efficiency and effectiveness of regulation (OECD nd). Lobbying, on the other hand, denotes the effort to influence decisions made by legislators and officials in the government in a strategic and systematic way. In addition, and especially in the EU, lobbying is characterized by permanent engagement with the political institutions, by a constant tracking and covering of policy-making, because single event activities only have a low chance of impact due to the complexity of the process of EU policy-making and due to the multitude of actors participating. The questions we analyze in this paper arise from the interplay between consultation and lobbying. We investigate (1) whether and how consultation instruments of the Commission's new consultation regime factually serve as lobbying instruments; and (2) if, how and why participation in consultation instruments differs in composition as regards functional and territorial interests. Both questions have implications for the evaluation of the Commission's consultation regime as a means to enhance the democratic legitimacy of European policy-making. Due to the empirical database of this paper, which concentrates on participation patterns in the Commission's consultation instruments, the focus here is limited to one aspect, the participatory deficit, and the findings obtained thus relate to the Commission's two self-implied criteria of openness and inclusiveness.

The theoretical framework of this paper is the conceptualization of interest intermediation, under which we subsume both consultation and lobbying, as an exchange. The Commission offers interest representatives to participate in and impact on EU policy-making in exchange for information that is crucial for the EU policy-making process (Bouwen 2002, 2004; Henning 2004) but also in exchange for political support and legitimation offered by interest groups. Participation patterns in consultation instruments are thus a result of (1) the Commission offering certain chances to get involved into EU policy-making, but also actively reaching out to different actors by inviting some actors rather than others to participate in more exclusive consultation formats; and (2) of interest representatives competing for involvement in certain instruments rather than others. Our *hypothesis* is that differences in the participation structure of consultation instruments can be explained by differences between consultation participants in the endowment with resources (see Eising 2009 on resource dependence). As different interest representatives are vested with different resources (information, economic relevance, contacts and representativity), they are at different phases of the policy cycle of different interest to the Commission, but they also have different possibilities and a different interest to participate (regularly) in consultations depending on their financial and human resources, their subject-specific expertise, etc.

Our analysis is structured as follows: first, the Commission's consultation instruments are shortly characterized with regard to their possible qualities as lobbying instruments. In a second step, the composition of participants in different types of consultations is examined, followed by an analysis of participation patterns with regard to the whole spectrum of consultation instruments throughout the consultation cycle, i.e., whether participation of different territorial and functional interests in different consultation instruments follows a specific path. Finally, in the conclusion our findings are summarized.

Consultation Instruments as Lobbying Instruments

Attractiveness of Consultation Instruments for Lobbyists

Our analysis of the question, why certain interest representatives participate in one form of consultation rather than in another is guided by a 'rational approach of participation' as theoretical fundament. We assume that the 'hierarchy' of attractiveness between the different instruments is the same for all interest representatives, and that it is determined by the probability to actually influence EU policy-making through participation in a specific consultation format. In this, we assume that interest representatives participate in consultations not only to express their position, but to advocate their interest. Indeed, different consultation instruments have a different quality with regard to their 'value' as an instrument of interest representation. In general terms it can be assumed that the more exclusive a consultation instrument, the higher it is valued as a means of interest representation or lobbying because of the limited number of participants and closer contact to policy-makers. Further, exclusiveness often goes hand in hand with a selection process, controlled or at least supervised by the Commission, which indicates that participants are selected for specific reasons like representativity, expertise, societal and/or political weight, etc.

Rather exclusive instruments of stakeholder consultation are various kinds of working groups with an official mandate from the European Commission like workshops, consultative/advisory groups, policy forums (Broscheid and Coen 2002), and platforms (an analysis of the functioning of a platform is offered by Jarmann in this issue). Although these forms of consultation, which we subsume under the heading *workshops and forums*, usually include a wide spectrum of stakeholders as regards diverging interests like business representatives, NGO and trade unions, their composition is regulated by the Commission. While the spectrum of represented interests is mostly balanced (Quittkat 2011b), the number of participants is limited and for interest groups participation in consultative (or advisory) groups, policy forums and platforms certainly presents a privileged way of interest representation.

Consultation instruments oriented towards the wider public, like conferences and online consultations, present a different category of consultation instruments, and are quite dissimilar as a means for interest representation. It is clear from the outset that both conferences and online consultations do not necessarily need to be open to the wider public but can also have a much narrower focus, addressing only the 'informed public', specific stakeholders or specialists.

Online consultations were introduced in 2000 with the intention to attract representatives of different types of interests and to lower the threshold for individual citizens to access EU level consultation processes. They are highly formalised and have high standards as regards inclusiveness, openness, and transparency (Quittkat 2011a). Not only are written contributions to online consultations published, but online consultations also end with a report on the consultation results. Thus, for interest representatives online consultations on the one hand offer a good possibility to lay down their arguments and demands on a specific subject, but on the other hand due to their openness are far from offering preferential access to the policy-making process (see also Fazi and Smith 2006, 29).

Conferences again have another orientation: As for their 'consultation quality', it is obvious that conferences are mainly oriented towards dissemination of policies and the raising of support for them, a fact that makes being speaker a valuable activity. Being rather a forum where stakeholders can meet than a place of deliberation, for interest representatives, participating in conferences is not a means of *direct* lobbying but of networking and coalition-building. As regards the quality of conferences as lobbying instrument in practice, conferences will attract mainly those actors, which under conditions of limited (human and financial) resources, have a stake in the subject. It is also plausible to assume that the Commission's conferences, which often take place in Brussels, are highly frequented by EU level interest representatives due to the networking function of conferences. Similar to forums and platforms, with regard to *conference speakers*, conferences also include a selection process: The selection of conference speakers usually is in the hands of those hosting the conference, i.e., the Commission, and its result is often a 'diplomatically' negotiated compromise between opposing interests. It can be assumed that mainly those known as specialists, highly relevant stakeholders, and those with rather mainstream positions to the questions at hand will have preferential access to the speaker role.

Yet, the characteristics of the consultation instruments are merely one factor which impacts on their usage as lobbying instruments. It is also the specific sequence throughout the policy cycle by which they are applied, which impacts on their quality as instruments of lobbying. In the EU system of multi-level governance the agenda-setting phase and the early phase of policy formulation are decisive; later phases of the policy cycle offer only very limited possibilities to lobbyists to impact on public policies (Schmidt 1999). Thus, the attractiveness of a consultation instrument as an arena for EU lobbying is defined by the instrument's characteristics as well as by its (early) application in the course of the policy cycle. Numerous empirical studies on EU interest intermediation have demonstrated that due to the Commission's monopoly over policy initiation, the European multi-level system of governance, and the multitude of actors the most promising lobbying strategy are activities at the early stages of the policy process, i.e., at the agenda setting and policy formulation stage (Bouwen 2002; Coen and Richardson 2009; Cram 2001). And indeed, our own research has shown that the Commission's consultation regime is marked by a complex yet structured interplay of various consultation instruments (Quittkat 2008): Online consultations are used in the agenda-setting phase and in the early stage of policy formulation. The further process of policy formulation is accompanied by conferences on more specific facets of the issue at stake. An important supplement to stakeholder and/or public involvement is expert input through expert seminars or expert groups. In addition, for some issues the Commission establishes policy forums or platforms which complement the policy-making process throughout the policy cycle (Quittkat 2011b). For our analysis, the practical relevance of these arguments implies that while open online consultations are too inclusive to be of unequivocal use for lobbying, they are still attractive because they are early in the policy cycle, when the theme is framed and the relevant actors for later stages of EU policy-making are identified. Based on this reasoning we hypothesise that being active in online consultations is a means for interest representatives to gain visibility, which can then be used to gain access to more exclusive forms of consultations like workshops and forums or as conference speakers.

This overview of the Commission's consultation instruments shows how instruments diverge regarding their attractiveness and usability as an instrument of lobbying. Our analysis encompasses exclusive consultation instruments like workshops and forums, differentiates between the highly exclusive group of conference speakers and the more general and thus more inclusive group of conference participants, and we will consider highly inclusive online consultations.

Methodological Remarks

Our empirical analysis is based on a database containing all consultation instruments directed towards 'civil society' (online consultations, conferences, forums and platforms, seminars, etc) by Directorate General Employment, Social Affairs and Equal Opportunities (DG Employment) and Directorate General Health and Consumers (DG SANCO) and all institutional and organisational participants of these various consultations. For data collection we relied on the information provided by the Commission's homepage. The starting points were two links at the homepages of both DGs: 'Events' and 'consultations'. These two sources concentrate on those activities of the European Commission which are geared towards wide participation, like online consultations, conferences or policy forums. This enables us to focus on those instruments which are — contrary to 'old' formats of interest intermediation — designed to achieve both broad participation and acquirement of stakeholder/expert knowledge, i.e., are intended to have also a legitimizing function. The cut-off date for the database is 30 June 2007. DG Employment and DG SANCO were selected as test cases due to their visible openness to 'civil society' and thus (presumably) offering a 'best case scenario' with regard to participation patterns of different actors in various consultation instruments.

In line with the above arguments, we propose to distinguish participants in consultations in two groups: (1) those that only participated in one single consultation instrument regardless of the issue ('one-time-participants'); and (2) those that apply a strategy of systematic (issue) lobbying and appear at least twice in consultations on the same specific issue ('lobbyists'). Given that the number of consultations on a specific issue is rather small (on average between four and eight consultations), we take repeated participation as an indication that an actor puts an effort into being present throughout the policy process, which matches the standard notion of a lobbyist. It is well known from other studies that 'professional' lobbyists constantly track the policy process, monitor the political agenda and try to present their views on every stage of the policy process (Coen and Richardson 2009; Eising 2009; Saurugger 2008b).

Differentiating between two levels of activity with regard to consultation participation allows us to analyse whether and how consultation instruments of the Commission's new consultation regime serve as lobbying instruments, are occupied by lobbyists, and whether this approach differs with regard to functional and territorial interests.

Lobbyists and One-Time-Participants in the Commission's Consultation Instruments

The Commission's consultation regime has a clear purpose, namely to reach out to other actors than those involved in the regular policy-making process, to increase civic participation and to widen the spectrum of different (and diverging) interests. Yet, differences between the various functional interest representatives in terms of resources and professionalisation remain and it is an empirical question, whether consultations manage to reach out to 'amateurs' in EU policy-making, or whether they are the playing-ground of professional EU lobbyists. Similarly, we analyze the role of territorial interest representatives in the context of the Commission's consultations: On the one hand the EU political system provides for the participation of member states and sub-national public authorities in European policy-making through various institutions like the Council of Ministers or the Committee of the Regions; on the other hand — and similar especially to EU level associations — national governments and sub-national public authorities represent large 'constituencies' and thus might have preferential access to the Commission's consultations. Thus, with regard to the theme of this special issue we ask: What functional and territorial representatives participate, whether consultations are a forum where a new set of actors such as NGO and sub-national actors can raise their voice, and what role territorial interest representatives play in the context of the Commission's consultations.

In general terms we find that the Commission's consultation instruments reach out to a large variety of actors. The number of different actors participating in the 89 online consultations, conferences, workshops and forums of DG Employment and DG SANCO from 2000 to June 2007 was 2.528. Keeping in mind that the new consultation regime was established to increase the involvement of interest groups others than the social partners into the policy-making process, as well as the heated debate on the inclusion of public authorities into the register of interest representatives, the composition of consultation participants is quite remarkable. Participants include functional as well as territorial interest representatives with NGO (27.6%) and business associations (21.1%) taking the lead, followed by companies (14.4%), public authorities (12.2%), and trade unions and professional organisations (11.9%). Taking into account the organisational level of interest representatives, the largest group participating in the Commission's consultations are national NGO (16.1%), companies (14.4%), national business associations (11.3%), national trade unions and professional organisations (8.1%), EU level business associations (7.5%) and national public authorities (6.4%).

The composition of overall participation shows that the Commission's consultation regime — mainly thanks to online consultations — today reaches out to all categories of actors, to all kinds of functional and territorial interests, and to all organizational levels (see Table 1). Indeed, from the Commission's perspective the participation of local level and sub-national interests in its consultation instruments is a remarkable success, in particular with regard to the traditional picture of the EU dealing predominantly with EU level associations (Eising 2009). However, this success only applies to public authorities and NGO, while labour und business interests, both functional sectors with a highly integrated and hierarchical associational system, obviously delegate EU consultation participation to national level and EU level associations.

Table 1. Participants in DG Employment's and DG SANCO's consultation instruments (2000–June 2007)

Organisational level		Public authorities	NGO	Labour interests	Business interests (incl. companies)	Others	Total
International	N	10	50	9	19	8	96
	%	0.4%	2.0%	0.4%	0.8%	0.3%	3.8%
European	N	21	136	60	189	39	445
	%	0.8%	5.4%	2.4%	7.5%	1.5%	17.6%
National	N	163	406	205	285	116	1175
	%	6.4%	16.1%	8.1%	11.3%	4.6%	46.5%
Sub-national	N	52	47	17	34	14	164
	%	2.1%	1.9%	0.7%	1.3%	0.6%	6.5%
Local	N	62	59	9	6	29	165
	%	2.5%	2.3%	0.4%	0.2%	1.1%	6.5%
No level attributed (companies, research)	N	0	0	0	364	119	483
	%	0.0%	0.0%	0.0%	14.4%	4.7%	19.1%
Total	N	308	698	300	897	325	2.528
	%	12.2%	27.6%	11.9%	35.5%	12.9%	100.0%

Table 2. One-time-participants in DG Employment's and DG SANCO's consultation instruments (2000–June 2007)

Organisational level		Public authorities	NGO	Labour interests	Business interests (incl. companies)	Others	Total
International	N	6	32	5	10	4	57
	%	0.3%	1.8%	0.3%	0.6%	0.2%	3.1%
European	N	11	80	35	89	27	242
	%	0.6%	4.4%	1.9%	4.9%	1.5%	13.3%
National	N	93	316	155	190	96	850
	%	5.1%	17.4%	8.5%	10.5%	5.3%	46.8%
Sub-national	N	33	43	14	32	9	131
	%	1.8%	2.4%	0.8%	1.8%	0.5%	7.2%
Local	N	54	56	7	5	22	144
	%	3.0%	3.1%	0.4%	0.3%	1.2%	7.9%
No level attributed (companies, research)	N	0	0	0	294	97	391
	%	0.0%	0.0%	0.0%	16.2%	5.3%	21.5%
Total	N	197	527	216	620	255	1.815
	%	10.9%	29.0%	11.9%	34.2%	14.0%	100.0%

What does the data tells us regarding our question whether consultations are used as lobbying instruments? Despite the broad range of actors reached, there is a clear gap between those actors who participate only in one single consultation, with the one-time-participants making up the majority (72%), and those actors who engage more extensively in consultations on a specific issue, which we denote as lobbyists. Further, out of the 1.815 one-time-participants, 1.807 participated in an online consultation; this underlines again the success of online consultations as regards their ability to reach out to actors which might otherwise remain excluded from EU policy-making (the composition of the one-time-participants is given in Table 2).

Obviously, for one-time-participants, participation is rather driven by concernment and input provision than by a *systematic* EU level lobbying approach. Nearly all one-time-participants engage in preparing a submission for an online consultation, in itself a demanding task, but do not send personnel to workshops, forums or conferences. Indeed, the composition of the group of one-time-participants compared to lobbyists shows that using consultations as lobbying instrument is a strategy rather applied by national and EU level interest representatives than by sub-national and local actors. Many one-time-participants were small and medium size companies and research institutes (391) as well as local and sub-national public authorities (87) and NGO (106), all of which, of course, have a different focus in their daily work than EU level interest intermediation (on the question of role assignment see also Barron, this issue). Thus, a first result of our analysis is that the Commission's consultations, especially online consultations, reach out to a wide spectrum of actors from all territorial levels, which implies that the 'participatory turn' bears its fruits. But the differentiation between one-time-participants and those more often present in the Commission's consultations also points to the sensitive structure of the Commission's consultation regime, which is an arena for lobbying to about a third of participants.

Patterns of Participation: Lobbying via Consultation Instruments?

In the following we investigate more closely how different consultation instruments are used as lobbying instruments, how participation in different consultations is interlinked and how actor characteristics impact on the role of consultation instruments as instruments of lobbying.

Issue Lobbying

Turning to those actors, who appeared at least twice in a range of consultations on the same specific issue (our 'lobbyists'), we find that the usage of consultations as a lobbying instrument varies with the issue at stake (see Figure 1). Some issues are significantly more dominated by lobbyists than others. Differentiating for our analysis between the main policy issues, namely public health, food safety and consumer affairs in the case of DG SANCO and between corporate social responsibility (CSR), demography, equality and labour in the case of DG Employment, the finding is astonishingly clear: Regular participation in consultation instruments as a means of

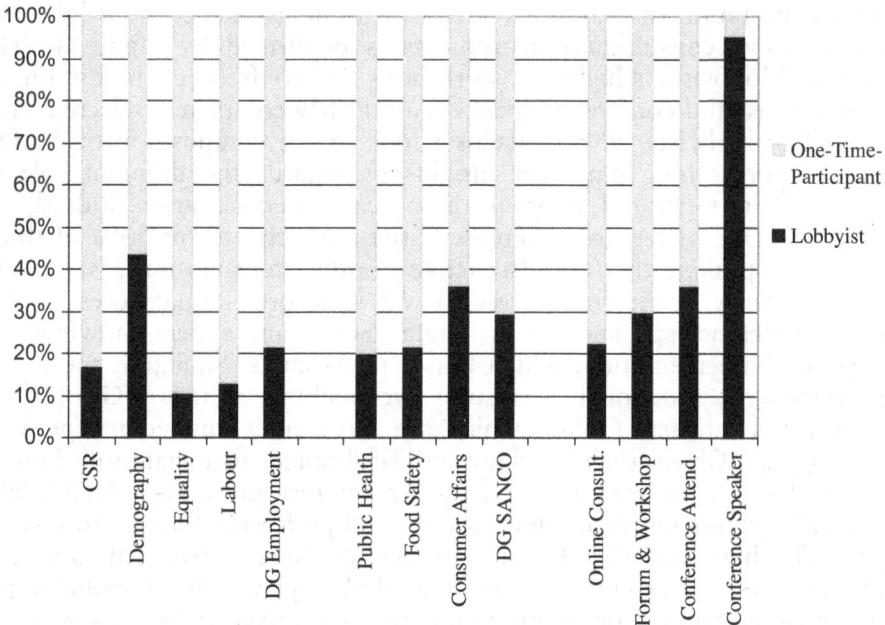

Figure 1. Shares of 'lobbyists' and one-time-participants by issue and instrument

interest representation is a strategy mainly applied to those issues which are either new on the Commission's agenda, like demography, or which are in the process of being re-defined, as it was the case with European consumer rights in the noughties (Figure 1). Whereas stable issues like labour or equality are marked by consolidated interest cleavages in addition to well-established relations between policy-makers and interest representatives outside of the consultation regime, which therefore does not become the (main) arena for influence-seeking, in cases of issue formation or re-definition of issues, consultations are not only a platform to transport input, but offer interest representatives new possibilities of self-positioning.

Exclusive Versus Inclusive Consultation Instruments

As noted above, consultation instruments differ with respect to their accessibility, but also with regard to their attractiveness as regards their quality as a lobbying instrument: We expect to find a higher proportion of lobbyists in exclusive consultations than in inclusive consultations, assuming that participation in exclusive instruments is considered to offer more chances of effective influence than participation in inclusive instruments. To test this assumption, we differentiate between online consultations and conferences on the one hand which both have a rather low participation threshold, and between workshops and forums as well as the composition of conference speakers on the other hand. The latter group presents instruments with a highly exclusive character which are from the perspective of lobbyists despite (or exactly because of) the hurdle of a selection process highly attractive for interest representation since they offer preferential access to EU policy-making and to EU policy-makers.[2]

Our expectation that more exclusive instruments attract more lobbyists than inclusive consultation instruments is confirmed by Figure 1. The fraction of lobbyists is higher in workshops and conferences than in online consultations, and conference speakers are nearly completely selected from the pool of lobbyists (95%). A closer look at the composition of conference speakers offers important insights as regards the different role of functional and territorial actors in the process of consultation. Indeed, the high percentage of territorial representatives, which present 53% of those conference speakers that are also active in other consultations, is remarkable. Obviously, territorial representatives have preferential access to the role as conference speakers for their relevance in and expert knowledge of EU policy implementation, which lies in their hands. Similarly, the distribution between functional interests is eye-catching, as it is NGO (20%), not business interests (16%), which are more often invited to speak at conferences.[3] Given their background of limited financial and human resources — in comparison to business interest groups — NGO, like territorial interest representatives, are offered preferential access to conferences. The high rate of NGO conference speakers shows that advocacy and public interest groups have become relevant players in EU policy-making, which are valued for opening up new perspectives on policy issues.

The Interplay of Participation in Different Consultation Instruments

As argued above, in general terms we assume consultation instruments to differ as a means to influence European policy-making, with exclusive instruments ranking higher than inclusive instruments as forums for possible influence. Yet, there is one institutional aspect which needs to be taken into account: The most inclusive instrument is online consultations which require nothing more from lobbyists but to register in order to participate. While not necessarily of interest per se due to their inclusiveness, online consultations offer interest representative the opportunity of (self-)presentation as a well-informed, serious, professional and reliable consultation 'partner'. In fact, by registering and participating in online consultations interest representatives become part of a pool from which the Commission selects participants for other, more exclusive consultation formats. Further, as mentioned, online consultations mark the beginning of a policy-making cycle and actors therefore might participate in order to get noticed by the Commission early on.

And indeed, regression analysis shows (Table 3) that participation in online consultations is significant for participation in other consultation instruments and robustly so. Thus, the data strongly confirms our hypotheses: There are strong and significant effects of the frequency of participation in online consultations for the frequency of participation in workshops and forums and in conferences, and also for actors being invited as speaker at a conference. This effect is robust against the inclusion of other actor features, i.e., it is activity per se which matters. If an interest representative is highly visible by participating in many online consultations, the representative's chances of becoming a conference speaker as well as a participant in the more exclusive consultation formats

Table 3. Determinants of participation behaviour

	Online consultation[1]	Workshops and forums[1]	Conference attendance[1]	Conference speakers[2]
Frequency of participation in online-consultations		0.040***	0.414***	0.463***
Public actor	1.473***	0.066*	0.268***	0.978**
European level	0.646***	0.017	0.083	0.667
National level	0.115	−0.176***	0.010	−0.865*
Sub-national and local level	−0.567**	−0.182***	−0.126	−2.261***
EU-15 member	0.129	0.038	0.003	0.318
EU new member	0.137	−0.021	0.179	0.091
Company	−0.424*	−0.150***	0.257**	−0.197
Labour interest	0.236	−0.016	−0.154*	−0.763
Business interest	0.545***	−0.019	−0.252***	−1.108**
NGO	0.213	0.010	−0.051	−0.312
Constant	1.005***	0.095***	−0.342***	−3.221***
Explained variation[3]	0.07	0.118	0.508	0.252
N = 2542				

Notes. Remark: (1) OLS regression; conference attendance includes both, listeners and speakers; (2) logistic regression for chance of being speaker at a conference; (3) explained variation is Pseudo R^2 for being speaker at a conference, and R^2 for the other three variables.

increases. The low explanatory power of actor properties for the frequency of participation in online consultations indicates that such properties, and thus implicitly the resource endowment of an actor, matters little for participation in online consultations. This is to say that if interest representatives invest in visibility by participating regularly in online consultations, which have a rather low threshold, they increase the probability of gaining access to exclusive consultation instruments and can, in principle, equalize the advantages other actors have.

The Impact of Resources on Participation

As for the properties of participants, which enable them to gain access, it can be argued that for exclusive consultation instruments participants are either selected for what they are or for what they are known. For instance one might expect that the Commission has a preference for EU level associations and member state public actors as these both represent large 'constituencies'. Regarding territorial interest representatives, notably in the case of member state governments, public authorities additionally have the resource of formal power in the EU setting, making them presumably even more likely to be invited to exclusive consultations. Regarding functional interest representatives, business associations and labour associations both share the property of representing functional constituencies via a highly hierarchical structure, giving much weight to their contributions in a consultation process due to their representativity. Finally, (large) companies are well endowed with financial and human resources, but even more so with technical expertise: Financial and human resources allow them to participate more often in consultations, technical expertise as a resource also makes them highly attractive interlocutors from the Commission's perspective.

Table 3 gives the results of regressing certain forms of participatory behaviour on properties of the actors and shows that some properties of actors like organisational level, origin from an old or a new member state, and type of interests represented, significantly affect participation in exclusive consultation formats. As for the organizational level, it comes to no surprise that it has a significant effect: National level and in particular sub-national and local level actors are at a disadvantage compared to EU level actors regarding all our instrument categories, and the disadvantage is the stronger, the more exclusive the consultation instrument. As expected, EU level actors participate in the more exclusive consultation formats more often not because they participate more often in online consultations as a means to create visibility, but because there exists a bias towards EU level actors on the side of those being in charge of participant selection, i.e., the Commission, this effect being strongest for the speaker role in conferences.

Geographic origin on the other hand has no effect on consultation participation: Associations and public actors from the old EU member states do not enjoy better access, a presumption one might hold due to the expectation that the Commission knows these actors for a longer time than representatives from the new EU member states. Nor do actors from the new member states or from Central and Eastern European member states enjoy a kind of 'attention bonus' in that they are invited more often to be a conference speaker or to participate in a workshop or forum. However, although not clearly significant, actors from new member states or Central and Eastern European member states attended more often conferences than actors from EU–15 member states. This can easily be attributed to the wide range of conferences by DG Employment focussing especially on the accession countries and EU harmonisation in order to ensure smooth integration.

Regarding the differentiation between territorial and functional interests, the regression analyses reveal further significant differences in participation patterns. To start with, being a public authority has a significant effect, indicating that for public actors the requirement to be 'visible' in consultations is less relevant. Thus, public actors use consultations less systematically as lobbying instruments than functional interests. Given that those public actors participating more often in workshops and forums and speaking often at conferences are mostly representatives of the member states' governments, this finding is little surprising: National level public actors are invited by the Commission to exclusive consultations for being what they are and in order to prepare and ensure the implementation of EU policies and their acceptance in the member states.

But we also find significant effects for other types of interest representatives. When comparing participation in workshops and forums, there are few differences between the various functional interests. All three main types of functional interests — labour, business and NGO — are to a similar extent present in these exclusive instruments. Business interests, however, are only represented in workshops and forums by business interest associations, not via individual companies, which participate significantly less often. This displays the logic of these instruments which are conceived of as compromise-seeking working groups and thus reflect the Commission's preference for those actors who aggregate interests. Similarly, contributions to online consultations are the task of business associations rather than companies. Conference attendance shows quite the opposite pattern of participation: In the audience we find single companies rather than business interest associations, and representatives of trade unions and professional organisations are also significantly less often found in conferences than in other consultations, a pattern which needs to be attributed to the high level of organisational integration of the social partners. Finally, as regards the speakers' role at conferences, we find that NGO, labour interest representatives as well as companies are at par as regards invitations by the Commission. However, business interest associations are invited significantly less often than other interest representatives. Thus, if business interests are invited as speakers, the Commission chooses representatives from companies rather than from business interest associations: First-hand presentations of specific cases offer valuable illustrative material regarding the impact of EU policy.

Conclusion

Summarizing our main findings, the composition of participants shows that the Commission's consultation regime today reaches out to a wide variety of actors, including functional and territorial interests from all organisational levels into the European process of policy-making. However, participation patterns indicate a substantial distinction between those who participate only once in the Commission's consultations and those, who participate more often in consultations and do so on a specific policy issue. Further, we find that it is mainly thanks to online consultations that the new consultation regime attracts a wide spectrum of actors and thereby increases diversity (which is expected to enhance the democratic legitimacy of the Commission's policy-making; see Jarmann and Knodt, this issue). Online consultations allow for the participation of actors which may care very much about a specific issue, but do not track the policy-making process or the issues of a DG on a permanent basis. This suggests that those reached by online consultations are indeed those the Commission wants to reach: Stakeholders, i.e., sub-national, local, and national public and private actors as well as the 'usual suspects', well-known (functional and territorial) lobbyists orbiting EU institutions. Indeed, online consultations are the instrument which despite its deficits manages best to collect input from civil society and which to a considerable degree is able to capture the plurality of views and stakes in society and fulfils the intentions underlying the consultation regime (Hüller 2010, Kohler-Koch and Quittkat 2011).

As regards the question whether the new consultation regime opens up new strategies of lobbying, we find supporting evidence. The number of actors participating at least twice in consultations on a specific issue, i.e., the number of lobbyists, is significantly higher for those issues, which are either new on the Commission's agenda or which are in the process of being re-defined, than for established issues, which are marked by consolidated interest cleavages and well-established relations between policy-makers. We also find that the consultation system offers pathways for systematic interest representation: Participation in inclusive online consultations, often the starting point of a new policy-making cycle, increases participation in other, more exclusive consultation instruments, where participants are selected by the organisers, i.e., the Commission.

But here we are confronted with an inconsistency of the Commission's consultation regime: Access to online consultations is easy, albeit not a low cost effort, and in principle this implies that everybody can, by investing in visibility via participation in online consultations, also gain access to more exclusive consultation formats like workshops and forums or to the group of conference speakers. Thus, on paper, this strategy should allow 'outsiders', lacking resources for conventional interest representation, to gain access to EU policy-making. However, for the time being, exclusive consultation instruments are indeed the playing ground of those interest representatives which engage in systematic lobbying; but conference audiences, workshops and forums, and the exclusive group of conference speakers are dominated by a specific group of actors, namely EU level interest groups as well as national (member state) public authorities (see Greenwood, this issue), well-connected and resourceful actors.

Our findings on the effects of actor properties on participation behaviour indicate that the Commission's consultation instruments offer a new route for lobbying only for those with a very specific profile. Although the new consultation regime is characterised by its openness towards civil society (organisations) and its assignment to reach out to civil society at all organisational levels, it is territorial interest representatives as well as EU level functional interest groups which are in a favourable position, having access to consultation instruments for what they are, namely transmission belts and institutions of interest aggregation, and not for what they do.

Finally, regarding the contribution of consultations to the Commission's intention to enhance the democratic legitimacy of European policy-making, we find that despite its self-implied criteria of openness, transparency, and inclusiveness the specific construction of the consultation regime hampers the attainment of the Commission's normative goals: In the course of the policy cycle the Commission's consultation instruments become more and more exclusive and exclusive instruments attract more lobbyists than inclusive consultation instruments. Thus, as regards the Commission's objective to address the participatory deficit, we perceive the effects to be limited: The only instrument reaching out to society is online consultations, but this is the instrument with the least direct impact on EU policy-making.

Notes

1. For an overview on the EU lobbying research see for example Beyers, Eising, and Maloney (2008), Coen (2007), Coen and Richardson (2009) Eising (2008).
2. However, we want to underline that access is not to be equated with higher influence. On the question of power and influence of interest groups in the EU see Dür (2008).

3. Out of the 16 conference speakers who did not participate in any other consultation instrument on the same issue half came from research institutes and none represented a company, the remainder being evenly split among the other actor groups.

References

Balme, R., and D. Chabanet. 2008. *European governance and democracy. Power and protest in the EU*. Plymouth: Rowman and Littlefield.

Bernhagen, P., and B. Trani. 2009. Who gets what on British politics? Analyzing media reports on lobbying around government policy 2001–2007, paper presented at the 67th Annual National Conference of the Midwest Political Science Associations, Chicago, IL, 2–5 April.

Beyers, J., R. Eising, and W. Maloney. 2008. Researching interest group politics in Europe and elsewhere: much we study little we know? *West European Politics* 31, no. 6: 1103–28.

Boussaguet, L., and R. Dehousse. 2008. Lay people's Europe: a critical assessment of the first EU citizens' conferences. *European Governance Papers (EUROGOV)*, No. C-08-02, http://www.connex-network.org/eurogov/pdf/egp-connex-C-08-02.pdf (accessed 24 February 2011).

Bouwen, P. 2002. Corporate lobbying in the European Union: the logic of access. *Journal of European Public Policy* 9, no. 3: 365–90.

Bouwen, P. 2004. Exchanging access goods for access: a comparative study of business lobbying in the European Union institutions. *European Journal of Political Research* 43, no. 3: 337–69.

Broscheid, A., and D. Coen. 2002. Business interest representation and European Commission fora: a game theoretic investigation. *MPIfG Working Paper*, 02/7, July.

Coen, D. 2007. Empirical and theoretical studies in EU lobbying. *Journal of European Public Policy* 14, no. 3: 333–45.

Coen, D., and J. Richardson. 2009. *Lobbying the European Union: institutions, actors, and issues*. Oxford: Oxford University Press.

Cram, L. 2001. Whither the Commission? Reform, renewal and the issue-attention cycle. *Journal of European Public Policy* 14, no. 3: 384–403.

Dür, A. 2008. Interest groups in the European Union: how powerful are they? *West European Politics* 31, no. 6: 1212–30.

Dür, A., and D. De Bièvre. 2007. The question of interest group influence. *Journal of Public Policy* 27, no. 1: 1–12.

Eising, R. 2008. Interest groups in EU policy-making. *Living Reviews in European Governance* 3, no. 4, http://www.livingreviews.org/lreg-2008-4 (accessed 2 February 2011).

Eising, R. 2009. *The Political Economy of State-Business Relations in Europe. Interest mediation, capitalism and EU policy-making*. London/New York: Routledge.

Fazi, E., and J. Smith. 2006. Civil dialogue: making it work better. *Civil Society Contact Group (CSCG)*, http://act4europe.horus.be/module/FileLib/Civil%20dialogue,%20making%20it%20work%20better.pdf (accessed 24 February 2011).

Greenwood, J. 2004. The search for input legitimacy through organised civil society in the EU. *Transnational Associations/Associations transnationales* 2, no. 1: 145–55.

Greenwood, J. 2007. Review article: organized civil society and democratic legitimacy in the European Union. *British Journal of Political Science* 37, 333–57.

Henning, C.H.C.A. 2004. Modelling the political influence of interest groups: theory and empirical evidence from European agricultural policy. In *Governance in Europe: the role of interest groups*, eds. A. Warntjen and A. Wonka, 93–111. Baden-Baden: Nomos.

Hüller, T. 2008. Demokratisierung der EU durch Online-Konsultationen? *Forschungsjournal Neue Soziale Bewegungen* 21, no. 2: 73–82.

Hüller, T. 2010. Playground or democratization? New participatory procedures at the European Commission. *Swiss Political Science Review* 16, no. 1: 79–109.

Kohler-Koch, B., and C. Quittkat. 2011. *Die Entzauberung partizipativer Demokratie. Zur Rolle der Zivilgesellschaft bei der Demokratisierung von EU-Governance*. Frankfurt: Campus.

Mahoney, C., and F.R. Baumgartner. 2008. Interest group research in Europe and America. *West European Politics* 31, no. 6: 1253–73.

OECD. nd. *Background document on public consultation*. Paris: OECD, http://www.oecd.org/dataoecd/4/43/36785341.pdf (accessed 11 February 2011).

Persson, T. 2009. Civil society participation and accountability. In *The illusion of accountability in the European Union*, eds. S.K. Gustavsson and T. Persson, 122–33. London: Routledge.

Quittkat, C. 2008. Wirklich näher am Bürger? Konsultationsinstrumente der EU-Kommission auf dem Prüfstand *Forschungsjournal Neue Soziale Bewegungen* 21, no. 2: 64–72.

Quittkat, C. 2009. The Europeanization of professional interest intermediation: national trade associations in a French–German comparison. In *Interest groups and lobbying in Europe. Essays on trade, environment, legislation, and economic development*, ed. C. McGrath, 125–60. New York: Edwin Mellen Press.

Quittkat, C. 2011a. The European Commission's online consultations – a success story? *Journal of Common Market Studies* 49, no. 3: 653–74.

Quittkat, C. 2011b. Die Konsultationspolitik der Kommission in der Praxis: Eine Tiefenanalyse. In *Die Entzauberung partizipativer Demokratie. Zur Rolle der Zivilgesellschaft bei der Demokratisierung von EU-Governance*, eds. B. Kohler-Koch and C. Quittkat, 98–124. Frankfurt/Main: Campus Verlag.

Saurugger, S. 2008a. The participatory turn and the professionalisation of interest representation in the European Union, paper prepared for the 4th ECPR Pan-European Conference on EU Politics, Riga, Latvia, 25–27 September.

Saurugger, S. 2008b. Interest groups and democracy in the European Union. *West European Politics* 31, no. 6: 1274–91.

Schmidt, V.A. 1999. National patterns of governance under siège: the impact of European integration. In *The transformation of governance in the European Union*, eds. B. Kohler-Koch and R. Eising, 155–72. London: Routledge.

Steffek, J., and M.P. Ferretti. 2009. Accountability or 'good decisions'? The competing goals of civil society participation in international governance. *Global Society* 23, no. 1: 37–57.

Wright, S. 2007. A virtual European public sphere? The Futurum discussion forum. *Journal of European Public Policy* 14, no. 8: 1167–85.

Strategies of Territorial and Functional Interests: Towards a Model of European Interest Intermediation?

MICHÈLE KNODT

Technical University Darmstadt, Institut für Politikwissenschaft, Germany

ABSTRACT   Research on interest representation in EU governance has addressed different kinds of actors in somewhat different and independent discourses. This contribution will start from the specific requirements is demanding as well as opportunities the European multi-level system is offering to territorial and functional interest representation. The main question will be whether differentiations or similarities can be found in the comparison of functional and territorial interest representation. The contribution will elaborate on this question in the following section and assume that there are more similarities than differences within the use of strategies by territorial and functional interests. The contribution elaborates two explanations for the similarities and differences found. Empirical evidence is given in the second part of the contribution. It will be shown that we even find convergence within territorial and functional interest intermediation and how actors have learned from each other. In addition it will be revealed that other factors than the type of interest are responsible for persistent differences. A third short chapter points out that both types of interests work with complementary strategies to succeed within the European multi-level system. All in all, the contribution will speculate about whether it is possible to identify certain elements of a European model of interest intermediation across the different actor categories.

Introduction

Research on interest representation in EU governance has addressed different kinds of actors in somewhat independent discourses. A broad overview of functional interest representation has recently been provided by special issues and single articles on the 'state of the art' (see Beyers, Eising, and Maloney 2008; Coen 2007; Dür and De Bièvre 2007; Woll 2006). These publications present different approaches and research questions central to the analysis of EU functional interest intermediation. However, the contributions exclusively draw attention to business interest groups, social movements and NGOs, and do not address either territorial interest intermediation or the comparison with functional interest intermediation. The literature on territorial interest intermediation has developed separately and has been shaped by the discourse on the 'Europe of the Regions' of the mid-1980s (see Keating and Jones 1985; Anderson 1990; Borras-Alomar, Christiansen, and Rodriguez-Pose 1994; Boschma and Schobben 2000). The representation of regional interests within the multi-level system of the EU was a central topic analysed by several large-scale research projects on regional interest representation (see a.o. Kohler-Koch et al. 1998).

Thus, findings of the research community on functional interests have not yet been compared to analyses of territorial interest intermediation. The strategies of functional actors have been researched in detail (see Coen 1998; Bouwen 2002; Quittkat 2002, 2004, 2008; Eising 2004, 2007) and at least some literature on territorial strategies is also available (see Kohler-Koch et al. 1998; Knodt 1998, 2010; John 2000). But what can be said about these strategies in comparison? Hardly anything yet. Even in contributions which address both functional and territorial interest intermediation (Balme and Chabanet 2008), the question of a systematic comparison of interest intermediation strategies is not posed. Here, the double-sided construction of territorial interests — as legitimated constituencies of democratic systems on the one hand and actors within multi-level systems that pursue lobbying on the other hand — is not recognized. Rather the distinction between territorial and functional representation within democratic nation states is maintained. Functional interests are supposed to represent their specific profit- or non-profit-oriented interests through any channel possible for lobbying depending on their resources (see Piattoni, this issue). Territorial interests are defined as representatives of national or sub-national constituencies. Thus, they are supposed to represent their interests in the first place through their national representative institutions and in European institutions which represent national interests. But in multi-level systems such as the EU, marked by a lack of institutionalised representation for sub-national interests, territorial interests are also forced to represent their interests differently, i.e., via lobbying. Most obviously this was the case in the late 1980s when regions opened their 'representations' in Brussels (see below), which drew a corresponding scientific interest. But there exists no systematic research yet that looks at territorial interests as actors which have to represent their interests via both internal institutional structures and via external lobbying, and how they perform the latter in comparison with functional interests. This is because the 'manner in which territorial and functional (interests)... are represented in the EU does not quite fit our analytical and normative maps, which are normally drawn by reference to the nation-state' (Piattoni, this issue). Thus, the special challenges of the multi-level context for territorial and functional interest intermediation in comparative perspective is not yet present in the literature.

This contribution will start from the specific requirements which the European multi-level system demands, as well as the opportunities it offers to territorial and functional interest representation. The main question will be whether differences or similarities can be found in the comparison of functional and territorial interest representation. The contribution will elaborate on this question in the following section and assumes that there are more similarities than differences between the strategies of territorial and functional interests. Possible explanations for the similarities and differences found will be presented, which open up new demand for research in this field. Empirical evidence is given in the second part of the contribution. It will be shown that we find convergence within territorial and functional interest intermediation and that actors have learned from each other. In addition it will be revealed that other factors than the type of interests are responsible for persistent differences. A third short chapter points out that both types of interests work with complementary strategies to succeed within the European multi-level system. All in all the contribution will reflect about whether it is possible to identify certain elements of a European model of interest intermediation across the different actor categories.

Analysing Similarities and Differences in Territorial and Functional Interest Intermediation

Because a detailed description of the EU as an interactive and communicative system of multi-level governance is developed in the introduction, some general remarks on its characteristics will be sufficient at this point. Governance in the European multilevel system, as elaborated by Hooghe and Marks (2001) and many others consecutively, is seen here as an 'interpenetrated system of action' (Grote, Knodt, and Larat 1996), which is characterised by various interlocking levels of governance. It is a polycentric system, containing various centres of decision-making formed by functional networks. Different public and private actors cooperate in multiple, overlapping arenas in order to generate binding decisions (Benz 2000, 152; Hooghe and Marks 2001). The organising principle of political relations within the European system is based on consensus, which helps actors to manage heterogeneity within political communities. Thus, EU policy-making is consensus-oriented and gives priority to problem-solving strategies rather than bargaining (Scharpf 1999). Combined with individual interests as the legitimate political unit of action, the governance of the EU could be categorised as 'network governance' (Kohler-Koch 1999, 23). Consensual policy-making relies heavily on interaction and communication between its entities (Knodt 2002b). Therefore, accumulation of knowledge, collective learning, and the exchange of ideas and concepts are significant. Within the management of interaction and communication in multiple arenas and networks, the European Commission plays a prominent role as a policy entrepreneur (Knodt 2004). The Commission gathers information and develops guiding principles and ideas. For doing this, however, i.e., for communicating and interacting with representatives of regions, cities, business and civil society actors, the Commission performs an important broker function. Governance in the interpenetrated European system of action should be both efficient and legitimate. There is a deficient legitimizing mechanism of parliamentary representation. This has resulted in the dual role of sub-national territorial interests as well as in various attempts to establish alternative means of legitimizing the EU involving both territorial and functional actors. Suggestions range from a model of post-parliamentarianism consisting of loosely coupled arenas (Benz 2000), deliberative (Schmalz-Bruns 1999; Cohen and Sabel 1997; Eriksen and Fossum 2000) up to participative models (Heinelt 2002; Grote and Gbikpi 2002). Participative models, in particular, have been incorporated into political concepts.

If we acknowledge the special context of the multi-level system the first question that arises is whether differences or similarities can be found in the comparison of functional and territorial interest representation.[1] Do territorial and functional interests represent their interests in a similar or different way? Do they use similar strategies, or, is there even some kind of convergence of strategies? Having worked on either functional or territorial interest intermediation within the European multi-level system for many years (see Knodt 1998, 2005; Knodt and Finke 2005; Knodt and Quittkat 2004) it is reasonable to assume that there are similarities within the strategies and instruments used by both of the two types of interests. But it is also quite likely that we find similarities and differences beyond the distinction of territorial and functional interests. The present paper offers first empirical insights regarding the comparison of functional and territorial interest representation on the basis of available data; a comparative database for this research question is still missing.

If we can find similarities and differences which can not be explained by the type of interest, this would already be a first step to show that both categories are acting in the same way within the multi-level system of the EU. The question will be how to explain differences and similarities beyond the functional and territorial interest representation divide.

The first step towards an explanation is to have a look at different ways interests are incorporated in the decision-making process. Thus, it is argued in the logic of those authors who conceptualise the decision-making process and its windows of opportunities as external factors having an impact on interest representation. This perspective is taken by Streeck and Schmitter (1981) and their notion of the logic of influence as well as by the concept of the 'structures of political opportunity', addressed by Princen and Kerremans (2008), which map the types of access and participation within the EU.

From this perspective it can be observed that the European Union has tried over the past several years to develop strategies for the involvement of civil society actors (in a broad sense) that would increase the legitimacy of the European Union and provide additional expertise. By analysing various policy fields, it has become apparent that inclusion takes on different forms and that tension exists between the demand for legitimacy through involvement and the reality of inclusion. Various authors have addressed the EU efforts to provide legitimacy through civil society involvement. Thus, different forms of involvement have been identified and categorised. Steffek and Nanz (2008) came up with several criteria of civil society participation which multi-level institutions have to meet in order to provide legitimacy within the EU. Jarman (in this issue) categorizes different types of involvement by distinguishing a consultative and a collaborative model. Kohler-Koch and Quittkat (2011) identified different consultation regimes. Yet, these efforts do not sufficiently stress the different quality of types of participation. For the purpose of this paper, two different models of involvement will be distinguished (see Knodt 2005). The models are constructed according to five dimensions and their distinctive values: (a) the access of civil society actors to the European level; (b) governance mechanisms in the sense of political versus societal steering mechanisms (Kohler-Koch and Knodt 1999); (c) the conception of civil society actors; (d) their function within the political process; and (e) the function of the public for civil society participation. Each of these dimensions can have two values and therefore can be merged into two ideal types (for details see Knodt 2005).

In the first mode — in the sense of a Weberian ideal type — the consultative mode, involvement is for the purpose of consultation. In this case, decisions about the access of civil society actors to policy-formulation are made ad hoc and selectively. The dominating governance mechanism is sovereign governance with the selective inclusion of societal actors. Civil society actors are of interest merely for their resources and qualities (such as expertise, according to Schmitter's 'holder' concept; Schmitter 2002). Their inclusion should improve the qualities of decision-making and facilitate the implementation of policies. Moreover, civil society actors are intended to act as mediators to the public and work to gain support for the political decisions reached. In this context, the public is the arena for the mobilization of support for decisions at international level (Knodt 2005). In the second mode (deliberative communication mode), intended more for communication and deliberative procedural provisions of involvement, civil society actors experience broad inclusion in political decision-making processes. Thus, the mode is based on the communicative theory of Habermas (1998). The mode is characterised by the codification of inclusion and the existence of institutionalized access to inclusion procedures. Sovereign governance is therefore closely connected to societal governance. The interaction of political and societal actors is thus characterized by an understanding-oriented approach and civil society actors are considered to be advocates of legitimate interests (Schmalz-Bruns 2002). Special value is given to the integrative forums for the exchange of all good arguments, marked by their open and deliberative character (Habermas 1998, 166;

Habermas 1992, 23). It is assumed that this procures common welfare and that the quality of decisions is improved. As an overall achievement of this procedure, the legitimacy of the decision is increased. The public is, in this context, the arena for deliberative communication for the public exchange of reasoning and explanations (Trenz 2005). This ideal type is therefore closely associated with the criteria of political decision-making in deliberative arenas developed in democracy theory (Schmalz-Bruns 2002; Steffek and Nanz 2008) and can partially help dispose of demand for supposed lacking legitimacy (Knodt 2005).

The European Commission is trying to enhance its legitimacy in propagating the deliberative communication mode of involvement, especially within its White paper on 'European Governance' from July 2001. In this paper, the European Commission strongly argues in favour of stronger interaction with regional and local governments as well as civil society (in a broad sense). Even if it sees the member states as being mainly responsible for the achievement of stronger interaction, the Commission, for its part, would like to establish a more systematic dialogue with the representatives of regional and local governance as well as civil society organisations through national and European associations at an early stage of policy-making (European Commission 2001, 4). Therefore, wide participation should be ensured throughout the policy chain, from design to implementation (European Commission 2001, 10). This claim of the European Commission for strong deliberative and communicative involvement based on the principle of participation is undermined by its routine approach to gathering expertise, which mainly follows the consultative mode (Knodt 2005).[2] The use of the involvement mode just described depends to a great extent upon the Commission's decision how to create the dialogue and varies between functional arenas and policy fields. The mode of involvement has an impact on the strategies of the different actors who want to represent their interests at the European level. The more the Commission follows the consultative mode, the more the actors have to represent their interests in an aggregated manner. Thus, the networks of integrative social networks (as platforms) and the umbrella associations have good chances of getting their common interest represented, which has an impact on their strategies of interest intermediation. The more selective the mode of involvement, the more important it is for interests to establish access points to the European institutions, or even better, to penetrate them. The strategies resemble the inside venue, as explained by Beyers (2008) in reference to Kollman (1998) and Grant (2001). Beyers distinguishes two arenas: The inside venue which aims at the world of advisory bodies and committees is not or only partially visible to a larger audience, whereas outside venues refers to 'the communication among interest groups, policy-makers and citizens' and 'becomes visible to a broader audience' (Beyers 2008, 1189). The distinction between the inside and outside venue fits very well with the consultative and communicative mode of involvement and therefore should be treated together in the following. The strategy of secondment (which will be presented later in detail) could be seen as one end of a continuum from not being invisible to being partly visible to a larger audience in regards to the participation of interests groups within advisory bodies and committees. In addition, the horizontal coordination of interest actors to improve their action and direct representation has to be seen as part of this inside strategy. The communication mode would lead to outside arenas being used as interest intermediation strategies, namely as 'venues where the communication among interest groups, policy-makers and citizens becomes visible to a broader audience' (Beyers 2008, 1189). Here, strategies will especially include the use of institutionalized access points like the European Economic and Social Committee (EESC) and the Committee of the Regions (CoR), as well as the participation in the consultation instruments of the EU.

At this point, the question is whether functional and territorial interests react in the same way to the involvement of the European Institutions or if they use the potential strategies differently? The hypothesis is that the distinctive types of interest — functional or territorial — are not reflected in the different strategies of interest representation within the European multi-level system. There is no causal relation between the use of strategies and the type of interest. Rather the mode of involvement has an impact on the strategies and instruments used. Within a mode of involvement we expect to find convergence in the strategies and instruments, whereas divergences are expected to occur between different modes of involvement. Thus, the convergence of the functional and territorial interest strategies can be explained by the opportunity structure of the European multi-level system, and in particular the two different involvement strategies which seem to enable the use of similar strategies within one mode by territorial and functional interests.

A second variable which explains convergence between territorial and functional interest intermediation are learning processes. Learning processes are conceptualized here as processes of diffusion, as elaborated by Levi-Faur (2005). Levi-Faur points out that individual and collective action has to be interpreted as striving for external 'structural forces' as well as 'contagious diffusion'. He stresses the point that structural force alone cannot explain change. Diffusion can be described as a process 'by which an innovation is communicated through certain channels over time among members of a social system' (Rogers 1995, 5). The outcome of processes of diffusion and structural forces can be clustered behaviour or convergence (Levi-Faur 2005). This discussion is closely linked to the models of policy learning, rooted in the field of policy-analysis. Here the model of the 'lesson drawing' model of Rose (1991) should be taken up. It provides the possibility to focus on strategies. Rose identifies different kinds of lesson-drawing: (1) copying, i.e., the implementation of a program that is already in effect; (2) adaptation, which is nearly the same thing but adjusts the program or strategy to fit the new context; (3) 'hybrid' creation through combining elements of programs from two different places; (4) synthesis, which is nearly the same thing, but combines programs from many different places; and (5) inspiration to create something new (Rose 1993, 30). This model is abstract enough to cover policy programs and actor strategies, and can explain how different strategies can diffuse from one interest type to the other. By examining the development of strategies, it can be assumed that it is likely that the different actor types have learned from each other, thus revealing a convergence of their strategies.

Different Strategies of Interest Intermediation within the European Multi-Level System

Looking at the strategies of interest intermediation of different actor types — territorial and functional — there are several main strategies that can be identified within the two main involvement strategies and the related inside and outside venues as described above.

(1) Strategies for Interest Representation in inside Venues of the EU through Consultative Involvement

A strategy within an inside arena that is completely invisible from the outside is secondment. The exchange of personnel between different administrations, known as secondment, has been more or less ignored as a strategy of functional interest intermediation in the EU by existing literature although this form of very informal access can be extremely effective. This instrument is only acknowledged in literature regarding policy-making at the national level or EU interest representation at the regional level — if at all. Especially in some German regions, the direct sending of regional administrative staff into the European Commission has to be seen as a strategy that has been successfully used for many years (see Knodt 1998, 2002a). It is particularly helpful in working out and implementing measures of regional politics, as well as research and technology politics. The civil servants sent into the Commission work there for a certain time span and their salaries continue to be paid by the region. Afterwards, they go back to their regional state service. In the case of Bavaria, this exchange is two-way, in that civil servants of the Commission work in Bavarian ministries for a certain amount of time. Mainly constitutionally strong regions out of the regionalised or federal member states have been using this strategy for some time.

The German functional actors in particular have started to copy this strategy. Since the mid-1990s, representatives of companies and associations have also been working in the Commission and have remained almost unnoticed by the public. The seconded business actors appear as regular Commission staff. The European Commission differentiates between 'seconded national experts' (SNEs) on the one hand, and 'special advisers' on the other. The latter are visible from the outside the Commission as business actors. The legal foundation for SNEs is a Commission Decision that was published in the beginning of 1998 (C(97)3402). Article 1 states:

> 1. The present Rules are applicable to national experts on detachment to the Commission and to national and international civil servants and private-sector employees serving with the institution under the staff exchange scheme. 2. The detached national experts covered

by these Rules shall remain in paid employment in an international, national, regional or local administration or in a salaried position in a private-sector firm throughout the period of detachment. (European Commission 1998)

This definition was modified in a new Commission Decision (C(2008) 6866) issued in 2008, making it harder but not impossible for functional actors to second employees into the Commission (European Commission 2008).[4] The number of SNEs varies — in 2000 the Commission stated in response to another parliamentary request (2001/C163E/116), that the number of SNEs rose to 655, whereas 32 belonged to the private sector. The strongest countries of origin represented herein were (in this order) France, Germany and UK (European Parliament 2000).

The strategy of secondment is in the meantime pursued by both territorial and functional actors. Here it can be shown that functional actors have learned from the long-term experience of territorial actors. The German functional actors were among the first to apply the secondment strategy (Adamek and Otto 2008). Thus, it can be assumed that they first adopted it from the German territorial actors. There is close cooperation between functional actors and the German regional representation offices in Brussels. The diffusion from the territorial to the functional actors took place through the exchange of personnel between regional administration and the business community (Adamek and Otto 2008). Some of them even have functional representation offices incorporated within their representations, such as Baden-Wurttemberg. In addition, functional actors in the German national administration have practised secondment since 2002, which might have reinforced the diffusion of this strategy into the functional realm at the European level.

As another strategy, both actor categories try to construct transnational communication arenas[1] that also serve as lobbying instruments mainly within an inside venue which is partly visible and part of the consultative involvement. The European regions and municipalities thus cooperate beyond national boundaries. Their motivation is twofold: On the one hand, common problems need to be identified and solved; on the other hand, the co-operation serves better coordination and strengthening of interest representation on the European and, to a lesser extent, the national level. This is a main difference to the functional transnational co-operations which are centrally aimed at strengthening interest representation. Bundling and thereby strengthening their interests is a very important strategy within the consultative involvement type of the European Commission. Functional as well as regional and local actors represent their interests collectively at the EU level through European associations. The transnational European business associations, as well as NGO representations, are usually responsible for the EU level. Since most European associations have a very high degree of representation, they are best positioned to present an aggregated and — where possible — profound opinion of their companies to the European institutions, most specifically the Commission, which is crucial for a successful interest representation within the consultative type of involvement.

The Commission itself exerts influence on the European organisational structure through its clear preference for European interest representation. The Commission makes use of the Euro associations as a source of information for technical and economic questions. Through their filter function, Euro associations can offer information in their respective area of expertise to the Commission, which is already the outcome of an internal decision-making process of the national member associations (Knodt and Quittkat 2004). Thus, they are perfectly suited to fulfil their consultative function, as expected by the Commission within the consultative type of involvement. A single interest without a majority within the European association does not find its way to the European level, as would be requested by the communicative type of involvement.

Territorial interests are also collectively represented on the European level. On the regional level these are the 'Assembly of European Regions' (AER), as well as the conferences 'Europe of the Regions' (Heinelt and Niederhafner 2008) which where brought up during the discourse of a Europe of and with regions starting in the 1980s. The AER sees its function as a common decision body of the regions based on a broad foundation for its common actions within the EC context. The conference 'Europe of the Regions' contains a more ad hoc character and can be considered as a forum of the legally and materially strong regions. For local actors this would be the international co-operation within the International Union of Local Authorities (ILUA) and the Council of European Municipalities and Regions (CEMR) or the city network EUROCITIES, in which municipalities themselves are organised.

As some of the territorial actor associations were founded in the 1950s without being related to the European Communities, we witness a parallel strategy of interest representation with regard to the different actor types. Thus, we cannot find clear diffusion processes in the overall strategy. However, we can find some strategies used by territorial actors only, such as the co-operation of regions that are far apart from each other to represent their common interests as well as to strengthen the region in their own national states and the European system. The most prominent example is the working group 'Four Motors for Europe', made-up of the four regions, Baden-Wurttemberg, Rhône-Alps, Lombardy and Catalonia, which have been cooperating on different issues since 1988 (see Knodt 2002a). For local actors we can observe the inter-linkage of problem resolution, information generation and lobbying. Thus, local networks mainly serve for the exchange of knowledge and diffusion of innovative practices in city politics on the one hand, and offer support in the application for European funds as well as assertion of local interests as lobbying bodies, on the other hand (Zimmermann 2008, 19; Knodt 2010). The same holds true for the cross-border co-operation, which dates back to the 1970s and is especially carried out within the European structural funds through the Community initiative INTERREG.

However, this strategy of constructing transnational communication arenas as such can also be used by both actor categories as a strategy of communication involvement and an outside venue, if these arenas are used for campaigning. This can be witnessed in the case of NGOs as well as business and territorial actors (see Knodt and Finke 2005).

Direct interest representation at the European level is one of the strategies used by both actor categories within the consultative involvement, which is also partly visible within the inside venue. It seems to be the most visible strategy because the representation offices at the EU level also have to demonstrate their work to the outside.

Direct representation of interests by functional actors can be witnessed since the beginning of the European Community. Firms employ dedicated representation in Brussels to lobby the European institutions. Nevertheless, national differences are found between member states; whereas lobbying by firms was comparatively rare in the 1990s in Germany, it has always been common in France and Great Britain (Van Schendelen 1993; Quittkat 2002; Eising 2007). On the European level, only multinational companies can afford direct lobbying because the resource expenses for a representation in Brussels are high. Even though there is the danger of independent company lobbying intruding with the filter and aggregation function and the associability of European and national associations, many associations do not consider the independent lobbying activities of their members as problematic; moreover, some regard it as complementary to their own efforts. This is due to their specific 'information-competence', which is inherent to the different actors. Multinational companies, in particular, are considered to have special expertise concerning national legal, tax and social law systems because they are most affected by the differences between the member states (Knodt and Quittkat 2004). Hence, they provide the demanded expertise within the consultative involvement. National associations also have direct contact to the EU level in the course of interest intermediation. This direct contact is important as the filter function of the Euro association screens out nationally concentrated minority opinions within the European association's position, so that these remain disregarded. Moreover, national associations exert more competence concerning legal questions and the assessment of political consequences because they are more familiar with the respective legal systems as well as the political atmosphere in their countries. Companies and national associations are following the whole policy cycle on the European level and try to insert their interests as early as the agenda-setting phase (Knodt and Quittkat 2004).

Territorial actors later started to directly represent their interests at the European level and copied their functional examples. Since the mid-1980s, regions have made an effort to reach the European level directly (see Greenwood, this issue; Knodt, Große Hüttmann, and Kotzian 2009). Hereby, regions in federal and regionalised states established a complementary structure to their involvement through the national state. It is important to note that this new strategy runs in addition to the interest representation of institutions of federal and regionalised states, and has at no time replaced these. Through the direct representations, regions in these states gained the possibility to introduce their interests into European politics for the first time, while additionally strengthening their position within the national state. Constitutionally weak regions used this strategy to get their interests represented directly within the EU and also used this to fight for more constitutional rights within their national states, like the most prominent examples of the British and Spanish regions (see Lange 1998).

On the one hand, direct representation of regions serves to improve information about European politics, and on the other hand, their regional lobbying in Brussels (see Greenwood, this issue). The regions' information and liaison offices in Brussels are important instruments in this regard. The first of these were established in the mid-1980s. Opening these information and liaison offices provoked fierce controversy as they were seen as 'secondary foreign politics'. In the meantime, the direct representation of regional interests is accepted by all member states. Today, almost every region, irrespective of its constitutional setting within member states, is represented through its own office. Nowadays, cities and municipalities also go for direct representations in order to be better informed about European politics and fulfil a lobbying function in Brussels. These are being established at an increasing rate since the late 1990s and are being copied from the regions (John 2000; Knodt 2010).

Comparing the territorial interest representation of today with its beginnings, a considerable shift has taken place as shown by the new research that analysed the representation offices of the German Laender in comparison (Knodt, Große Hüttman, and Kotzian 2009). Taking the policy cycle of agenda-setting, policy formulation, decision-making and implementation, it can be observed that the functions of early warning systems and active networking with EU institutions gained most importance. These are both functions that are needed mostly to influence agenda-setting, policy formulation and decision-making. Through these developments, a shift from a concentration on the implementation phase to the early phase of agenda-setting and policy formulation took place in the function of Laender representatives. Thus, territorial actors now perform the development that functional actors have been exerting since the early phases of the EU, or at the latest, since the deepening of integration through the Maastricht Treaty — thus showing a learning process in which they have copied the functional strategy. The diffusion of these practices again seems to have come from the functional realm and been carried by staff who was recruited from firms and business associations by the regional representation offices (Knodt, Große Hüttman, and Kotzian 2009).

(2) Strategies for Interest Representation in Outside Venues of the EU through Communicative Involvement

A very visible strategy within the communicative involvement is the institutionalized participation through the institutional setting of the EC/EU. Territorial as well as functional interests are provided with European channels of institutionalised participation by the European Economic and Social Committee (EESC) and the Committee of the Regions (CoR), even though they are only consultative bodies. The EESC is the oldest institution for interest representation, established by the 1957 Rome Treaties. It was especially set up to involve economic and social interest groups in the establishment of the common market and to provide expertise for the

European Commission and the Council of Ministers on European Community issues relevant at the time. Its role was reinforced by the different Treaty revisions and its organisational set up was up-dated. But its main purpose as an institutionalised channel for functional interest intermediation has not been changed (see Smisman 2000). Copying this model of the EESC, territorial actors pushed for their own committee at the beginning of the 1990s. With the negotiations of the Maastricht Treaty revision, the discussion around the representation of regional interests on the European level reached its peak. The regions' demands had achieved entry into the Maastricht Treaty (see Hrbek 2000; Christiansen and Lintner 2005). As one of the main demands, the Committee of the Regions (CoR), a regional consultative body, was created after the ideal of the EESC (Art. 198, Maastricht Treaty). Within the CoR, regional and local authorities can represent their interests directly and independently to the Council and the Commission, i.e., not through the governments of the member states. Even the German local actors have three representatives in the CoR, who are sent by the national municipal associations. However, it fulfils a merely consultative function, as well; its competencies are confined to the right of hearing and the right to submit statements (Hrbek 2000). The CoR has also changed over time. The Lisbon Treaty strengthens the CoR as it obliges the European Commission to consult with local and regional authorities and their associations across the EU as early as in the pre-legislative phase. Both bodies presumed to be representative and consultative bodies for common interests of specific types of actors rather than an effective way of getting the interests of single actors represented.

Influenced by the discussion to enhance the EU and especially the Commission's legitimacy, the Commission enriched its set of involvement strategies, as elaborated above. Thus, it has come up with a variety of instruments out of the communicative involvement such as online forums and policy forums as well as European Citizens' Conferences which are used by actors to represent their interests. As these instruments are analysed in detail by Christine Quittkat and Peter Kotzian in this issue, it need only be mentioned here that public authorities and their associations are also as functional interest taking part in these instruments, even if this is not their main strategy (for detailed participation pattern see Quittkat and Kotzian, this issue).

Conclusion

This contribution has identified new trails in comparing territorial and functional interest representation. It has been shown that both actor categories make use of similar strategies and that these strategies have converged over time despite still existing minor differences of actor specific strategies. Rather, the strategies were aligned at the involvement types of the EU. Within this contribution, two types of involvement were distinguished — a consultative and a communicative type. These types were linked to a more inside and more outside venue of interest intermediation. Functional and territorial interests applied different strategies according to these types of involvement. Both actor categories nowadays make use of the strategy of secondment, construct transnational communication arenas and apply strategies of direct representation as part of an inside venue within the consultative involvement. The communicative involvement shows the strategies of both actor categories using institutionalized access points (EESC and CoR), joining online consultations and campaigning.

It has also been shown that the different actor categories are learning from each other and that the ideas of different strategies have diffused. For example, for territorial actors, the strategy of secondment depicts a customary strategy, whereas for functional actors, it is a new strategy. Thus, over time, both categories of interest intermediation have converged to a great extent.

Overall, it has been shown that both actor categories deploy all strategies and channels at the same time and thus work with complementary strategies. In the EU interactive multilevel system of action, operating at only one level or relying on one strategy does not lead to the intended effect. This does not mean that territorial and functional interests are interchangeable in analytical terms. Piattoni (this issue) provides us with fundamental knowledge about the differences of these two categories that coexist in their efforts of interest representation and with the specificities of territorial representation. Moreover, it is common sense that through their constitutional setting, regions are equipped with different competencies and are, therefore, more (e.g., Belgium and Germany) or less (e.g., France and the United Kingdom) involved in EC policy-making via the central state. However, this contribution should have made clear that both actor categories apply mainly the same strategies if they want to represent their interest successfully. Thus, a kind of European model of interest intermediation has been developed, which is shaped by the different types of involvement of the EU institutions and the challenges the multi-level system poses to territorial and functional interests. It is based much more on consultative inside venues than outside venues, according to the communicative mode of involvement. It applies strategies for both arenas in a complementary way because neither territorial nor functional actors count on one single strategy to represent their interests within the European multilevel system.'

Notes

1. The analysis will especially look at sub-national actors as territorial interests.
2. The data used here is derived from the research projects 'The Europeanisation of Interest Representation' (EUROLOB — Eising; Kohler-Koch; Quittkat) and from the VW-Project 'Regions as unities of action in European politics' (REGE; see Knodt 1998; Kohler-Koch et al. 1998).
3. 68,8% of Euro associations represent 75% of its potential members (according to their statute), whilst only 55,5% of national associations in France, Germany and Great Britain have a similarly high degree of representativity (Knodt and Quittkat 2004).
4. For an example see the various projects of the 'Oberrheinkonferenz', where the chambers of commerce and the chambers of crafts are involved, http://www.oberrheinkonferenz.org/de/themen-und-projekte/wirtschaft/projekte/ (accessed 26 August 2010).
5. See http://ec.europa.eu/civil_service/job/sne/index_en.htm (4 June 2010).

References

Adamek, S., and K. Otto. 2008. *Der gekaufte Staat. Wie Konzernvertreter in deutschen Ministerien sich ihre Gesetze selbst schreiben.* Köln: Kiepenheuer & Witsch.

Anderson, J.J. 1990. Skeptical reflections on a Europe of Regions: Britain, Germany, and the ERDF. *Journal of Public Policy* 10, no. 4: 417–47.

Balme, R., and D. Chabanet. 2008. *European governance and democracy. Power and protest in the EU.* Lanham: Rowan and Littlefield.

Benz, A. 2000. Entflechtung als Folge von Verflechtung: Theoretische Überlegungen zur Entwicklung des europäischen Mehrebenensystems. In *Wie problemlösungsfähig ist die EU? Regieren im europäischen Mehrebenensystem*, eds. E. Grande and M. Jachtenfuch, 141–64. Baden-Baden: Nomos.

Beyers, J. 2004. Voice and access. Political practices of European interest associations. *European Union Politics* 5, no. 2: 211–40.

Beyers, J. 2008. Policy issues, organisational format and the political strategies of interest organisations. *West European Politics* 31, no. 6: 1188–211.

Beyers, J., R. Eising, and W. Maloney. 2008. Researching interest group politics in Europe and elsewhere: much we study, little we know. *West European Politics* 31, no. 6: 1103–28.

Borras-Alomar, S., T. Christiansen, and A. Rodriguez-Pose. 1994. Towards a 'Europe of the Regions'? Visions and reality from a critical perspective *Regional Politics and Policies* 4, no. 2: 1–27.

Boschma, R., and R. Schobben. 2000. Special issue: Europe and the regions. The issue of governance. *Regional and Federal Studies* 10.

Bouwen, P. 2002. Corporate lobbying in the European Union: the logic of access. *Journal of European Public Policy* 9, no. 3: 365–90.

Christiansen, T., and P. Lintner. 2005. The Committee of the Regions after 10 years: lessons from the past and challenges for the future. EIPAScope 1, 7–13.

Coen, D. 1998. The European business interest and the nation state: large-firm lobbying in the European Union and member states. *Journal of Public Policy* 18, no. 1: 75–100.

Coen, D. 2007. Empirical and theoretical studies in EU lobbying. *Journal of European Public Policy* 14, no. 3.

Cohen, J., and C. Sabel. 1997. Directly-deliberative democracy. *European Law Journal* 3, no. 4: 313–42.

Dür, A., and D. DeBièvre. 2007. The question of interest group influence. *Journal of Public Policy* 27, no. 1: 1–12.

Eising, R. 2004. Multilevel governance and business interests in the European Union. *Governance* 172, 211–45.

Eising, R. 2007. Institutional context, organizational resources, and strategic choices: explaining interest group access in the European Union. *European Union Politics* 11, no. 3: 329–69.

Eriksen, E.O., and J.E. Fossum. 2000. *Democracy in the European Union.* London: Routledge.

European Commission. 1998. Rules applicable to national experts on detachment to the Commission, 07.01.1998, C(97) 3402.

European Commission. 2001. European governance. A White Paper, Brussels, 25.7.2001, COM (2001), 428 final.

European Commission. 2008. Commission gecision of 12.11.2008 laying down rules on the secondment to the Commission of national experts and national experts in professional training, 12.11.2008, C(2008) 6866 final.

European Parliament. 2000. Written question E-3403/00 by Monica Frassoni (Verts/ALE) to the Commission, 07.11.2000, 2001/C 163 E/116.

Grant, W. 2001. Pressure politics: from 'insider' politics to direct action. *Parliamentary Affairs* 54, no. 2: 337–48.

Grote, J., and B. Gbikpi. 2002. *Participatory governance. Political and societal implications.* Opladen: Leske + Budrich.

Grote, J., M. Knodt, and F. Larat. 1996. *Convergence et variation des styles régionaux de politique dans le cadre des politiques communautaires.* Mannheim : Arbeitspapier des Mannheimer Zentrums für Europäische Sozialforschung, AB III 17.

Habermas, J. 1992. Drei normative Modelle der Demokratie: Zum Begriff deliberativer Politik. In *Die Chancen der Freiheit. Grundprobleme der Demokratie*, ed. H. Münkler, 11–24. München Zürich: Piper.

Habermas, J. 1998. Die postnationale Konstellation und die Zukunft der Demokratie. In *Die postnationale Konstellation. Politische Essays*, ed. J. Habermas, 91–169. Frankfurt am Main: Suhrkamp.

Heinelt, H. 2002. Civic perspectives on a democratic transformation of the EU. In *Participatory governance. Political and societal implications*, eds. J. Grote and B. Gbikpi, 97–120. Opladen: Leske + Budrich.

Heinelt, H., and S. Niederhafner. 2008. Cities and organized interest intermediation in the EU multi-level system. *European Urban and Regional Studies* 15, no. 2: 173–87.

Hooghe, L., and G. Marks. 2001. *Multi-level governance and European integration*. Lanham: Rowman and Littlefield.

Hrbek, R. 2000. Das Subsidiaritätsprinzip in der EU. Bedeutung und Wirkung nach dem Vertrag von Amsterdam. In *Jahrbuch des Föderalismus 2000. Föderalismus, Subsidiarität und Regionen in Europa*, ed. Europäisches Zentrum für Föderalismus-Forschung, 510–31. Baden-Baden: Nomos.

John, P. 2000. Europeanization of sub-national governance. *Urban Studies* 37, no. 5/6: 877–94.

John, P. 2001. *Local governance in western Europe*. London: Sage.

Keating, M., and B. Jones. 1985. Regions in the European Community. Oxford: Clarendon.

Knodt, M. 1998. *Tiefenwirkung europäischer Politik. Eigensinn oder Anpassung regionalen Regierens?* Baden-Baden: Nomos.

Knodt, M. 2002a. Europäisierung regionalen Regierens: Mit Sinatra zum 'autonomieorientierten Systemwechsel' im deutschen Bundesstaat. *Politische Vierteljahresschrift* 2, no. 2: 211–34.

Knodt, M. 2002b. Regions in multilevel governance arrangements: leadership versus partnership. In *Participatory governance. Political and societal implications*, eds. J. Grote and B. Gbikpi, 177–94. Opladen: Leske + Budrich.

Knodt, M. 2004. Governance in an expanded multi-level system. *Journal of European Public Policy* 11, no. 4: 701–19.

Knodt, M. 2005. *Regieren im erweiterten europäischen Mehrebenensystem — die internationale Einbettung der EU*. Baden-Baden: Nomos.

Knodt, M. 2010. Kommunales Regieren im europäischen Mehrebenensystem. In *Die EU-Reflexionsgruppe Horizont 2020–2030: Herausforderungen und Reformoptionen für das Mehrebenensystem*, eds. G. Abels, A. Eppler and M. Knodt, 153–68. Baden-Baden: Nomos.

Knodt, M., and B. Finke. 2005. *Europäische Zivilgesellschaft. Konzepte, Akteure, Strategien*. Wiesbaden: VS-Verlag.

Knodt, M., M. Große Hüttmann, and P. Kotzian. 2009. Direkte Interessenrepräsentation der deutschen Länder in der EU. In *Europapolitik und Europafähigkeit von Regionen*, eds. K.-H. Lambertz and M. Große Hüttmann, 123–35. Baden-Baden: Nomos.

Knodt, M., and C. Quittkat. 2004. Interessenvermittlung im europäischen Mehrebenensystem. *Politische Bildung* 37, 64–79.

Kohler-Koch, B. 1999. Evolution and transformation. In *The transformation of governance in the European Union*, eds. B. Kohler-Koch and R. Eising, 14–35. London: Routledge.

Kohler-Koch, B., et al. 1998. *Interaktive Politik in Europa: Regionen im Netzwerk der Integration*. Opladen: Leske + Budrich.

Kohler-Koch, B., and M. Knodt. 1999. Konzepte der politischen Steuerung in einer globalisierten Welt. In *Facetten der Globalisierung. Ökonomische, soziale und politische Aspekte*, ed. U. Steger, 235–56. Berlin: Springer.

Kohler-Koch, B., and C. Quittkat. 2011. *Die Entzauberung partizipativer Demokratie. Zur Rolle der Zivilgesellschaft bei der Demokratisierung von EU-Governance*. Frankfurt/Main: Campus.

Kollman, K. 1998. *Outside lobbying. Public opinion and interest group strategies*. Princeton, NJ: Princeton University Press.

Lange, N. 1998. *Zwischen Regionalismus und europäischer Integration. Wirtschaftsinteressen in regionalistischen Konflikten*. Baden-Baden: Nomos.

Levi-Faur, D. 2005. The global diffusion of regulatory capitalism. *Annals of the American Academy of Political and Social Science* 598, 12–32.

Princen, S., and B. Kerremans. 2008. Opportunity structures in the EU multi-level system. *West European Politics* 31, no. 6: 1129–46.

Quittkat, C. 2002. *Europäisierung der Interessenvermittlung. Französische Wirtschaftsverbände zwischen Beständigkeit und Wandel*. Wiesbaden: VS Verlag.

Rogers, M.E. 1995. *The diffusion of innovations*. New York: Free Press.

Rose, R. 1991. What is lesson-drawing? *Journal of Public Policy* 11, no. 1: 3–30.

Rose, R. 1993. *Lesson-drawing in public policy*. Chatham, NJ: Chatham House.

Scharpf, F. 1999. *Governing in Europe. Effective and democratic?*. Oxford: Oxford University Press.

Schmalz-Bruns, R. 1999. Deliberativer Supranationalismus. Demokratisches Regieren jenseits des Nationalstaates. *Zeitschrift für Internationale Beziehungen* 6, no. 2: 185–244.

Schmalz-Bruns, R. 2002. The normative desirability of participatory democracy. In *Participatory governance in multi-level context. Concepts and experience*, eds. H. Heinelt, et al., 59–74. Opladen: Leske + Budrich.

Schmitter, P.C. 2002. Participation in governance arrangements: is there any reason to expect it will achieve sustainable and innovative policies in a multilevel context? In *Participatory governance. Political and societal implications*, eds. Jürgen J. Grote and B. Gbikpi, 51–70. Opladen: Leske + Budrich.

Schmitter, P., and W. Streeck. 1981. *The organization of business interests. A research design to study the associative action of business in the advanced industrial societies of western Europe*. Discussion paper IIMV/Arbeitsmarktpolitik, Wissenschaftszentrum Berlin.

Smismans, S. 2000. The European economic and social committee: towards deliberative democracy via a functional assembly. *European Integration online Papers (EIoP)* 4, no. 12.

Steffek, J., and P. Nanz. 2008. Emergent patterns of civil society participation in global and European governance. In *Civil society participation in european and global governance: a cure for the democratic deficit?* eds. J. Steffek, C. Kissling, and P. Nanz, 1–29. Houndmills, Basingstoke: Palgrave Macmillan.

Trenz, H.-J. 2005. Zivilgesellschaft und Öffentlichkeit im europäischen Integrationsprozess: normative Desiderate und empirische Interdependenzen in der Konstitution einer europäischen Herrschaftsordnung. In *Europäische Zivilgesellschaft. Konzepte, Akteure, Strategien*, eds. M. Knodt and B. Finke, 55–78. Wiesbaden: VS-Verlag.

Van Schendelen, M. 1993. *National public and private EC lobbying*. Aldershot: Dartmouth.

Woll, C. 2009. Trade policy lobbying in the European Union. In *Lobbying the European Union: institutions actors and issues*, eds. D. Coen and J. Richardson, 277–297. Oxford: Oxford University Press.

Zimmermann, K. 2008. Cities for growth, jobs, and cohesion. Die implizite Stadtpolitik der EU. In *Lokale Politikforschung heute*, eds. H. Heinelt and A. Vetter, 79–102. Wiesbaden: VS Verlag.

Actors of the Common Interest? The Brussels Offices of the Regions

JUSTIN GREENWOOD

Robert Gordon University, Aberdeen Business School, Aberdeen, UK

ABSTRACT The absence of a formal place in representative democracy at EU level casts sub-national authorities more as actors of EU participatory democracy. Where they have specific interests to pursue their Brussels offices act in the same way as 'lobbyists', but public authorities are also capable of acting on broader interest sets. This analysis is geared to understanding variation in the extent to which the diversely constituted Brussels offices of the regions can act on a broad spectrum of civil society interests, and thus have potential as actors of European integration in connecting civil society with EU institutions. Differences in the orientation of offices towards either highly defined or broad agendas can be conceived in qualified principal–agent terms, in which the autonomy of offices to develop activities is the critical explanatory factor. This autonomy can be derived more from the structure of principals and from degrees of purpose they have than from asymmetries of power between principals and agents, which in turn can be drawn from typologies of degrees of devolved authority present in different member states. It predicts that territorial offices from member states with medium degrees of devolved authority have the greatest potential to act on a broad range of civil society oriented interests.

As the first two contributions to this special issue elaborate, the passage of functional interest representation through territorial channels at EU level raises a variety of intriguing issues. There are no direct links between regions and the EU Committee of the Regions (CoR), because it is member states which propose CoR members via the Council of Ministers. Appointed CoR members act as 'experts' in regional matters (Knodt this issue) rather than as delegates, while the CoR only has advisory status. Whilst there are established arrangements which permit member states to designate regions to act for them in decision-making in the Council of Ministers, these arrangements primarily concern member states which are federal or quasi-federal, are limited in scope, and ultimately depend upon member state agreement. In terms of the Lisbon Treaty, sub-national authorities are thus more actors of participatory democracy than of representative democracy. Yet as public authorities acting in their own back yards, they are familiar with the roles of representative democracy, aggregating demands from civil society and seeking to reconcile competing claims. They are not required by EU decision-making structures to do these things, but they can do, and need to conform to expectations that they do so by the populations they serve. These factors place them in a distinct position in EU interest representation, sentiments which are expressed in the following excerpts:

> Concerning the question of legitimacy, the local government organisations are distinct from other interest groups. As the elected government bodies nearest to the people, they are able to express the interests and concerns of the broad citizenry and do not represent just the concerns and demands of certain (self-interested) stakeholders. (Heinelt and Niederhafner 2008, 175)

> Brussels can indeed be considered the world capital of lobbying for local and regional authorities. The activities of their representations in Brussels, present, however, a specific profile that partly distinguishes them from classic interest groups and lobbies. The activities of regional representations in Brussels are broader and not focused solely on direct lobbying and interest representation. (Huysseune and T. Jans. 2008, 10)

Yet sub-national authorities can and do become 'lobbyists' for their own distinct interests as public authorities, responding in similar ways to other producer interests so as to diffuse the costs of regulation of their service provision (such as responsibilities for waste collection from electronic equipment) to other parties. In such circumstances, they act as 'lobbyists' would, taking collective action and seeking where possible to appeal to public interest advocates for tactical alliances likely to carry the broad support necessary for EU public policy-making. Where EU public policy produces distributive and re-distributive benefits with territorial effects (such as funding schemes or where there is reliance upon a particular industry), territorial authorities also have interests to maximise, which may structure patterns of collective action. Many sub-national authorities now have offices in Brussels in pursuit of such goals. Yet when public authorities do not become direct stakeholders in the distribution of costs and benefits, they have the opportunity to become players in wider systemic goals, with the potential to act as agents of EU democratic legitimacy by bridging territorial civil society with EU institutions. The key question addressed by this article is: Which of the territorial Brussels offices are likely to act as wider agents of EU democratic legitimacy?

The ambivalence in the role of sub-national authorities at EU level is reflected in the European Transparency Register. The first version (2008) set apart public authorities from 'lobbyists' by declaring that 'public authorities of any level or geographical origin are not expected to register' (European Commission. 2008, 2). In a change of direction, the proposals for a revised version of the scheme (2011) expect representative offices of such authorities to register. Are the Brussels offices of the regions somehow a category apart from 'special interest groups' (and thus have the capacity to act as wider agents 'of the broad citizenry')? What significant differences arise between different sub-national representations in Brussels to act as such agents, and why? Are some preoccupied with using the Brussels venue for other purposes? Do some offices have more potential than others to act as agents of wider civil society (rather than of particularistic types of — primarily producer — interests)? And if so, what are the predictive factors, and how are these operationalised? Such questions matter, because the potential for sub-national actors to act as two way conduits between the populations they serve and EU institutions has long been recognised in EU initiatives oriented towards popular legitimacy, most notably in the 2001 White Paper on Governance.

Such questions about the role of the Brussels offices of the regions inevitably draw upon issues of 'principals' (those who fund such offices, and in turn those to whom these funders answer), and 'agents' (the offices and their employees). Instead of following well-trodden pathways about degrees of homogeneity amongst principals, and mechanisms linking agents to principals, an alternative frame is the degree to which the principals start off with distinct goals. Where principals have distinct goals, so it may be expected that offices act as tightly controlled 'mandated delegates', with mechanisms deployed to keep agents tied to those goals. Where there are more generalised factors in the establishment of offices, so agents would have considerable structural autonomy to develop activities of their own choice, provided they can be 'sold' to principals as generating value. In such a scenario, agents would not be treated as mandated delegates. If employee agents are recruited from the EU 'circuit' rather than solely from the ranks of regional administrations, they may be more likely to develop activities which build European integration by linking territorial civil society with EU institutions.

Characteristics of the Population: The Brussels Offices of the Regions

A detailed interrogation of the most recent edition of a *repertoire* produced by the Committee of the Regions (CoR) of 'Associations/Bureaux de Representation Regionale et Communale a Bruxelles' (CoR 2009) reveals a population of 215 sub-national territorial representations in Brussels from the member states. While this population is diverse, most of the organisations listed are territorial public authorities within the member states. In a survey by Marks *et al.*, two-thirds of the Brussels offices of the regions represented a single sub-national government (Marks *et al.*, 2002). There are also collective units of local and regional authorities drawn from a distinct concept and created for the purpose of pooling resources for Brussels representation.

Some of the Brussels territorial representations have a more diverse range of direct stakeholders than sub-national territorial governing authorities. One such type is the public–private partnership. Some of these are a concept which (as discussed later) reflects historic national controversies in the very concept of the establishment of a territorial 'representation' in Brussels. Some public–private partnerships are more pragmatic creations which are orientated towards funding, partner-searching, and branding a region. Another concept is a widely drawn stakeholder membership model, embracing public authorities and regional development agencies alongside territorial organisations drawn from business and commerce, trade unions, universities, public agencies, organisations of the professions, and 'third sector' organisations. This latter model is common among UK offices, which often provide a range of 'member services'. Whereas offices tied to a regional authority have the preoccupations of that authority, usually with political guidance, offices based on serving members are likely to have a wider range of activities which reflects membership diversity. Table 1 summarises the population data extracted from the CoR *repertoire* chosen as the focus of analysis here.

Balme and Chabanet note how EU mobilisation has been particularly strong among 'medium range subnational authorities' (62), and in particular the UK and the Nordic countries, where offices were established at an early stage, and in the case of Nordic countries ahead of accession. Their explanation for this is because more powerful regions from federal or quasi-federal states are caught up through their domestic linkages in a consensus between national governments and the Commission not to address domestic political issues (Balme and Chabanet 2008). Conversely, regional authorities from 'medium' devolved countries have a particular niche which makes them well placed to take up a broad set of issues related to European integration.

The variation between territorial offices in size of establishment is very marked. Unsurprisingly, offices from countries with high territorial devolution are well populated among the top size quartile in the Marks *et al.* survey of 2002. Those from Germany, Austria, Belgium and Spain spent an average of €447,000 each year, with some occupying 1000m^2 space (Marks *et al.* 2002) and a budget in excess of €1m (Vleva 2008). The German Länder together employ 400 staff, as opposed to 150 in the German permanent representation (Moore 2006); some of their representations have the feel of sizeable diplomatic missions, complete with bier kellar cabins and gardens for entertaining. At the other end of the spectrum, the lowest quartile of all offices in the Marks *et al.* survey had budgets of less than €150,000 and floor space of less than 80m^2, where a local government or small group of localities in the same region might employ a single person on a shared-time basis.

There are very few territorial representative offices in Brussels from centralised countries. Portugal, Greece, and Ireland, had virtually no presence during the 1980s and 1990s, highlighting the weakness of linkage between funding receipts and a Brussels presence. The small number of territorial representative offices from these countries arrived at a later time, often led by a regional development agency. Most central and eastern European countries remain highly centralised, with the partial exception of Poland and Hungary. From 2004 accession countries, Poland has the greatest presence of territorial offices in Brussels, with a small office for each of its eighteen administrative regions. These are undertakings of typically one–three staff, exercising minimal functions such as information tasks, and working under some degree of co-ordination assistance from the national permanent representation (Riedel 2010). These offices also provide a means of EU oriented training for future civil servants, often relying upon internships for their staffing. 'Offices' from some of the other accession countries have proved somewhat more transient. In worst-case scenarios, there are symbolic directory entries listing no more than a Brussels postal address box.

Classifying countries by degrees of devolved authority to the regions is a cottage industry in itself, with a variety of complexities, but a variety of sources yield a 'rough and ready' broad consensus as to the following contemporary degrees of classification.

Only regions from 'Medium' and 'High' devolution countries have offices with sufficient capacity to be a focus of analysis here. The extent of competence of territorial authority will always be a key, though not sole, factor, in shaping the nature of Brussels regional offices (Marks *et al.* 2002). The categories of 'low' and 'medium' and 'high' to some extent overlap, with the possibility to create sub-categories such as 'high-medium' and 'medium-low' based on a variety of indicators which structure centre-regional relationships (Watts 2006). Nonetheless, as is discussed below, the concept of categories of devolution, with a broadly based distinction between 'medium' and 'high', does help to predict which types of offices are most placed to develop broad agendas connected with European integration. The starting point for this is that offices tied to a single regional authority are the norm for countries with a high level of devolved authority apart from Belgium, where Flanders and Wallonia have spawned public/private partnership models. Belgian 'exceptionalism' is discussed later.

Variance in Goal Specificity: Which Factors Explain the Emergence and Development of the Brussels Territorial Offices?

Offices from the regions started to appear in Brussels in the mid 1980s, the first in 1984 and rising in number to almost 100 ten years later, and to 170 in 2001 (see the review in Mamadouh 2001). Some aspects of the development of these follow EU milestones which seemed likely to boost the 'regional agenda' in future years. These general stimuli included: The creation of the Committee of the Regions; the Treaty on European Union clauses on subsidiarity; permitting the representation of member states by sub-national authorities in the Council of Ministers (BELO 2009); and significant investment in structural and research fund instruments.

The establishment of some territorial offices in Brussels related to these events seems to have lacked specific focus other than a growing sense of the need to be where the action seemed to be happening, a recognition that a Brussels representative office had become the norm among territorial authorities (Riedel 2010), a response to a competitor region establishing a representative office, a status symbol, or to 'signpost' a region. The Brussels cocktail circuit flourished while some offices were seeking to develop their role, with regional delights freely proffered. Where there was a lack of focus, offices needed to find useful things to do and attract constituencies of support along the way aimed at organisational maintenance. This latter pathway of development is of particular significance to this enquiry, because in such offices lay the autonomy to develop activities with wider connections to European integration, rather than following more specific goal pursuits laid down by principals.

When the Committee of the Regions failed to develop beyond a model of 'experts about the regions' into a model of political representation in EU decision-making, some Brussels territorial offices found their feet with more focused agendas (Marks *et al.* 2002; Huysseune and Jans 2008), generating workloads which demanded office expansion. Tatham argues that 'first league' regions (from countries with high devolution) became oriented towards influencing public policy, while 'second league' regions with less significant domestic powers primarily chased funding orientated goals (Tatham 2008). For 'first league' regions, the possibility to represent a member state in the Council of Ministers meant the need to focus their resources accordingly, rather than seeking a role which might lead them into developing activities related to European integration. Among the German Länder, Knodt saw also an initial orientation towards the structural funds, and later as a response to poor information flows from federal ministries (Knodt 2002); there is now a 'Länderbeobachter' office in Brussels whose sole mission is to observe and report to the Länder on meetings of the Council of Ministers. All these activities therefore denote goals which were highly defined by principals, but other offices had some autonomy to define other roles for themselves.

In the case of 'second league' regions, the establishment of an office in Brussels might have been a symbolic measure to help support claims of local political leaders to have played a part in 'winning EU funding', despite the reality that such funds are primarily distributed as a result of decisions made by national governments in putting forward regional candidates (Greenwood, Levy, and Stewart 1995; Marks *et al.*, in Keating 2006; Olsson 2009). Once the symbolic function had been fulfilled, so offices had to find ways to develop their roles further. In funding pursuit mode, offices saw their role as being linked to economic development, becoming 'network brokers' for SMEs and universities so as to enhance the capacity of a region to access targeted funding instruments, looking to stimulate new cross-national partnerships. Once offices had gone as far as they could with funding, so offices sought to create other agendas to justify their existence, creating potential for the development of agendas related to civil society.

The act of devolving authority carries with it significant potential for centre–region power struggles (Watts 2006). The degree of this naturally varies according to the extent of alignment of domestic governing parties between the centre and the regions, but the potential for structural conflict is generally higher with greater degrees of devolved authority, in which Brussels inevitably became the latest venue in the ongoing battleground of relations between territorial authorities and central government. The issue came to greatest prominence in cases surrounding the establishment of offices from the German Länder, the Spanish Communidad Autonomas, and regions with special autonomous status in Italy. The presence of these offices in Brussels raised substantial national sensitivities about who had the right of external representation, leading to national constitutional court test cases to establish whether a regional 'representation' in Brussels was compatible with national law, or *ultra vires*. The cases themselves, and the structural tensions in centre–regional relations which underlie them, significantly shape the degree of purpose which the Brussels regional offices from these countries have, and the roles they undertake, and therefore here to assess their potential to undertake actions linked to European integration. Territorial offices locked in ongoing power struggles with central government, or with an institutionalised role in the EU policy process, have highly focused agendas which tie the workload of staff.

In Germany, the legal issues resulted in an early compromise whereby territorial offices initially chose low-key names such as 'information bureau' (Moore 2006). Once the right to a Brussels office was recognised, the result was the establishment of 'representative missions to Brussels' up to a substantial size, varying from municipalities to state level. Territorial presences in Brussels from Spain and Italy, typically had to operate under camouflage within the offices of a chamber of commerce mission, until such time as the court rulings went in favour of the regional authorities (Badiello 1998). The final outcome was that the regional authorities from high devolution countries, typically representing a regional government, could establish larger and more prominent capacities in Brussels in which a significant part of their activities were taken up either by protect/promote their own political agendas in EU or in domestic politics, or/and acting as 'watchdogs' of their member states in Brussels. This is also reflected in the nature of relationships with permanent representations. In countries of 'medium' devolved authority, where centre/regional relations are less fraught than in 'high' devolution countries, there is typically an informal working relationship between the regional office of the country concerned and the national permanent representation in Brussels, with notably close ties on dossiers of mutual interests to be found in the Dutch, British, Swedish and Finnish cases. In 'high' devolution countries, such as Germany and Spain, this relationship can be more formal, and sometimes tense, and in the case of Germany some of the municipal authority offices have no access to the permanent representation.

Territorial authorities from high devolution countries typically staff their Brussels offices from amongst their own pool of employees, rather than looking to rely upon recruitment from the pool of EU orientated staff to be found in Brussels who might be more orientated towards agendas about European integration. When these staff are sent as secondees to Brussels on limited life appointments, it increases the control of the 'principal' over the 'agent', and reduces the likelihood over time that the agent might 'go native' in Brussels. For regional governments it has been a common (but not exclusive) arrangement to second civil servants to their Brussels office for a limited duration; from Germany, a norm is for periods of up to four years (see also Moore 2006, who gives a figure of two–three years). A variation is the regional offices from Italy, which employ a mixed model of office staffing based on a core of 'civil servants' sent by, and tied to, the regional authority, but supplemented by a number of 'consultants' working on fixed duration EU funded projects who are recruited from the pool of EU specialists in the Brussels job market. These latter staff may bring with them a set of interests and experiences which are not tied to those of a specific regional authority, but more European in orientation. In tandem with arrangements for staff deployment is that the work of offices from countries with regional governing authorities is overseen by a deputy of the President of the region (see also Badiello 1998).

Employment related conditions can thus ensure that the principals have the means to keep their agents true to their goals, and restrict the ability of agents to develop a wider range of activities (such as those related more to European integration). In Pitkin's terms, these civil servants are more 'delegates' than 'agents' with significant degrees of autonomy (Pitkin 1967), operating to specific instructions from 'head office', and there is therefore limited scope for agents to stray from agendas designated by principals. The cumulative effect is that the roles of Brussels offices from 'high' devolution countries are more orientated towards interest agendas prescribed by regional authorities than wider agendas connected to European integration.

Where the staff of Brussels offices are not career public servants on limited period secondments from a sender authority back home, but come instead from a general pool of 'EU experts' on the Brussels scene, so they are more likely to have orientations towards European integration. There is just such a cadre of career mobile, Brussels based staff with strong EU connections, typically with a multi-lingual (and sometimes multi-national) background, and extensive knowledge of how the EU works. The cadre of *anciens* from the College of Europe are typical members of this pool, and some of the regions have specific schemes to fund scholarships at the College. They have a strong European orientation, are highly networked, and have interests in working on issues which are European in nature rather than tied to a remit of a principal sending authority. Such individuals can be identified among the pool of Brussels offices, with remits including citizenship and e-participation health, social policy, youth and education. In Pitkin's terms, these qualify as 'agents' rather than 'delegates' (Pitkin 1967). These staff are disproportionately more likely to be found in the offices of countries of 'medium' devolution where the working language is one of the main languages of the EU.

Saurugger sees the presence of such EU professionals in a somewhat problematic way, in that the 'professionalisation' of EU interest representation denotes the distance of organised civil society from 'grass roots' civil society (Saurugger 2006), characterised by a narrow, almost private dialogue in which 'Brussels talks to Brussels'. Saurugger's thesis has echoes of the rather hostile treatment of professionals in 'public choice' traditions, where the pursuit of private interest is seen as a core problem resulting in damage to wider public interests, and the solution is in finding ways of increased accountability to principals. Another interpretation is of a 'new class' with the capacity to perceive and represent common interests, a kind of emancipatory force as a result of their distance from the 'old classes' of capital and labour, with a liberal 'culture of critical discourse' (Gouldner 1979). Such a tradition applied here would place emphasis upon a cadre of European orientated, Brussels based professionals working for territorial offices who use their relatively autonomous positions to create civil society-wide agendas.

Another issue with the potential to impact upon the extent of functions performed by a Brussels territorial office is whether it represents a single or multiple municipalities. Multiple authority offices (most frequently found from the Netherlands) have been found to be much more oriented towards seeking to exercise political influence than are single locality offices (Marks *et al.* 2002). Over time, some territorial offices have consolidated into a model which involves some degree of collaboration so as to operate from the same address. Such scales of collaboration might involve sharing back-office facilities, through to a concept designed to facilitate functional collaboration on topics of common interest. In the Dutch 'G-4' Brussels office, an individual represents one each of the large four Dutch cities (Amsterdam, The Hague, Rotterdam, Utrecht), but share a collective office identity. These distinctions may carry implications for the type of work an office will undertake. In principal–agent terms, the dilution of control among multiple principals might result in a higher degree of autonomy for agents. But give that the establishment of such offices require a degree of purpose in their establishment between multiple funding principals, the scope to develop activities beyond these those defined by principals might be limited.

Thus, some extent of difference between the remit of Brussels territorial offices cannot be explained by comparing national degrees of decentralisation. Differences can be found among the remit of offices from individual countries. Xxxx, for instance, finds that competition between Länder helps explain differences in the capacities of their Brussels offices, noting differences in their abilities to interact strategically with EU authority on the basis of their involvement in networks. Using network analysis, she finds Baden Württemberg's participation in EU networks to be 'tighter' and 'denser' when compared to Lower Saxony (xxx.2002; see also Article x in this issue). Network participation can be expected to influence the extent to which an office is likely to become drawn into corresponding activities;

as is described later, Brussels territorial offices participate in a variety of networks with orientations towards citizen interests. But the variation between Brussels territorial offices is greatest when comparing offices by degrees of decentralisation, in which national traditions are a foremost factor.

Thus far, a proposition seems to be emerging; that *territorial offices from member states with a 'medium' degree of decentralised authority may have had sufficient autonomy and agenda space to develop self-generated activities which cover broad segments of civil society interests, and which may therefore have the potential to contribute to deepening EU democratic legitimacy*. To develop this further, some analysis is undertaken of the activities and structures of offices from member states with 'medium' degrees of devolved authority.

Brussels Territorial Offices as Actors of the Common Interest

A key issue in assessing differences of activities among Brussels territorial offices is the way in which the purposes of the individual offices are defined and interpreted by those concerned with their governance. In turn, the preceding discussion has indicated a number of ways in which the structure of 'principals' will influence the agendas of their agents. Some types of Brussels offices of the regions have been agents relatively free to use their station to create diverse agendas and activities.

The survey by Marks *et al.* confirms that the population as a whole undertake an eclectic range of activities, in which the offices rated just about every type of activity reviewed above as of some importance in their overall workload (Marks *et al.* 2002). These activities might be summarised as helping to connect the region — and the interests embedded within it — with Brussels, as well as Brussels with their region. However, in a (2008) survey of the Directors of 40 Brussels offices, Olsson notes a great variation in the extent to which the offices communicate 'the regional goals achieved in Brussels to the constituents at home' (Olsson 2009, 26). Olsson notes that most of the interviewees saw it as their role to 'bring Europe closer to the elites at home' (Olsson 2009, 26). Many had invested time in bringing local elites to Brussels; in a survey involving the participation of 123 of the Brussels regional offices, Huysseune and Jans report that an office hosts an average of 635 visitors each year (Huysseune and Jans 2008). Brussels office specific websites of the territories are full of news about a visit by a regional political figure, but also about visits by stakeholder groups in their own territories.

Whilst the agendas of most of the Federal countries are dominated by institutional participation, and centre–local relations, the Belgian regions are less pre-occupied with monitoring central government. This is because the centre is too weak relative to the regions, with the regions undertaking national functions for EU representation; thus, the Brussels Capital office is located within the Belgian permanent representation (Goergen 2006). The result is that Belgian regions having the space to develop agendas beyond domestic power struggles, which can be citizen oriented. Thus, the

EU agency of Flanders includes within its mission 'interface with Flemish civil society' and 'raising awareness among the general public' (Vleva 2008, 4), while its Annual Report advises the EU institutions to 'find a different way of listening to the European citizens, in order to decrease the democratic deficit' (ibid., 8).

Among 'medium' devolution countries, similar orientations are evident. The Association of Finnish Local and Regional Authorities, which first secured a Brussels presence in 1992, defines one of the benefits of its EU policy that 'public discussion about EU affairs is deepened' (LOGON 2002, 98). There is a dense collection of civil society orientated networks in which the Brussels offices of the territorial authorities participate, many of which were created on the initiative of one, or a small cluster, of offices. Examples include: The European Network of Social Authorities (ENSA); the European Local Inclusion and Social Action Network (ELISAN); the Social Inclusion Regional Group (SIRG); the European Association of Regional and Local Authorities for Lifelong Learning (EARLLL); ERRIN, the European Regions Research Innovation Network, which has a sub-committee structure which includes a Health Network; Euro Health Net; European Regional and Local Health Authorities' (EUREGHA) network. These networks are disproportionately populated by regional offices from countries with 'medium' devolved authority, while SIRG, ENSA, and EARLL, were all established from an initiative taken by one such office, and the Health network of ERRIN is led by another. ENSA has ongoing projects involving disability and inclusion, care of the elderly, and youth inclusion, as well as past projects focusing on immigrants' integration, foster carers, and child protection. The health networks have civil society orientations, including the prevention of suicide among young people. EUREGHA includes among its objectives 'to improve the collaboration among Brussels Regional Offices' as well as 'to cooperate with relevant stakeholders such as NGOs' (Euregha 2011). And ELISAN declares itself 'towards a social Europe that fulfils the citizens needs' (Elisan 2011).

Examples of social related agendas are apparent from the websites of the Brussels territorial EU offices. Stockholm region showcases its involvement in the Interreg (IV C) funded 'People Project', aiming 'to reinforce the cohesion and social welfare in the participating regions and find solutions to address some of the consequences of the economic down turn' (People Project. 2010). One strand of this involves 'Civil Society empowerment', involving 'all those organisations through which citizens participate in social life,' (PEOPLE handbook, 110) in which such organisations are invited to participate in interventions aimed at their capacity building. The North West (of England) Brussels Office, which includes the North West Health Brussels Office (NWHBO), a partnership of the principal public sector health agencies in the territory, is a member of the EU NGO the European Public Health Alliance (EPHA). The NWBHO's '10 Areas for Action' to 'Prioritise our Health' (North West Health Brussels Office. 2010) are very similar to those of the EPHA. Similarly, the Veneto office incorporates a unit of health policy staff which have participated in an EU funded project aimed at addressing health inequalities.

Whilst network participation is drawn from offices from a mixture of 'high' and 'medium' devolution countries, the majority of examples are drawn from the 'medium' category. It is nonetheless important not to over-state the case, and there will be exceptions to generally observed trends. In the case of medium devolved authorities, the website of a Brussels territorial office from a Finnish region states that it's 'website is not a general information site for the public at large, but rather a communication tool between the EU office and the region' (Tampere Central Region 2010). Nonetheless, it is apparent from a scan of some of the 'most likely cases' drawn from countries with medium degrees of devolved authorities (plus the special case of Belgium, discussed earlier) that there are a broad range of civil society oriented activities undertaken, as well as more narrowly constituted economic development type actions. Conversely, there are examples to be found from regions in high devolution countries of attempts to link civil society with the EU, but these initiatives are more to be found in the regions themselves (such as the Catalan 'Horizon Europe') than among the Brussels representative offices of regional government from high devolution countries.

Further discussion and conclusions

A qualified version of principal–agent theory seems to offer some interpretative clarification once adapted to the circumstances of the Brussels territorial offices. Waterman and Meier (1998) apply it to the circumstance of bureaucratic politics. The starting point is summarised by Gosnell (in Pitkin 1967), that 'any specialisation of function involves representation'. The central tenet of principal–agent theory is that there is an inevitable loss of control once a principal delegates a task to an agent, and that goal conflict arises between the parties in which the degree of information asymmetries can be modeled as to where the power resides. In turn, this can help explain policy related outcomes. As Waterman and Meier explain, this is a somewhat blunt instrument in that there are many different relationships between principals and agents, with highly varying degrees of potential conflicts. In particular, they point to critical variations in goal symmetry between principals and agents, among the number of principals, and the degree of information sharing (Waterman and Meier op. cit.). One scenario outlined by these authors is that of goal sharing between principals and agents, in which agencies are delegated a task with a goal and then left to get on with it'; 'principals require regular reports, and if nothing is out of line they do nothing' (ibid., 191). These have been applied in circumstances of relationships between a 'central' and a regional office of public administrations (see, for instance, Schmidt 2002), but are also applicable here by connecting with Pitkin's work on representation.

For Pitkin, the key distinction to draw is that between a 'delegate' with a specific mandate to carry out, and an 'agent' with higher degrees of discretion and autonomy to carry out a task (Pitkin 1967). This latter role could involve a role in helping the principal to identify their goals where there is a high degree of asymmetry of expertise (Philips 1995). This variation — between 'mandated delegate' at one extreme and quasi-autonomous actor at the other — seems to capture the variation in both the structure and the working conditions of the Brussels offices. An outpost of a specific public territorial administration where staff work towards highly directed goals will create entirely different working agendas to one where agents are left with the ability to develop their own activities. Whilst agency 'problems' arise in every type of traditionally defined principal–agent relationships, the impact of autonomy make it worthwhile emphasising the different outcomes through use of the (Pitkin derived) nomenclature 'delegate' in order to distinguish the wide gulf between one working in a highly mandated environment with little scope for autonomous activity, and another working with a relatively high degree of discretion.

The main departure here from the model presented by Waterman and Meier is also one over clarity of goals. For these authors, the clarity of goals is a given, with agents working with more or less autonomy towards these goals in shared goal situations. In the case of the Brussels regional offices, the degree of goal-setting by principals is highly variable; the federal states have significant regional authorities whose Brussels offices serve them with specific goal sets, whereas those from countries with medium degrees of devolved authority tend towards a different model. In the latter cases, offices were either established with little specific original focus, or as a public/private partnership model with member services, whose diversity of principals enable offices to develop a wide range of activities. This diversity also creates structural autonomy for agents, either to exploit by pursuing their own interests which are then 'sold' to a member within the cognate field. In these high autonomy/discretion circumstances, the explanatory drivers are not those of goal conflict or information asymmetries, but more the range of principals, the degree of purpose established by the principal/s, as well as the structural autonomy of the office from its principal.

The varying extent of activities of the Brussels offices of the regions can thus be explained by the degrees of devolved authority with which they operate. The workload of those from regional governing authorities endowed with considerable devolved authority have become orientated towards specific goals, such as formalised input into the EU policy process, and as stations reflecting their domestic power struggles viz. central government. Offices from Germany, and Spain, provided clear-cut examples of such cases. Consequently, these principals have created mechanisms designed to retain their ability to control and prescribe the agendas and activities of their Brussels offices, such as the use of staff on limited time secondments. The latter actors are better captured by the nomenclature 'delegate', denoting the limited scope for 'agency problems' (in principal–agent terms) compared to agents with the autonomy to define their own agendas, because the impact of the difference is so substantial.

Thus, an altogether different model arises in the case of principals which are sub-national territorial entities from countries with 'medium' degrees of devolved authority. These tend towards diverse constitution, meaning that their energies have not been preoccupied with specific purposes such as domestic power struggles, or routine participation in the decision-making fora of the EU institutions. Here, agents have been able to cast their agendas diversely, enabling them to pursue a broad range of civil society-wide activities, rather than those tied to particular interest stakeholders. Offices in 'medium' devolved authority states can thus bring Europe to the regions and localities, rather than just representing the interests of territories to EU institutions, often in more than just a superficial way. *Inter alia*, some offices see their role as explaining to the region the impact of 'Europe' upon it, and involving territorial civil society with 'Europe'. Here, autonomy is the key variable, in which the 'asymmetry' in favour of the 'agent' is defined not so much by the ability of the principal to exercise control, but the inclination to do so. Brussels territorial offices with significant autonomy are most likely to have developed activities which seek to connect territorial civil society with the EU, and it is the offices from countries with medium degrees of devolved authority which are most likely to have such autonomy. Thus, the Brussels territorial offices from countries with medium devolved authority have the most potential, among the entire population of offices, to help connect the EU with wider civil society.

References

Badiello, L. 1998. Regional offices in Brussels: lobbying from the inside. In *Lobbying, pluralism and European integration*, eds. P.H. Claeys, C. Gobin, I. Smets and P. Winand, 328–44. Brussels: European Interuniversity Press.
Balme, R., and D. Chabanet. 2008. *European governance and democracy: power and protest in the EU*. Lanham: MD: Rowman and Littlefield.
Brussels European Liaison Office (BELO). 2009. Local and regional representations: a recent development, http://www.blbe.be/default.asp?V_DOC_ID=1867 (accessed 3 March 2011).
Committee of the Regions. 2009. Associations/Bureaux de Representation Regionale et Commuale a Bruxelles: Repertoire. Brussels: Committee of the Regions, available as pdf via Google title search http://www.yonet.org/IMG/pdf/bureaux_regionaux.pdf (accessed 1 February 2010).
Elisan (European Local Inclusion and Social Action Network). 2011. Presentation, http://www.elisan.eu/presentation.asp?lg=en (accessed 2 February 2011).
Euregha (European Regional and Local Health Authorities). 2011. http://www.euregha.net/home/index.php?option=com_content&task=section&id=4&Itemid=28 (accessed 2 February 2011).
European Commission. 1992. An open and structured dialogue between the Commission and special interest groups, 93/C 63/02, http://ec.europa.eu/civil_society/interest_groups/docs/v_en.pdf (accessed 3 February 2010).
European Commission. 2001. European governance: a white paper, COM(2001) 428 of 25.7.2001, http://ec.europa.eu/civil_society/ngo/docs/communication_en.pdf (accessed 10 February 2010).
European Commission. 2008. European Transparency initiative — frequently asked questions on the Commission's register for interest representatives, http://ec.europa.eu/transparency/docs/reg/FAQ_en.pdf (accessed 3 February 2010).
Goergen, P. 2006. *Lobbying in Brussels: a practical guide to the European Union for cities, regions, networks and enterprises*. Brussels: EBN.
Gouldner, A. 1979. *The future of intellectuals and the rise of the new class*. London: Continuum.
Greenwood, J., R. Levy, and R. Stewart. 1995. The European Union structural fund allocations: 'lobbying to win' or recycling the budget? *European Urban and Regional Studies* 2, no. 4: 317–38.
Heinelt, H., and S. Niederhafner. 2008. Cities and organized interest intermediation in the EU multi-level system. *European Urban and Regional Studies* 15, 173–87.

Huysseune, M., and T. Jans. 2008. Brussels as the capital of a Europe of the regions? Regional offices as European policy actors. *Brussels Studies*, 16, 25 February, http://www.brusselsstudies.be/PDF/EN_57_BruS16EN.pdf (accessed 2 February 2010).

Keating, M., and L. Hooghe. 1996. 'Bypassing the nation-state? Regions and the EU policy process'. In *European Union: power and policy making*, ed. J. Richardson, 216–29, chapter 13. Oxford: Oxford University Press.

Knodt, M. 2002. 'Regions in multilevel governance arrangements: leadership versus partnerships'. In *Participatory governance: political and societal implications*, eds. J. Grote and B. Gbikpi. Opladen: Leske & Budrich.

Leonardi, R. 1993. *The regions and the European community*. London: Frank Cass.

LOGON (Local Governments Network of Central and Eastern European Countries). 2002. *LOGON report 2002: lobbying in Europe*. Vienna: Association of Austrian Cities and Towns.

McAteer, M., and D. Mitchell. 1996. Peripheral lobbying! The territorial dimension of euro lobbying by Scottish and Welsh sub-central government. *Regional and Federal Studies* 6, no. 3: 1–27.

Mamadouh, V. 2001. The regions in Brussels: subnational actors in the supranational arena. *Tijdscrift voor Economische en Sociale Geografie* 92, no. 4: 478–87.

Marks, G., F. Nielsen, L. Ray, and J. Salk. 1995. Competencies, cracks and conflicts: regional mobilisation in the European Union. Typescript, Department of Political Science, University of North Carolina-Chapel Hill.

Marks, G., R. Haesley, and H. Mbaye. 2002. What do subnational offices think they are doing in Brussels? *Regional and Federal Studies* 12, no. 3: 1–23.

Moore, C. 2006. Schloss Neuwahnstein? Why the Länder continue to strengthen their representations in Brussels *German Politics* 15, no. 2: 192–205.

North West Health Brussels Office. 2010. Prioritise our health: 10 areas for action, http://www.northwesthealth.eu/cms/default2.asp?active_page_id=199 (accessed 5 February 2010).

Olsson, A. 2009. Euroscepticism revisited — regional interest representation in Brussels and the link to citizen attitudes towards European integration. Paper prepared for delivery at the 11th Biennial Conference of the EU Studies Association, Los Angeles, April 23-25.

PEOPLE handbook. 2009. Civil society empowerment, http://www.peopleproject.eu/useful_docs.php (accessed on 5 February 2010).

People Project. 2010. People news, http://www.peopleproject.eu/index.php (accessed 2 February 2011).

Phillips, A. 1995. *The politics of presence*. Oxford: Clarendon Press.

Pitkin, H. 1967. *The concept of representation*. Berkeley: University of California Press.

Riedel, R. 2010. Silesian representations in Brussels — objectives, performance, evaluations. Paper presented to the International Political Science Association International conference, 'Is there a European model of governance', Luxembourg, 18–20 March.

Saurugger, S. 2006. The professionalisation of interest representation: a legitimacy problem for civil society in the EU? In *Civil society and legitimate European governance*, ed. S Smismans, chapter 12. Cheltenham: Edward Elgar.

Schmidt, D. 2002. Politicization and responsiveness in the regional offices of the NLRB. *American Review of Public Administration* 32, 188–215.

South Denmark European Office. 2010. South Denmark European Office in English, http://www.southdenmark.be/Default.aspx?alias=www.southdenmark.be/english (accessed 5 February 2010).

Tampere Central Region. 2010. Mission and tasks, http://www.tamperecentralregion.eu/tampere-central-region-eu.html (accessed 5 February 2010; website now superseded by http://www.tampereregion.eu/in-english/mission-tasks/).

Tatham, M. 2008. Going solo: direct regional representation in the EU. *Regional and Federal Studies* 18, no. 5: 493–515.

Vleva. 2008. Annual report, http://www.vleva.eu/en/files/annualreport_2008.pdf (accessed 5 February 2010).

Waterman, R., and K. Meier. 1998. Principal-agent models: an expansion? *Journal of Public Administration Research and Theory* 8, no. 2: 173–202.

Watts, R. 2006. Origins of cooperative and competitive federalism. In *Territory democracy and justice*, ed. S. Greer, 201–23. Basingstoke: Palgrave Macmillan.

Social Movements and the European Interest Intermediation of Public Interest Groups

CARLO RUZZA

Department of Sociology, University of Leicester, Leicester, UK

ABSTRACT It is argued that, in the EU environment, social movements are important actors and acquire distinctive traits in terms of coalitional activities, inter-institutional relations, modes of financing, and representational activities. They put forward an often utopian vision of desirable policy changes that other non-state organizations and institutional activists can utilise as a negotiating standards, whilst recognising, however, that they may be unachievable. This role is appreciated by institutional activists — bureaucratic and political actors sympathetic to movements — who typically attempt to channel funds, legitimacy and visibility to social movement organizations, both for reasons of ideological congruence and to engage in processes of bureau-shaping and budget maximising from which they benefit. The relative absence of strong policy steering on the EU level enables them to do so to a larger extent than in national polities. This is however more likely to occur when there is a specific legal base that legitimises movements' support.

In studying processes of interest representation, analysts use typologies to help identify, define and examine recurrent features that encapsulate the modes of operation of specific political actors. Recurrent categories of interests include the distinction between private, public and territorial interests, or the distinction between national and supranational interests. Distinctions that focus on modes of financing, governance level and mechanisms of functional representation can also apply to public interest organizations. However, given the wide range of types within civil society, more subtle distinctions are also needed to capture important differences. Within the field of civil society organizations, a distinction is commonly drawn among churches, service delivery NGOs, and public interest groups. These typically have different resource bases, relations with political sponsors and social institutions, and visibility in the public sphere.

An often neglected category is 'social movements'. This is because, although at EU level movements often include organizations that behave as public interest lobbies, they have other distinctive features that are salient but not evident in highly institutionalised policy environments like the EU: for instance, the propensity of social movements to engage in disruptive protests, or their strong identity and the emotional commitment of their members. Because of these features, they have distinctive styles of interaction with the public and the political arena that make their interest representation features often effective but different from the dominant modes of interest representation. As some of these features are not easily observable in the EU environment but occur within member states, these organizations are typically not conceptualized as a distinctive category. Yet social movements are widely represented and influential at EU level, and their contribution should be examined.

There are several such organizations in Brussels that are somewhat difficult to define: for instance, a group like Greenpeace is somewhat unconventional among the associations lobbying the European institutions. On the one hand, they perform some of the functions generally undertaken by interest groups: they provide information to the policy process and exert legal advocacy and persuasion. On the other hand, unlike many public interest groups, they generally refuse to accept money from the Commission. Their general stance is confrontational and they are ready to engage in disruptive protest events, even if not necessarily in Brussels. They devote a great deal of effort to achieving and retaining visibility in the media addressed to the general public, and they are often more effective than many NGOs. They have a distinctive following of highly motivated activists, some of whom are willing to engage in high risk actions. They are therefore somewhat different from other NGOs, which often have weaker political identities and different action repertoires. Similar considerations apply to several anti-discrimination groups, such as anti-racist organizations, which focus on conventional interest group goals but also engage in protest activities, again not necessarily in Brussels. They may also focus on exerting influence to strengthen legislation in fields such as ethnic relations, gender, sexuality and disability, and they may do so in conjunction with other NGOs and public interest groups. For instance, anti-racist groups are part of umbrella groups, for example the European Network against Racism, which comprise several conventional public interest associations. However, there are various organizations that maintain a strong confrontational role and engage in protest initiatives such as demonstrations, boycotts, sit-ins and other forms of symbolic politics. They may attempt to acquire resources from European institutions: for instance, funds for pilot projects or service delivery resources to benefit their constituencies. However, at the same time they retain a base of committed activists ready to engage in protest actions, sometimes at EU level, and more frequently in member states. Their EU interest representation activities should therefore be understood as part of a set of differentiated aims pursued through a multifaceted action repertoire.

This paper will argue that the best way to understand groups such as these is to use the concept of 'social movement coalition', and that this concept, and more specifically its transformation at EU level, affords better insights than other social-scientific categories. It will be argued that the social movement form needs to be reconceptualised to understand its adaptation to the EU supra-national environment. The paper will consist of (1) a section on the specificity of social movements at EU level in relation to other civil society organizations, (2) a section on their goals and strategies of interest representation, (3) a section on their characteristics, structure and role in multi-actor networks, and (4) a section on their role in governance arrangements. Methodologically, the paper is based on a set of over 50 in-depth interviews conducted over the last ten years with social movement activists in the fields of environmental policy, anti-racism and migration, language protection, gay rights, human rights and the consumer movement. A similar number of interviews have also been conducted with relevant civil servants in EU institutions and MEPs. The interviews were intended to clarify patterns of collaboration, exchanges of resources, ideological similarities and differences, and to identify reputational networks.

It will be argued that social movement organizations exhibit a set of distinctive traits in the EU environment. These will be described, and other intervening variables that qualify their appearance will be identified. Social movements will then be characterized as relevant actors at EU level. Three features stand out and need to be emphasized from the outset. Firstly, movement-related associations are present in Brussels to interact with EU institutions, and as such they are, by necessity, less prone to disruptive action than social movements in member states. This is because nation states provide clearly defined authority structures and clearer mechanisms with which to acquire media visibility which make disruptive action more consequential. They often relate to parallel associations in member states. Secondly, to the extent that they do so, they are therefore part of a governance structure which connects them across different states and different levels of government. However, some organisation such as the Alter-EU[1] mainly or only exist at the supranational level, and in that context they provide a new and alternative organizational type (Mathers 2007). Thirdly, although they pursue different goals, like-minded organizations such as most anti-discrimination organizations are also often interconnected in broad umbrella groups which give structure to their associational field and constitute an associational ecology in which both competition and conflict occur at the same time, and in which a division of labour takes place between cooperative and conflictual groups. They therefore act as parts of broad multi-purpose coalitions (Ruzza 2004).

As defined by the literature, social movements are a set of opinions and beliefs in a population which represents preferences for changing some elements of the social structure and/or reward distribution of a society (McCarthy and Zald 1982, 1217). They typically address a policy paradigm in normative terms challenging existing normative structures and proposing radical alternatives that are historically situated and embedded in social networks (Diani 1992). In their moralisation of policy they are then different from interest groups even when these take radical positions. Interest groups can on occasion adopt extreme policy positions as negotiating stances, whereas for movement groups policy positions are generally part of a normatively held and shared vision that spans across single organizations. Social movements are therefore broader than social movement organizations and may include activists that are not part of specific organizations, or not part of the organizations active in a specific location, such as Brussels. Many movements produce organizations of different types, including NGOs, which have a legal status independent of governments. In Brussels one thus finds both social movement organizations and individual social movement activists, some of whom belong to other types of organizations but will on occasion collaborate with social movement organizations, such as for instance the social platform (Cullen 2010). In Brussels we then typically see coalitions bringing together a variety of civil society organizations, such as movement organizations, general social organizations sympathetic to movement goals, and unaffiliated activists and sympathisers, some of whom may be based in EU institutions.

In their attempt to exert influence, they address a variety of other organizations, including political and social ones like parties and state bureaucracies, and also civil society organizations, which thus constitute targets and allies alike, as well as being domains of contestation in which conflicting policy visions are debated (Cullen 2010). In organized environments, social movements can exert influence through their impact on other civil society organizations or through specific oppositional movement organizations. However, even when addressing EU institutions directly, they have generally adapted to the supranational environment, so that their stance is not necessarily confrontational, and consequently distinct from their action repertoire at member state level. Their organizations may also collaborate on a stable basis with institutional actors committed to the movement's goals and able to pursue them from a base within state institutions, such as elected officials and civil servants committed to those same goals. In other words, they engage in a relation which is often simultaneously cooperative and conflictual (Giugni 2004). To the extent that they engage in the strategic coordination of goals and tactics with other political actors, they become part of coalitions with different levels of formalization and duration. In these terms, groups like certain environmentalist organizations active in Brussels fully qualify as social movement organizations. They, and other organizations similar to them in other policy areas, would evidently belong to the more formalized and institutionalised range of social movement groups. Formalization and coalition activities of certain social movement groups, of course, are not necessarily distinctive of the supranational environment. There is no doubt that several European social movements, for instance the 'new movements' of the eighties, have followed an institutionalisation trajectory so that they today represent a new form of political participation. Scholars have referred to this process as the NGO-isation of social movements, even if they have often distanced themselves from such a blanket assumption since the emergence of the No Global movement (Della-Porta 2009, 52). Nonetheless, this process has created a set of intermediate organizational forms that retain some of the features of social movements but have also acquired some of those distinctive of NGOs, for instance a degree of professionalization, service delivery roles, and better legal skills.

However, what has most characterized the last two decades is the greater ability of social movement organizations to operate in transnational environments and to become 'norm entrepreneurs' (Keck and Sikkink 1998, 1–4). However, only seldom has the social movement literature considered how these institutionalization-related and governance-related trends play a role at the EU level. On the other hand, nor has the interest groups literature sufficiently focussed on public interest groups originating from social movements. These are seen as pertaining to a general category of associations, and important distinctive features — such as their propensity for conflictual stances, their stronger identities and their denser networks — are considered of little relevance by a literature that typically focuses on other issues, such as policy impact and mechanisms of consensus aggregation, even if these distinctive social movement features can have an impact on their policy outcomes. To fill this gap, it is first necessary to describe how the social movement form has transformed in the EU environment.

Distinctiveness of Social Movements at the EU Level

Social movements are to a large extent the historically shaped outcomes of processes of nation building and state building (Tilly 1984). Processes of internationalised governance are therefore likely to affect the form assumed by a social movement. Whilst the political type of the 'social movement' is typically defined in terms of political protest at the national level, it takes on a different role once transferred to the international and supranational arena; and this, as Marks and McAdam argue, requires the revision of its conceptual definition (Marks and McAdam 1996), particularly since, even within the boundaries of nation states, movements increasingly interact in multi-level governance structures with supranational aggregations, of which the EU is probably the most successful example.

These changes require movement organizations to redefine and broaden the environment in which they make their calculations. They now often interact simultaneously at several levels of governance, deciding strategically where to express their grievances. Such broadening makes calculations of the cost-effectiveness of protest actions more difficult, and the identification of targets more variable. To be expected in such a context is extensive venue shopping, and the targeting of action on the specific features of different venues.

Secondly, besides aiming to have a direct impact on the political system, social movements attempt to persuade the population of the rightness of their views through cultural initiatives such as exhibitions and media campaigns. These strategies often have an impact on elected representatives, who are then expected to respond in the political arena. As movements become more global, their views will become more convergent across countries and will also become more similar to the views espoused by the EU-wide umbrella groups represented in Brussels.

A convergence of political frames and a consequent willingness to collaborate with other political actors has occurred not only because of governance-induced factors, but also because of changes due to the institutionalisation of movements over recent decades. This has, for instance, implied the creation and successful entrenchment in the machinery of the state of movement-parties, for instance green parties or certain ethnic parties with strong roots in, and continuing ties with, the social movement sector (Müller-Rommel and Poguntke 2002) but also connections with the mainstream political system in articulated coalitions. Coalition behaviour does not necessarily alter the main identity of movements. However, coalition behaviour is in itself an important source of policy change. In the EU environment, one needs to differentiate coalitions where no movement is present from coalitions that encompass social movement organizations. The latter exhibit some distinctive features.

Particularly at EU level, the crucial variable that distinguishes among social movement public interest coalitions is not the contentious action repertoire, which generally remains a resource of last resort; nor is it a strong collective identity, which in a multinational environment like the EU is difficult to develop. What mainly defines them is the propounding of a radically alternative policy plan supported by organized networks of political actors with bases in a variety of more or less institutionalised social and political organizations. Arguably, it is precisely these features of radical policy reformulation that make these public interest coalitions useful interlocutors in the consultation game that develops in and around EU institutions. Social movement coalitions are not necessarily successful in achieving their stated policy goals or in bringing about their acceptance as legitimate insiders in the policy-making arena, but for several reasons now explained, they are often readily integrated into the EU environment. Nonetheless, they retain a disruptive mobilising potential at member state level. As we shall see, the fact that they have potential recourse to disruptive action and to high media visibility alters their negotiating potential. They can rely on substantive human resources based on the moralised donation of time and energy by their dedicated and often broadly-skilled constituency base.

A well-documented example of these processes are the events which occurred in relation to Shell's failed attempt to dispose of the 'Brent Spar' oil platform at sea (Jordan 2001; Rice and Owen 1999). The mobilization of social movement organizations and notably Greenpeace was decisive in overcoming uncertain scientific evidence (Rice and Owen 1999, 7). Among the factors that helped Greenpeace was its ability to use the EU and its institutions as a hub for lobbying, and to gather and circulate information, and to recruit support for its transnational activism. In particular a decisive role was played by the support of Ritt Bjerregaard, the EU Commissioner for the Environment, who argued that: 'the dumping of the Brent Spar is not acceptable. The dumping of all old oil installations must be banned' (Rice and Owen 1999, 87). This occurred whilst a radically different policy involving alternative and more costly ways of decommissioning the platform were espoused by activists, and while their policy views were supported by a EU-wide boycott and direct action forms widely reported in the media. The moral conviction of the protesters, their courage and commitment, were positively perceived by the media and European publics (Rice and Owen 1999, 6). Whilst still in many ways at loggerheads with EU official environmental policy, Greenpeace continues to retain a visible presence in Brussels and to form coalitions with other environmental groups at EU level and more broadly with other left-liberal groups. Thus it forms a public interest coalition — the Green Ten[2] — with other environmental organizations. It is also part of broader cross-sectoral coalitions: for instance, it is linked with the EU Civil Society Contact Group (CSCG) which 'brings together eight large NGO sectors — culture, environment, education, development, human rights, public health, social and women'.[3]

Goals and Strategies of EU Movements: A Trajectory of Incorporation

Whilst there are some general features of the EU policy environment that are germane to all social movements, one must acknowledge the major role played by short-term changes in the political climate, and the differential impact of political cultures and institutional constraints in different policy sectors. Various factors can foster institutionalisation or conversely promote de-institutionalisation and the resurgence of contentious politics. One of them is the emergence of new political opportunities for movements. Political opportunities — a concept widely used in social movement research — include elites' tolerance for protest and the existence of supportive institutional allies (Della Porta and Diani 2006, 16). Conflicts among elites, and the fact that some elites need the support of external allies such as social movement personnel, can also stimulate attempts to co-opt social movements, and therefore foster their institutionalisation. Conversely, processes of radicalisation may occur when the political system is hostile to the incorporation of social movements' ideals and their cadres. For this reason, when examining the role of social movements at EU level, one must necessarily frame it in terms of the recent history of incorporation. This history varies from one social movement to another, but also it varies for the entire social movement sector. With reference to the latter, movements typically emerge, expand, and demobilise in cycles (Tarrow 1989). Cycles of protest produce several mutually reinforcing or conflicting social movements. As said, in recent decades in Europe, a major cycle of protest has occurred with the 'new movements' of the eighties, which addressed policy issues such as social policy with the feminist movement, environmental policy with the green movement, and more recently migration policy with the social justice movement. These movements are now institutionalised: that is, they have conquered stable niches in the institutional realm of most member states; social and political institutions recognise the legitimacy of their claims. But they have lost mobilisation capacity and to an extent some of their perceived social relevance. It is therefore out of necessity that they increasingly engage in tactics such as multi-actor public interest coalitions, judicial activism, and processes sometimes referred to as 'NGO-isation' which include fewer political protests, smaller but newsworthy action forms, and the acquisition of scientific, technical and legal competences. Notably, these transformations reduce the difference between social movements and interest groups. By now, the concerns of the movements of the 1980s have a solid legal base in anti-discrimination or environmental policy providing them with legitimacy and channels to acquire resources.

In fields such as environmental policy there is a strong and longstanding history of the incorporation of environmentalist ideas within the Commission and the Parliament, an ability of environmentalist-minded civil servants, parliamentarians and activists to collaborate across their organizational boundaries and to confront the values and policy preferences of opponents. Environmentalists have a respected and broadly institutionalised umbrella group — the European Environmental Bureau (EEB) — and, as mentioned, a body coordinating a range of movement-inspired groups — the Green 10. These umbrella groups are strongly institutionalised. They are largely funded by the European Commission and other governments, but they also interact on a stable base with less institutionalised groups. In some cases, such as that of Greenpeace, the social movement ethos it is fairly strong and direct. In other cases, for example that of Friends of the Earth, it is still directly relevant and is typically connected with an idealised allegiance to the values of left-libertarian movements. For instance, the FoE website states that its core values are 'Peoples' sovereignty, human and peoples' rights; Equity and environmental, social, economic and gender justice; The intrinsic value of nature and the inextricable link between nature and people; Participatory democracy and other forms of participatory decision-making processes' — thus ideally connecting the FoE ethos with the gender and human rights priorities of other movement groups, but also with the narrative of human rights as a distinctive institutional priority of the European Union. In other words, key social movement ideas such as environmental justice, or antiracism and human rights are now fully incorporated in the dominant institutional discourse of the EU and can be considered founding myths of the European Union (Della Sala 2010; Ruzza 2011).

The Actor Type: Structure, Financial Arrangements and Norms

Social movement organizations, like other civil society organizations, are financed by a complex mix of sources. They all rely on donations of time and energy by activists. But other elements in their financial arrangements differ. Some use membership fees; several compete for EU monies, which can be granted for ad hoc projects or more seldom for running costs. Sources can be EU institutions, but sometimes they can also be governments in member states. For instance the European Environmental Bureau is financed by government institutions such as the German, British, Swedish, Danish and Finnish environmental ministries and by a range of foundations.[4] The EU Commission prefers to fund them on a project basis, which officials think provides more accountability, whilst all civil society organizations prefer a running costs model. This is easier to achieve by recognised EU-level umbrella groups. In any event, the proportion of EU funds can often be substantial, representing the overwhelming majority of funds in some cases. The high level of public funds available to movements is then another distinctive aspect that characterises EU movements, which, as mentioned, is rooted in the contribution to information and to political legitimacy that they can bring to EU institutions.

In addition, at least in some cases, such as certain environmental groups, conspicuous donations may come from private donors and firms, a fact which potentially raises issues of cooptation and can be factious within movements because donations engender conflict between the institutionalised part of the movement and the uninstitutionalised part which rejects them. In terms of organizational structure, social movement organizations are present in Brussels as branches of transnational movements with bases in member states. However, relations between nationally-based activists and Brussels cadres are often problematic. As previously seen in the case of FoE, a key tenet of the ideology of movements persisting from the eighties — the main movements active at EU-level — is participatory democracy. But participation is often costly and unachievable in the short consultation time — often only eight weeks — allowed by the Commission for many policy consultations (Ruzza 2004). The selection of action forms is a second source of tension, with EU level movements naturally favouring a politics of expertise and member state-based movements preferring more contentious forms (Tarrow 2008, 172–173). This engenders structural strains with national-based branches. There is consequently often a disjunction between the EU level and other levels of governance, and therefore a distinctive de facto insulation of EU organizations from their grassroots.

This tension is particularly marked when social movement groups come to be incorporated in umbrella groups, which they often find excessively institutionalised and not appropriately representative of social movement constituencies. This, for instance, is the case of the relationship between national environmental groups and the EEB (Rootes 2005).

Paths of Interest Representation: Governance, Provision of Information, Claims of Representation and Threats of Disruption

Social movement organizations lobby both directly and indirectly. Direct representation takes place through associations, such as Greenpeace and Friends of the Earth, which are recognized participants of a movement — in this case the environmental movement. Indirect representation takes place through umbrella groups of various dimensions. A useful concept with which to frame alliances among social movements is that of 'social movement family', which becomes particularly relevant as movements decline and lose visibility (Della Porta and Diani 2006, 247). The 'family' can provide synergies and resources when these are scarce. Some resources can be shared or used by other social movement groups when the groups that originally gathered them are no longer able to utilise them. For instance, the peace movement is formed by a large coalition of campaigns which involve different organizations and individuals; but as some causes become politically less relevant, a transfer of resources takes place. The previously mentioned 'EU Civil Society Contact Group' is another example of such a family of movement groups.

Of the several social movement families active in Brussels, the most influential is the left-liberal one, and particularly the 'new social movements' family which gained especial prominence in the 1980s and includes the environmental movement and anti-discrimination movements. Particularly important among anti-discrimination movements are article 13 anti-discrimination groups and feminist groups. EU policy in the field of minority protection developed rapidly after approval of Article 13 of the Amsterdam Treaty, including two directives and an Action Programme against discrimination. Two directives against discrimination were enacted: one on grounds of race and ethnic origin (known as the Racial Equality Directive), and one on grounds of religion or belief, disability, age or sexual orientation (the Employment Framework Directive) providing a specific role for public interest groups. The No Global movement, as a newer and complex set of interconnected organizations, is also present in Brussels in various guises, ranging from anti-poverty efforts to organizations supporting causes in developing countries.

Ethno-nationalist movements constitute a separate movement family defined by their struggles for regional causes. Its members range from separatist and autonomist parties and movements to federalist groups. Extreme right and Eurosceptic groups are also present, although they are rather weak in the EU environment. The degree and effectiveness of networking varies across different movement families, and the degree of interaction with more institutionalised groups varies as well.

Clearly, the more groups collaborate in larger aggregations, the more the network is institutionalised and loses some specific movement features, such as the willingness to engage in political protest and to use the media for theatrical actions. This happens because, as a group becomes larger, internal negotiations of framing dynamics and action repertoires tend to marginalise the fewer social movement groups involved. Their cohesion is provided by a common ideological stance firmly set in the context of the left-liberal movement ideology and a congruent vision of Europe, rather than by common action repertoires.[5] Their documents emphasise the rejection of what they see as a dominant European vision based on neo-liberal values. They also typically reject what they see as a formalistic, hierarchical and non-participative strand in European democracies. And it is for this reason that the issue of political representation is often a special focus of attention.

As Pitkin points out, political representation is a complex issue with multiple meanings, which often coexist in the expectations of representatives and represented constituencies. This also applies to all social movements, which typically assert distinct representational roles and on this basis their legitimacy claims. Movements articulate their claims for representativeness according to their different ideological tenets, which often include distinctive visions of appropriate modes and arenas of representation. Some focus on representation in elected institutions, such as when environmentalists demand to be consulted by city councils, ministries or parliamentary committees. Others embrace a broader concept of representation which prominently includes representation of the claims, grievances and identities of their constituencies in the public sphere. In articulating their claims they also have to consider whether their goal is largely one of presence — that is, aiming for opportunities to (a) establish their political visibility as a group, (b) to publicise their perspectives and blueprints for change, or (c) one of effectiveness. Although these strategies often appear intertwined and change over time, they lead to different views of representation. These can be broadly summarised with reference to the typology of representation claims in the seminal work of Pitkin.

One key feature of several recent movements is a concern with social exclusion and 'voicelessness'. Representation is therefore justified in terms of providing a presence in decision-making arenas. They thus typically articulate Pitkin's type of descriptive representation, which refers to the view that elected representatives should represent not only the preferences of their electorate but also those of their personal and social features that are politically salient, such as their gender or ethnicity. This is however not always the case and it is an issue often discussed by movement groups. Groups such the European Women's Lobby select women as representatives (their executive board and secretariat are entirely female) implicitly espousing a theory of symbolic representation, while anti-racist groups (such as ENAR) do not necessarily only include racial or ethnic minorities.

Movements groups such as women's groups and anti-racists claim a right to presence in policy circles. This first involves an argument about their right to be present, which is generally based on the necessity to represent sectors of the population that would otherwise be disenfranchised, either because of their limited access to voting entitlements, as in the case of clandestine migrants, or because of educational or resource limitations on their social citizenship. Secondly, it involves an argument about the selection of the representatives. This is typically justified on the basis of likeness — that is, activists claim to be 'like' the minorities excluded from the political process (because of similar features). They may also claim that their presence is legitimated because they have received authorization from their excluded constituency through a formal selection process — in the latter case also articulating the Pitkin's typology of authorizing representation. These aspects of compensatory representation have also been recently emphasised by the literature in conjunction with an emerging emphasis on the multiplication of arenas of representation and actors (Warren and Castiglione 2004). It should be noted that when movements stress likeness, authorization is often seen as less necessary, because an essentialist homogeneity of the constituency may be assumed, so that it is sufficient for activists to be identified as group members, for instance in gender or racial terms.

A second type of representative claim is based on policy results achieved in favour of a constituency. This is a distinctly more frequent claim in the EU environment. It does not require essentialist assumptions of membership in specific communities; rather, it requires specific skills that have to be proven to the constituency. This view articulates Pitkin's type of substantive representation. This is more likely to be associated with conjunct authorising claims, unlike descriptive representation, which does not need accountability (Pitkin 1967). Authorising claims are typically of two types. On the one hand, they refer to mechanisms of delegation and selection by national organizations; on the other hand, they emphasise deliberative mechanisms. Deliberation can at times substitute for institutional mechanisms, particularly since the social movements of the eighties were often ideologically sceptical of delegation and preferred extensive deliberation and flat pyramidal structures. Thus frequent positive references are made to deliberation, which at EU level compensates for the difficulty of consulting national level organizations, as for instance policy consultations required by the Commission are often expected in eight weeks. This is a period too short to comprehensively liaise with organizations in member states but sufficiently long for extensive discussions.

Umbrella groups naturally stress that they represent organizations rather than individual citizens, and that they represent nations in governance arrangements. Thus, for instance, ENAR's website states that 'What unites these organisations is that they are all involved in the fight against racism, and as such are able to collectively represent the voice of the organised human rights and anti-racist civil society'.[6] It also states that 'ENAR's member organisations are represented through national coordinations in each of the EU member states'. It should be noted in this regard that processes such as the growing importance of supranational integration and the prevalence of governance structures have broadened and redefined what is topical in relation to issues of representation.

The representation role of non-state actors, which include social movements, has also permeated the awareness of the Commission and other EU institutions, which often appear to espouse both a descriptive and a substantive view of representation, given that non-state actors can provide both informational contributions and a vicarious presence of disenfranchised constituencies (Ruzza 2006). In addition, importantly, EU institutions appear to understand representation in a novel and expanded manner as an activity of two-way representation whereby EU institutions not only accept movements as representatives, but also represent themselves to marginalised constituencies through the intermediary role of social movements, which are recruited and sponsored to diffuse institutionalised European values, such as environmental sustainability and anti-racism, in society. A project of societal regulation is thus intentionally pursued, at least at the discursive level, with the help of social movement organizations which come to represent European institutions in member states and generally in the public sphere. In other words, on the basis of an implicitly held but consequential theory of societal representation that parallels electoral representation, EU institutions come to see movements as important allies in a process that represents the views of grassroots constituencies. They also come to see movements as means to reach out to the aggrieved social groups represented by movements, and for this reason they are more willing to support them.

Interactions with the EU Level: Policy Fields, Allies and Opponents

Social movement groups can provide the EU with information through their scientists and their grassroots bases which counterbalances the information provided by lobbyists, and which can complement the understanding of social and territorial issues. This information function, however, presumes that there is a need for information, that a policy field needs more balanced information, and that there are political and civil service actors willing to accept new and possibly radical information and, more generally, policy perspectives. The first condition — the need for information — is typically relevant when there is a solid legal base that makes legislative activities necessary, and therefore the acquisition of information important. This is typically the case of environmental policy.

At both local and supranational level, institutionalised environmental groups are often highly specialised and possess specific knowledge about complex sectors such as transport, agriculture, or energy. At the EU level, information is particularly valued because of two main factors. One is the relatively limited size of the EU civil service and its limited funds and powers to acquire original and pertinent information to aid decision-making. The second is that the long-standing ideological and administrative fragmentation of the European Commission makes scientific and technical expertise highly controversial. It therefore not infrequently happens that different directorates general (DG) will prefer to use the expertise of civil society organizations that they can trust as being sympathetic to their values and policy orientations. This has been the case in areas such as migration-related policy, environmental policy, and generally article 13 anti-discrimination policy, because over the years an influx of movement-sympathetic civil servants and political actors has permeated the EU institutional structure (Bell 2002). These institutional movement supporters can be conceptualised as institutional activists (Santoro and McGuire 1997). In structural terms they are actors who, from a position of power, attempt to transpose some resources from an institutional sector to the social movement sector. They also grant social movements the political legitimacy that they need. This act of institutionalised intermediation is not unique to the EU: it routinely takes place in local councils, for instance.

In addition to institutional activists, social institutions like churches and trade unions may also support a social movement. What characterises the

EU level, given the relatively small scale of the EU environment in Brussels, is often the extent of submerged networks which triangulate and coordinate their efforts across institutional domains, and the fact that this has taken place for long periods. For instance, sections of the environmental committee of the Parliament, EU officials in DG Environment and environmental activists have long been shown to coordinate their efforts (Judge 1992). Northern European civil servants acquired early prominence in EU environmental policy and acted as committed popularisers (Hildebrand 1993). A similar situation emerged with some UK MEPs in areas such as anti-discrimination policy (Ruzza 2004). Institutional activists then import the policy perspectives of social movements not only by aiding the impact of activists in policy-making circles but also by intermediating the transposition of movement-sympathetic public discourse in policy circles. Thus, the impact of movement on the public media is made relevant by EU level institutional actors.

Social Movements and Governance

The relation between social movements and the EU is shaped by events in member states, power shifts in EU institutions such as changes in composition of the EU Parliament, and overall changes in the social movement sector. In addition to the global process of social movement institutionalisation, special consideration should be made of changes pertaining to the increasing reliance on soft laws. The greater frequency of steering mechanisms based on soft laws developed partially outside the authority of states, but also of EU institutions, have marked policy-making in all sectors. Recent decades have seen increasing reliance on consensus-seeking coordination, both because of a decline in the legitimacy of EU policy-making and as a response to its weakly authoritative institutional framework. Whilst the early enthusiasm for policy approaches such as the Open Method of Coordination may have abated, the continuing relevance of some multi-level deliberative fora, like those taking place in the context of environmental regimes, gives a new role to social movements and their advocates. In these contexts, sectors of the EU civil service, social movements and civil society can work together in pursuit of shared goals. However, whilst the traditional preference among EU actors was to incorporate activists based in Brussels, in recent years there has been growing awareness that broader consultation procedures are necessary. This has resulted in increasing reliance on online consultations, which have in their turn empowered movements in member states (Bozzini 2007). Whilst, as mentioned, the relation between member state-based and Brussels-based activists remains problematic, the Commission's increasing reliance on good communication with nationally-based activists also indicates increasing awareness among activists of the importance of good vertical channels of governance. A similar realisation also emerges from institutional activists within the Commission and Parliament, for whom it is important to hear the 'real voice of the grassroots', and not just that of institutionalised Brussels spokespeople. Movements are thus recruited as devices of social regulation: they are means to diffuse in member states EU constitutionalised values such as anti-racism and environmentalism with the help of social movements.

Discussion

This paper has argued for the typological relevance and distinctiveness of the concept of 'movement coalitions' in the EU environment. It has maintained that the 'social movement' as a form of political participation takes new forms in a transnational environment such as the EU because it is more substantively shaped by coalition behaviour; it performs novel representative functions which are functional to the process of EU construction; it is more focussed and involved in deliberative roles than in protesting ones, whilst retaining access to protesting repertoires; it acquires a distinctive role in the global public sphere, and more than in other contexts, it is shaped by the funding and supporting role of institutional activists. It has then been posited the changing but continuing importance of the social movement form at EU level. As normative ideas strongly held by networks of individuals who seek social and political change using both conventional and disruptive methods of protest, they affect several areas of EU policy. But it has been argued that their features are modified by the constraints and opportunities of the EU environment.

More specifically: (1) given the policy imperatives of the EU environment, movements need to be involved more frequently in multi-actor coalitions marked by simultaneous cooperation and conflict over the allocation of resources, the definition of agendas and the negotiation of access to institutional actors. As mechanisms of representation (2) movements perform a novel function of both top-down and bottom-up representation along a chain of governance from grassroots movement organizations to the institutions of the EU. This supports and complements other forms of democratic representation. This extra-institutional and transnational type of representation increases the political power of movements, contributing to expanding the scope and arenas of representation in contemporary societies (Saward 2009). (3) Given the extensive reliance on consultation mechanisms mandated by the weak authoritative structure of EU institutions and by the ideological reliance on open mechanisms of policy coordination, movements are involved in deliberative roles more than in most member states. (4) In association with their function as institutionalised and supported representatives of EU entrenched political values, EU level movements also perform a function in the public sphere which legitimises EU institutions as important carriers of socially approved values. (5) Thus, bureaucratic mechanisms of recruitment, attrition, budget-maximising and bureau-shaping favour a movement-supporting role of some EU institutional actors. Movements are particularly valued within areas of the Commission, because they provide a way to improve their political legitimacy by counterbalancing what is perceived as the overwhelming influence of private interests by providing a voice for under-represented constituencies. (6) Because of processes of selection of activists that can effectively target the EU level with the appropriate linguistic and legal skills EU movements have become more institutionalised and professionalised and in that respect are more useful to EU institutions in providing needed information on the key policy domains in which their presence is relevant.

Notes

1. See http://www.alter-eu.org/ (website accessed 28 July 2011).
2. See http://www.green10.org/ (website accessed 28 July 2011).
3. See http://www.act4europe.org/code/en/default.asp (website accessed 4 March 2011).
4. For a description of EEB funding sources see http://www.eeb.org/index.cfm/about-eeb/our-donors/ (website accessed 4 March 2011).
5. This is for instance typically summarised in the following excerpt from the website of CSGT the Civil Society Contact Group previously mentioned: 'The EU Civil Society Contact Group defends a vision of the European Union that is an advocate for and guarantor of peace, solidarity, justice, equality for all, equality between women and men, non discrimination, sustainable development, protection and improvement of the environment, the eradication of poverty and observance of human rights to ensure a high quality of life and well-being for present and future generations within the EU and globally' (see http://www.act4europe.org/code/en/hp.asp website accessed 28 July 2011).
6. http://www.enar-eu.org/Page_Generale.asp?DocID=15279&la=1&langue=EN website accessed 28 July 2011).

References

Bell, M. 2002. *Anti-Discrimination Law and the European Union*. Oxford University Press.
Bozzini, E. 2007. The role of civil society organisations in written consultation processes: from the European Monitoring Centre to the European fundamental rights. In *Governance and civil society: policy perspectives*, eds. V.D. Sala and C. Ruzza, 93–109. Manchester University Press.
Cullen, P. 2010. The platform of European social NGOs: ideology, division and coalition. *Journal of Political Ideologies* 15: 317–30.
Della-Porta, D. 2009. Social movements and civil society: how emerging social conflicts challenge social science approaches. In *Conflict, citizenship and civil society*, eds. P. Baert, S. Koniordos, G. Procacci and C. Ruzza, 41–68. Routledge.
Della Porta, D., and M. Diani. 2006. *Social movements: an introduction*. Oxford: Blackwell.
Della Sala, V. 2010. Political myth, mythology and the European Union. *Journal of Common Market Studies* 48: 1–19.
Diani, M. 1992. The concept of social movement. *Sociological Review* 40: 1–25.
Giugni, M. 2004. *Social protest and policy change: ecology, antinuclear, and peace movements in comparative perspective*. Rowman and Littlefield.
Hildebrand, P. 1993. The European community environmental policy, 1957 to 1992: from incidental measures to an international regime? In *A green dimension for the European Community*, eds. D. Judge. London: Frank Cass.
Jordan, G. 2001. *Shell, Greenpeace and the Brent Spar*. Basingstoke, UK: Palgrave Macmillan.
Judge, D. 1992. Predestined to save the earth: the Environmental Committee of the European Parliament. *Environmental Politics* 1, no. 4: 186–212.
Keck, M.E., and K. Sikkink. 1998. *Activism beyond borders*. Ithaca, NY: Cornell University Press.
Marks, G., and D. Mcadam. 1996. Social movements and the changing structure of political opportunity in the European Union. In *Governance in the European Union*, eds. G. Marks, F. Scharpf, P.C. Schmitter and W. Streeck. London: Sage.
Mathers, A. 2007. *Struggling for a social Europe: neoliberal globalization and the birth of a European social movement*. Farnham, UK: Ashgate.
Mccarthy, J.D., and M.N. Zald. 1982. Resource mobilization and social movements: a partial theory. *American Journal of Sociology* 6: 1213–41.
Müller-Rommel, F., and T. Poguntke. 2002. *Green parties in national governments*. London: Frank Cass.
Pitkin, H. 1967. *The Concept of Representation*. Berkeley, CA: California University Press.
Rice, T., and P. Owen. 1999. *Decommissioning the Brent Spar*. Abingdon, UK: Routledge.
Rootes, C. 2005. A limited transnationalization? The British environmental movement. In *Transnational protest and global activism*, eds. D.D.P.A.S. Tarrow. Lanham, MD: Rowman and Littlefield.

Ruzza, C. 2004. *Europe and civil society: movement coalitions and European governance*. Manchester, UK: Manchester University Press.
Ruzza, C. 2006. European institutions and the policy discourse of organised civil society. In *Civil society and legitimate European governance*, eds. S. Smismans, 169–95. Cheltenham, UK: Edward Elgar.
Ruzza, C. 2011. The international protection regime for minorities, the aftermath of the 2008 financial crisis and the EU: new challenges for non-state actors. *International Journal on Minority and Group Rights* 18, no. 2: 219–34.
Santoro, W.A., and G.M. Mcguire. 1997. Social movement insiders: the impact of institutional activists on affirmative action and comparable worth policies. *Social Problems* 44: 503–19.
Saward, M. 2009. Authorisation and authenticity: representation and the unelected. *Journal of Political Philosophy* 17: 1–22.
Tarrow, S.G. 1989. *Struggle, politics and reform: Collective action, social movements and cycles of protest*. Ithaca, NY: Cornell University.
Tarrow, S. 2008. *The new transnational activism*. Cambridge: Cambridge University Press.
Tilly, C.H. 1984. *Big structures, large processes, huge comparisons*. New York: Russell Sage Foundation.
Warren, M., and D. Castiglione. 2004. The transformation of democratic representation. *Democracy and Society* 2: 20–2.

Interests, Influence and Information: Comparing the Influence of Interest Groups in the European Union

ADAM WILLIAM CHALMERS

McGill University, Montreal, Canada

ABSTRACT The purpose of this analysis is to present and test an information processing theory of interest group influence in the EU. While it has long been acknowledged that information is the currency of lobbying in the EU, a systematic examination of how interest groups gather, generate, synthesise, and transmit information to decision-makers is still missing. I posit that interest group influence is a function of a group's ability to efficiently process information. Conceptualising influence in this way not only brings the study of influence in-line with key insights from the larger interest group literature, but it also helps avoid some serious methodological issues related to measuring influence. Using data from a large-scale online survey and elite interviews I compare how information processing varies across six different types of interest groups. The results suggest that most types of interest groups in the EU have similar information processing capabilities and thus, that influence in the EU appears to be, on balance, fair and impartial.

Measuring the influence of interest groups is one of the most important but methodologically tricky problems in political science research. Assessing influence lends significant insight into the production of efficient policies and the conditions for both economic development and political legitimacy. The problem, however, is that measuring influence typically leads to a serious methodological dead-end. It is, put simply, incredibly difficult, if not impossible, to categorically attribute a policy outcome to a specific interest group activity (Dür 2008a, 2008b; Dür and De Bièvre

2007a; Beyers, Eising, and Maloney 2008). The present analysis puts forward a way out of this dead-end. I argue that improving our measurements or refining our indicators cannot accomplish this. Rather, doing so requires a fundamental rethinking of interest group influence itself.

The limited scholarly work that has attempted to measure influence head-on invariably begins with the assumption that lobbying is inherently conflictual: Interest groups, using traditional pressure and purchase tactics, try to change the minds of decision-makers in an effort to bring about specific policy outcomes. Examining influence in this way, however, is wholly out of step with what we know about interest group behaviour. First, there is overwhelming evidence that interest groups are less likely to try to change the minds of decision-makers who disagree with them than to support those who already do (Bauer, Pool, and Dexter 1963; Berry 1977; Potters and van Winden 1990, 1992; Hall and Deardorff 2006). Interest groups, in other words, tend to lobby friends, not foes. Second, interest groups are best understood as 'service bureaus', to speak with Hall and Deardorff (2006), offering a form of professional labour to friendly decision-makers. The service they offer is largely informational. Well-informed interest groups provide understaffed decision-makers with policy relevant information in exchange for legitimate access to the policy-making process (Ainsworth 1993; Austen-Smith 1993; Crawford and Sobel 1982; Hojnacki and Kimball 1999; Bouwen 2004).

I begin by taking these insights very seriously. First, influence is exercised primarily through the informational service that interest groups provide decision-makers. Second, since interest groups are unlikely to lobby foes, we cannot expect to see the evidence of influence in changed minds and policy outcomes. After all, lobbying friends entails having shared interests. I thus conceive of influence as a function of an interest group's ability to provide decision-makers with policy-relevant information. While the importance of information in the policy-making process has long been acknowledged in the literature, a systematic study of how groups gather, generate, make sense of, synthesize and transmit information — what I call 'information processing' in short — is still missing.

Drawing on 64 elite interviews and an online survey of 308 interest group representatives active in the European Union (EU), I measure information processing across two dimensions: Information gathering and information transmission. I posit that interest group influence is a function of efficient information processing in both dimensions. Information gathering refers to how interest groups anticipate and prepare to meet the informational needs of EU decision-makers. It consists of monitoring EU activities using a multitude of reliable information sources and generating policy-relevant information through various research strategies. Efficiency in gathering relates primarily to timing. This means prioritizing monitoring activities, obtaining early information, and implementing effective research strategies. Information transmission refers to the type of information sent to decision-makers as well as the tactics used to do so and the targets at which this information is aimed. Efficiency in transmission means having a large and flexible repertory of strategies for passing along information to decision-makers. Gathering data on these two indicators provides the means for testing the following hypothesis: *The more efficient interest groups are at information processing, the more influence they will have.*

Measuring influence as information processing provides the tools for a systematic comparison of different types of interest groups in the EU. A comparative study is important for assessing which types of interest groups shape the EU decision-making process and which are systematically excluded from it. Is the EU interest group system a type of elite pluralism, as many scholars suggest, where private interest groups have more influence diffuse groups (Coen 1997, 1998; Cowles 2001; Mazey and Richardson 1997; Hueglin 1999)? To get an accurate picture of lobbying in the EU, however, we need to extend our comparison beyond the usual private-diffuse dichotomy and to span the functional–territorial interest group gap. This means including, within a systematic comparative framework, a very broad range of different types of interests operating at the European level. To this end I have gathered data on eleven different types of interest groups in the EU: Professional associations, companies, law firms, public affairs consultancies, chambers of commerce, academic organisations, trade unions, NGOs and associations of NGOs, representatives of religions, churches and communities of conviction, think-tanks, and, lastly, public authorities like regions, cities and municipalities. The main finding of this analysis is that interest group influence in the EU is, on balance, fair and impartial. No single type of group or groups dominates the process and no groups are excluded. Importantly, this goes some way in challenging claims that the EU system of interest intermediation is best characterised as a form of elite pluralism. I begin this analysis will a brief overview of the existing literature on interest group influence. I then put forward an information processing theory of interest group influence. Next, I outline my research design and discuss the operationalisation of my variables. Finally, I present and assess results from an empirical analysis using survey results.

Measuring Interest Group Influence

Interest groups have long been recognized as major channels through which citizen preferences are expressed and legitimate policy is produced (Lazarsfeld, Berelson, and Gaudet 1948; Lindblom 1965; Grant 1989). At the same time, however, intense competition between interest groups or the dominance of just a few strong interest groups can lead to politically and economically inefficient policies affecting the overall economic development in a state (Olson 1982, 2000; Lowi 1962; Schattschneider 1960). In the EU context, scholars suggest that interest groups are not represented evenly at all. The EU has not adopted the neo-corporatist model of interest group intermediation of its most powerful member states (Germany and France), but rather appears to be a type of elite pluralism where private interests have privileged access to EU decision-makers and where diffuse interests are systematically excluded (Mazey and Richardson 1997; Coen 1997, 1998; Cowles 2001; Hueglin 1999).

While the institutional structure of EU lobbying and conditions for interest group access might reflect a form of elite pluralism in the EU, only by measuring influence directly can we get an accurate picture of lobbying in the EU. Importantly, the scant research that addresses the issue of interest group influence tends to conceptualize it in terms of a Weberian notion of power: 'The opportunity to impose one's will in a social relationship, even against resistance, without consideration to what this opportunity rests on' (cited in Woll 2007, 75). Similarly, for James March, writing in 1955, influence is the power of an interest group to force a decision-maker 'deviate from (his) predicted path of behaviour' (435). Robert Dahl's classic reformulation developed in his study of pluralistic power in New Haven helps clarify further: 'A has power over B to the extent that he can get B to do something that B would not otherwise do' (1957, 203). Or, as Dür and de Bièvre have more recently put it, influence is the control over outcomes when these outcomes bring interest groups 'closer to their ideal points' (2007a, 3).

Influence, however, remains a nebulous concept that is typically operationalised using a series of proxies for measuring both its causes and effects. As 'cause', or the ability to control outcomes, influence is usually related to interest group resources, group organisation and a related capacity for collective action as well as, to a lesser extent, the institutional setting of the policy process and the policy issue itself (Mahoney 2007, 2008; Michalowitz 2007; Eising 2007; Princen 2007). As 'effect', influence is evinced in the extent that an interest group is able to realize its own preferences. This is measured as the degree to which groups have changed the minds of decision-makers (Michalowitz 2007; March 1955) or the similarity of a group's initial aims and the end policy outcome (Mahoney 2008; Burnstein and Linton 2002). Recent work even uses textual analysis to measure the similarities between a group's stated aims, either deduced in interviews, policy reports or position papers, and the actual outcome of an issue (Klüver 2009).

Influence as Information Processing

Conceiving of influence through a Weberian lens of power, however, is out of step with recent insights from the interest group literature. First, there is overwhelming evidence that interest groups tend to lobby friends rather than foes. Lobbying consists of the exchange of information between well-informed interest groups and understaffed decision-makers (Crombez 2002; Dür and de Bièvre 2007). Sending information to foes in order to change their minds is too costly and the results too uncertain (Lowery 2007). Given their limited resources, interest groups therefore transmit information to those who are already most likely to support their cause (Bauer, Pool, and Dexter 1968; Crombez 2004; Heinz *et al.* 1993; Hojnacki and Kimball 1999). The goal of lobbying is, on balance, not to change the minds of those who do not agree with you, but rather to subsidize the work of those who already do. It is in this light that Hall and Deardorff have argued that interest groups are best understood as service bureaus that provide a professional informational service to allied decision-makers (2006, 72).

The informational nature of lobbying is particularly important in the EU. Indeed, the different decision-making institutions in the EU actively generate a huge demand for policy relevant information. Both informal and formal institutions mandate EU decision-makers in the Commission, for instance, to consult widely with interest groups during the legislative process (i.e., European Commission 2007). Indeed, all of the EU's decision-making bodies are deeply affected by the conditions of informational asymmetry and rely on interest groups for a steady supply of policy-relevant information (Bouwen 2009; Hayes-Renshaw 2009; Lehmann 2009).

In downplaying the informational nature of lobbying in the EU and assuming that lobbying is invariably conflictual, the task of measuring influence is unwittingly saddled with a series of methodological difficulties. First, it is difficult, if not impossible, to establish a one-to-one causal link between interest group activities and policy outcomes that categorically brackets off the (perhaps unintended) influence of other interest groups as well as a host of other exogenous and endogenous causal factors (Dür 2008b; Grant 1989). Second, measuring influence as realizing preferences in concrete outcomes requires establishing what these preferences are. It is not only very difficult to identify and catalogue interest groups preferences, but in many instances interest groups themselves are not always clear about their own preferences, (Dür 2008b, 568). Finally, the link between influence and the outcomes of influence lacks any consideration of how the former impact the latter. There are no causal mechanisms that translate factors of influence, like resources, political support, campaign contributions and a capacity for collective action, into specific policy outcomes or changed-minds (Potters and van Winden 1992; Heinz *et al.* 1993).

These methodological difficulties, however, only apply when we think about lobbying as inherently conflictual and when we look for the evidence of influence in changed minds and policy outcomes. When interest groups are understood as lobbying friendly decision-makers, however, then there are no minds to change and policy outcomes cannot be categorically attributed to interest groups. Lobbying friends, after all, implies that interest group and decision-maker preferences already convergence.

This analysis suggests approaching interest group influence by unpacking the informational nature of lobbying in the EU and taking seriously the possibility that interest groups tend to lobby friends not foes (and thus, that the evidence of influence is not found in outcomes). As such, I propose measuring interest group influence in terms of the informational service interest groups provide decision-makers in the EU. To be sure, it has long been recognized that information is the currency of lobbying in Brussels (see Broscheid and Coen 2007). Nevertheless, the research that does address the informational nature of lobbying in the EU tends to focus on the demand-side of this informational relationship, examining the institutional factors that draw EU decision-makers to consult with interest groups in the first place (Crombez 2002; Eising 2007; Bouwen 2004). What is missing from the existing research is a systematic consideration of the supply-side of this informational relationship between interest groups and decision-makers. How, for instance, do interest groups generate information, gather it, synthesize and make sense of it? What type of information do interests transmit to which decision-makers using which tactics? These are precisely the questions that frame the present analysis of interest group information processing in the EU.

Research Design

To measure interest group influence as a group's information processing ability I have collected data in 62 elite interviews and a large-scale online survey of 308 interest group representatives active in lobbying EU decision-makers.[1] I define interest groups as any group that seeks to influence the policy-making process but does not seek to be elected.[2] Importantly, this excludes politicians and mass movements but includes a vast array of different types of groups. Inclusiveness without concept stretching is central to the comparative dimension of this analysis. I have generated a list of different types of interest groups by drawing primarily on the European Commission's new 'Register of Interest Representatives'.[3] It includes: Professional associations, companies, law firms, public affairs consultancies, chambers of commerce, academic organisations, trade unions, NGOs and associations of NGOs, representatives of religions, churches and communities of conviction, think-tanks, and, lastly, public authorities like regions, cities and municipalities. For the survey, a list of potential respondents was generated using three sources: The European Commission's 'Register of Interest Representatives', the 2008 edition of the 'European Public Affairs Directory', and the 'Brussels–Europe Liaison Office' list of subnational offices in Brussels.[4] This last source was critical for the inclusion of public authority groups in this study. In total, a list of about 2000 interest groups was generated. I used a simple proportional sampling technique (systematically selecting every n*th* group for each type of interest group on the list to minimize sampling biases). From this, a sampling frame of 932 interest groups was established. 308 responses were collected, putting the response rate at about 33%. Distribution of responses by group type is detailed in Table 1.

I analyse the survey data using descriptive statistics. Low response rates for law firms, think tanks, chambers of commerce, academic organisations and representatives of religions means that this analysis is limited to assessing influence in the following six types of interest groups: Companies, professional associations, NGOs and associations of NGOs, trade unions, public authorities, and consultancies. Assessing how representative this sample is vis-à-vis the EU interest group population is very difficult. There is no definitive list of interest groups in the EU and there are only loose approximations of the number of groups that actively lobby at the European level (see Berkhout and Lowery 2008; Greenwood 2007). Without these specifics, assessing the representativeness of the sample is next to impossible.

As intimated above, information processing is measured across two dimensions: Information gathering and information transmission. Before presenting results, I will discuss each dimension in detail.

Table 1. Distribution of Responses by Interest Group Type

Interest Group Type	Frequency	Percent
Companies	44	14.29
Professional Associations	73	23.70
Public Affairs Consultancies	30	9.74
Trade Unions	28	9.08
Chambers of Commerce	4	1.30
Law Firms	0	0
Academic organisations	2	0.65
NGOs/Association of NGOs	78	25.32
Think-Tanks	4	1.30
Representatives of religions, churches and communities of conviction	1	0.32
Public Authorities (regions, cities, municipalities)	34	11.04
Other	10	3.25
Total	308	100.00

Information Gathering

Information gathering refers to how interest groups manage to keep up-to-date on EU policy initiatives by monitoring decision-maker activities as well as how they use various forms of research to generate information. The two are linked. Monitoring allows interest groups to anticipate the informational needs of decision-makers and research prepares interest groups to respond to these needs. Importantly, there is a premium on early, efficient and reliable information in the EU. Decision-makers value policy relevant information but only if it is received in time for it to be useful in the policy-making process. Too late, and information loses all of its value. Therefore, interest groups must use efficient monitoring tactics to quickly and efficiently determine what the issue is, what information is needed, and who requires it. In fact, as one representative interviewed for this analysis explained, 'keeping up to date is not enough. You must be able to anticipate what the agenda will be'.[5] It is to this end that interest groups act as veritable 'early warning radar systems', taking on the task of 'horizon gazing'[6] with the intention of 'being in right from the start'[7] of the decision-making process.

Monitoring requires groups to quickly and efficiently parse a great many information sources, ranging from newspaper and newsletters, to official EU documents and press releases, to information passed along informally through word of mouth. Having information at the earliest possible stages of the policy-making process facilitates horizon gazing. 'News papers', to speak with another interest group representative, 'are really just second-hand news', and the information they provide 'is already too late'.[8] By contrast, 'good information is information we get earlier than others. It is not only the quality of the information, but its exclusiveness'.[9] Since 'the key is to get information before it is even published', groups value so-called 'early information', 'black information', 'leaked information' or *'information limitée'*. This type of early and exclusive information, obtained through word of mouth and face-to-face meetings, is thus more conducive to efficient gathering than more formal information sources (like newspapers, newsletter, TV and radio news and even official EU documents, like Green Papers and press releases).

Information gathering also involves the use of various research strategies that allow groups prepare to meet the informational needs of decision-makers. Research can take the form of commissioning private research studies or carrying out the research themselves. Commissioned studies refer to research that has been outsourced to third parties like service providers or consultancies. Research done in-house, however, should not be considered less valuable or rigorous. In fact, while in-house research can involve the engagement of executives, policy officers, and even *stagiaires* in research related projects, it can also refer to trained research experts, like engineers, technicians and scientists working for an interest group or its members. Both are powerful research strategies and can imply the costly engagement of experts and the generation of original data. The value of research lies in the need for interest groups to couch their preferences in a cause–effect logic (see Austen-Smith 1993; Esterling 2004). The trend in EU lobbying, to speak with one interest group representative, is toward 'evidence-based policy-making'.[10] 'Serious lobbying has to based on facts and figures... the basis has to be science'.[11]

Using data from an on-line survey, I contend that efficient information gathering is a function of three related factors: (1) prioritizing monitoring activities, (2) prioritizing information sources that provide interest groups with the most timely information, and (3) prioritizing research strategies. Survey questions provide data on each factor of information gathering.

First, monitoring was tapped by asking respondents about the importance, on a scale of one to five (with one being 'not at all important' and five being 'very important') of 'monitoring EU activities'. Interest groups that place greater importance on monitoring are better able to keep up-to-date on EU activities. Second, respondents were asked to identify the importance, again on a scale of one to five, of three basic types of information: Formal sources (newspapers, newsletters, TV news, radio news, books/magazines), informal sources (conferences/exhibitions, face-to-face meetings, and word of mouth) and EU sources (EU press releases, EU White Papers, EU Green Papers). Groups that prioritize informal sources over both formal and EU sources, in that informal sources tend to carry early and leaked information, should be better able to anticipate decision-makers' informational needs. Third, research refers equally to commissioning private research studies and conducting research in-house. Both are powerful research strategies. As such, respondents were asked about the importance (again on a one to five scale) of conducting both research strategies. Interest groups that stress both should also be those groups that are best prepared when it comes time to address the informational needs of decision-makers. I combine responses for both types of research to form a single 'research' score.

Information Transmission

Information transmission refers to the actual process of sending information to decision-makers. Here interest groups are faced with a series of strategic options regarding information types, tactics and targets. First, what type of information do they send (i.e., technical information, legal information, information about policy outcomes), which tactics do they use to send it (i.e., inside strategies like writing letters and taking meetings or outside strategies like mobilizing citizen support) and, finally, at which decision-maker is the information targeted (i.e., the European Commission, European Parliament or European Council). I argue, following Baumgartner and Leech, that effective information transmission is not about being good at one strategy, but rather having the greatest repertory of strategies (1998, 148). Sending just one type of information in one way to just one decision-maker is, on balance, less efficient than having recourse to a vast range of different types of information, different tactics for conveying this information and a large number of decision-makers at which this information is targeted. To speak with one interest group representative, 'you have to have the right message for the right audience'.[12] Moreover, according to another representative, the audience determines the 'way we deliver the message too. The message can be the same, but it can be delivered in different ways depending on the audience'.[13]

To assess efficient information transmission I compare how different types of interest groups vary in terms of their respective strategic repertories regarding (1) information type, (2) information tactics, and (3) information targets. For type, tactics and targets, effective information transmission is really a matter of *more is better*.[14] Sending more types of information, using more tactics and to more targets reflects a group's strategic flexibility across all three factors of information transmission.

Data on types, tactics and targets was gathered by asking respondents the following questions. First, respondents were asked to identify how frequently (based on a one to five scale, with one being 'never' and five being 'very often') they provide decision-makers with the following six types of information: Legal information, information about public opinion, information about the feasibility of implementing a proposal, information about the economic impact of a proposal, information about the social impact of a proposal, and information that makes technical or scientific data understandable/relevant. Second, respondents were asked about the frequency with which they use the following six tactics to provide decision-makers with information: Write an e-mail, write a letter, make a phone call, participate in the open consultation process, face-to-face meeting, host a public event and start of media campaign. Third, respondents were asked how frequently they provided information to the following targets: The European Commission, the European Parliament, the Council of Ministers, and Coreper.

Results

Figure 1 plots the five indicators for information gathering on a bar graph. Entries are mean scores based on scales ranging from one to five measuring importance (with one being 'not at all important' and five being 'very important').

As the results on Figure 1 make clear, all types of interest groups in the EU appear to place a considerable amount of importance on monitoring activities. This confirms the expectation that for many interest groups in the EU, monitoring is not just one activity among others, but rather, to speak with one representative, their 'raison d'être'.[15] Anticipating the informational needs of decision-makers, and thus knowing what type of information to send where and when, requires efficient monitoring and skilled horizon gazing. Similarly, as expected, all interest groups prioritize informal information sources over formal sources. Acting as early as possible requires early and even leaked information. This information is not available through newspapers and newsletters but rather through decidedly social sources like word of mouth and face-to-face meetings. As one representative explained, a general rule of thumb for obtaining early information is this: 'The less time we spend in the office the better'.[16] Many interest groups even legitimize their presence in Brussels on the basis of the importance of early information gained through contacts and networking. Interestingly, however, EU sources are also considered to be very important by most interest groups (in four cases, slightly more importance is attributed to EU sources than informal sources). While EU sources do not provide exclusive or early information, they do communicate details about upcoming opportunities for consultations and serve as valuable primary sources for information on legislation, proposals and briefings. there is no trade-off between informal and EU sources. Instead, efficient horizon gazing is well served by balancing early and leaked information sources with reliable EU sources.

According to Figure 1, interest groups attribute far less importance to research strategies, especially when compared to monitoring activities. Companies, nonetheless, place slightly more importance on research

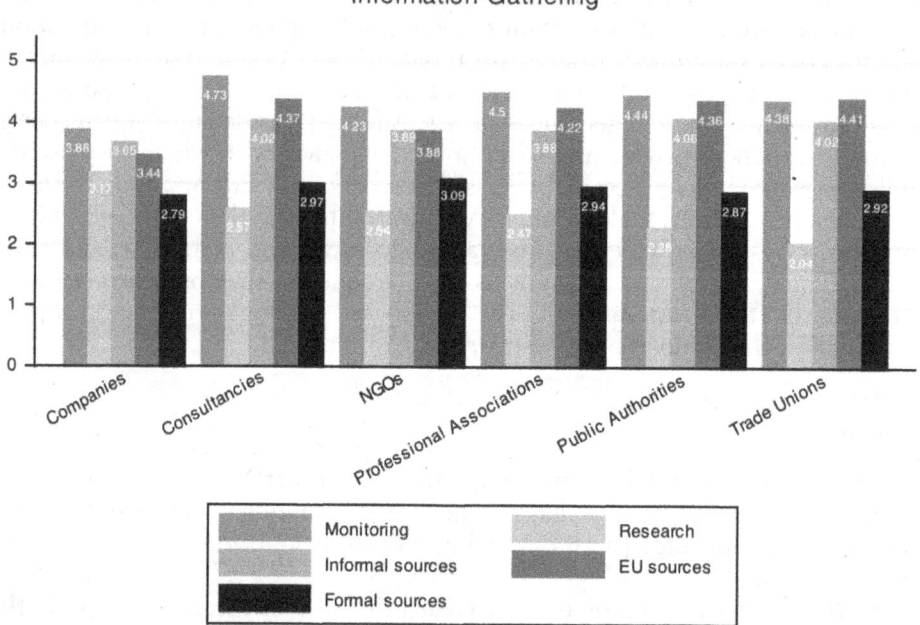

Figure 1.

strategies than other types of groups, perhaps reflecting their greater resources and thus their ability to commission research projects and employ skilled staff for conducting in-house research. The general results for research are surprising given the importance attributed to research as reported in interviews (see above). Importantly, monitoring already implies a type of research: Much of the information that tells an interest group when to act also provides it with the resources for preparing to react. Thus, by stressing research activities, companies might be making up for a lack of emphasis on monitoring (presented in Figure 1, above). Similarly, the considerable importance placed on monitoring by NGOs and public authorities, for example, might act as an *ersatz* (and perhaps more affordable) form of research, thus explaining the relatively low research scores for these types of groups. Of course, the type of interest being represented might also help explain these differences. Companies are commonly faced with very technical issues related to market, production and manufacturing issues that simply require more formal types of research. Companies also commonly commission research on consumer and market strategies for both internal and external use.

Figure 2 plots the three indicators for information transmission on a bar graph. Entries are mean scores based on scales ranging from one to five measuring frequency (with one being 'never' and five being 'very often').

High scores on types, tactics and targets imply a large 'repertory of strategies' at the disposal of a given interest group. Sending more types of information using a variety of different tactics and targeting many different decision-makers increases the chances of influencing policy. As the results in the Figure 2 suggest, most types of interest groups in the EU can indeed draw on rather larger repertories of strategies. NGOs, professional associations, public authorities and trade unions all have very similar high scores on types, tactics and targets, suggesting that all four types of interest group have a similar potential to impact policy in terms of information transmission.

Perhaps the most conspicuous results in both graphs are the relatively low scores for companies and the relatively high scores for consultancies. These results, coupled with the very similar information processing scores for trade unions, public authorities, NGOs and professional associations, beg the following two questions. First, do consultancies have considerably more influence than other types of groups? Second, do companies have less influence than other types of groups? Answering these questions provide the framework for the two main findings of the present analysis. I will discuss each finding in turn.

First, the results for consultancies should not be interpreted as their domination of the EU policy-making process. Consultancies, after all, do not represent their own interests but rather the interests of others — including, importantly, private interests but also diffuse interests and the interests of public authorities. Thus, the fact that consultancies are good information processors suggests that their clients have considerable influence on the EU policy-making process. Indeed, as Lahusen points out in his 2002 study of EU consultancies, these 'clients say something about the type of interests

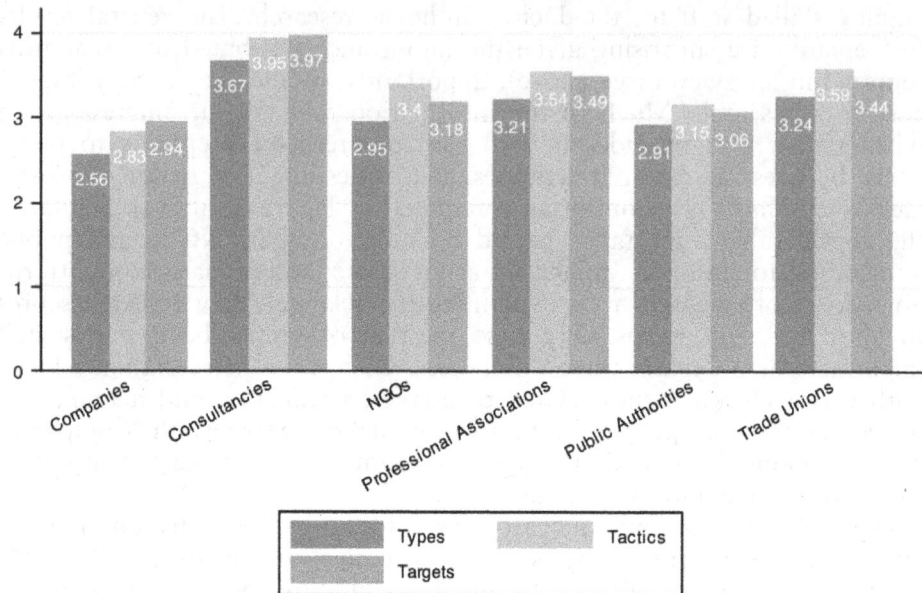

Figure 2

which consultancies tend to serve' (2002, 707). What Lahusen found was that consultancies tend to have a relatively diverse client base, ranging from trade associations, companies, NGOs and government institutions. When asked to rank the importance of their clients, however, most consultancies placed private interests (like companies) slightly ahead of trade unions, governmental institutions and NGOs, reflecting what Lahusen identified as the apparent 'predominance of economic and industrial interests in the EU' (707f.).

The high scores for consultancies might also explain the relatively lower scores for companies on monitoring and information transmission. Again, as Lahusen suggests, companies, more so than most other types of interest groups, are using consultancy services. It might well be the case, then, that companies are outsourcing monitoring tasks (including the gathering and parsing of information sources) to consultancies. Indeed, the two graphs above and Lahusen's study do seem to suggest this. Unfortunately, very little work on EU consultancies has been conducted and Lahusen's results need to be used cautiously. The parameters of 'importance' that consultancies attribute to clients in this study are not identified. It is unclear whether importance is based on the amount of time spent with a client, the amount of money the clients generates for the consultancy, or the perceived importance of a client in a given policy area?

The results presented in the two graphs seem to provide little evidence for elite pluralism in EU lobbying. Private interests, like professional associations, and diffuse interests, like NGOs and trade unions, all have relatively similar information processing capabilities. High consultancy scores appear to be balanced by low company scores on both dimensions of information processing. What is more, the results for public authorities show them as comparatively efficient information processors, operating in many regards like other interest groups. This result gives purchase to the vast literature on the role of sub-state actors in the EU legislative process (Hooghe and Keating 1994; Moore 2008). Importantly, by disaggregating between different types of private and diffuse interests and broadening the comparison to include other types of interest groups, like public authorities and consultancies, we get a much more accurate impression of which groups dominate the EU policy-making process and which are systematically left out. In the EU, no single type of group or specific set of groups appears to dominate at the expense of others. Rather, most types of interest groups in the EU have the potential for considerable influence in the EU policy-making process.

A second key finding of this analysis is also reflected in the relatively high information processing scores for consultancies. The rather diverse clientele of consultancies, even if slightly dominated by companies, reflects what several scholars recognise as the professionalization of lobbying in Brussels (Lahusen 2002, 2003; Lehmann 2009; Coen 2009). More and more, interest groups are seeking out the services of consultancies in the EU. The expanding complexities of EU law, the ever-changing nature of EU treaties, the extension of EU competencies into new policy areas and the EU's slow expansion to new member states creates a need for consultancy services. Consultancies offer professional clipping services that parse and filter information sources; they facilitate the formation of effective issue-based lobbying coalitions that bring together actors from private, diffuse and public authority interests; they conduct research and interpret the results in a user–friend (namely, client-friendly) way. More generally, the value-added of consultancies is reducing the complexities of lobbying in Brussels. 'Our competence', as a representative from a Brussels-based consultancy put it, 'is in understanding the system and being able to comment on the relative importance of things'.[17]

Conclusion

This analysis has presented an approach to measuring interest group influence that takes seriously the informational nature of lobbying in the EU as well as the near consensus in the literature that interest groups tend to lobby friends not foes. I have argued that conceiving of influence as inherently conflictual is out of step with these insights and has unnecessarily led to a series of methodological dead-ends. The way out of these dead-ends is not in improving our measures of influence but, rather, in rethinking the nature of influence itself. To this end I have conceived of influence as a function of an interest group's information processing capacity.

The comparative dimension of this study moved beyond the common private-diffuse dichotomy and spanned the territorial-functional gap, incorporating a broad range of interest groups in an analysis of influence.

A central weakness of this study, however, stems from low survey response rates from a number of key interest group types (law firms, think tanks, academic organisations, religious groups and chambers of commerce). Including more groups in an empirical analysis of information processing is necessary for making more definitive conclusions about which groups are influential and which are not.

The data collected here have nonetheless provided compelling evidence challenging long-held assumptions about the dominance of private interest groups in the EU. Rather than an elite pluralism, where only private interest groups influence the EU decision-making process, my findings suggest a much more balanced and unbiased form of influence coming from a wide range of different types of interest groups.

Broadening the comparison to public authorities and consultancies also provides some new insights into the nature of interest groups influence in the EU. The results for public authorities show them as comparatively efficient information processors, operating in many regards like other interest groups. The high scores for consultancies do not suggest that consultancies have more influence than other groups. Rather, they reflect the professionalization of interest representation in the EU. More generally speaking, the results of this analysis suggest not only that a theory of information processing provides a new way of understanding interest group influence but also that it provides new insights into the nature of the EU system of interest group intermediation. Insofar as the theory of information processing put forward in this analysis does away with long-held misconceptions of interest group influence, it gives a more accurate impression of the overall footprint of lobbying in the European Union.

Notes

1. Questions for the online survey were derived from information gathered from elite interviews with interest group representatives themselves as well as the relevant academic literature. To ensure a certain reliability and quality in responses, when possible surveys were sent to organization presidents, vice presidents, executive directors, upper level management or those legally responsible for the organization. While it is very difficult to remark on the effort given by respondents during the completion of the survey, especially considering that online surveys cannot be monitored, targeting these individuals directly should reflect a certain seriousness, care and thoughtfulness in the responses given.
2. On defining the interest group concept see Beyers, Eising, and Mahoney (2008).
3. The Register is available at: https://webgate.ec.europa.eu/transparency/regrin/welcome.do?locale=en.
4. The Brussels–Europe Liaison Office list (accessed in fall 2009) is available online at: http://www.blbe.be/directory/find.asp.
5. Interview, official, *Conseil regional d'Aquitaine*, Brussels, 12 October 2009.
6. Interview, Julian Carroll, Managing Director, *European* (The European Organisation for Packaging and the Environment), Brussels, 17 November 2010.
7. Interview, Martin Romer, General Secretary, *ETUCE* (European Trade Union Committee for Education), Brussels, 17 November 2010.
8. Interview, Dominic Rowles, European Officer, *Local Governmental Association*, Brussels, 16 October 2009.
9. Interview, Kerstin Duhme, Director, *FD Blueprint*, Brussels, 16 November 2010.
10. Interview, Paul Voss, Manger for Energy and Environment Policy, *AEGPL Europe*, Brussels, 16 November 2010.
11. Interview, Dr Marlene Wartenberg, Director, *Vier Pfoten*, Brussels, 19 November 2010.

12. Interview, Dr Marlene Wartenberg, Director, *Vier Pfoten*, Brussels, 19 November 2010.
13. Interview, Martyn Griffiths, Executive Officer, *Eurogroup for Animals*, Brussels, 15 November 2010.
14. Eising (2007) has made a similar point, providing evidence that sending more types of information to decision-makers results in greater access to the EU policy-making process.
15. Interview, Dominic Rowles, European Officer, *Local Governmental Association*, Brussels, 16 October 2009.
16. Interview, official, *South Finland EU Office*, Brussels, 14 October 2009.
17. Interview, Timo Schubert, Associate Director, *ADS Insight*, Brussels, 17 November 2010.

References

Ainsworth, S. 1993. Regulating lobbyists and interest group influence. *The Journal of Politics* 55, no. 1: 41–56.
Austen-Smith, D. 1993. Information and influence: lobbying for agendas and votes. *American Journal of Political Science* 34, no. 3: 799–833.
Bauer, R., I. de Sola Pool, L. Dexter. 1963. *American business and public policy: the politics of foreign trade*. New York: Atherton Press.
Baumgartner, F.R., B.L. Leech. 1998. *Basic interests. The importance of groups in politics and in political science*. Princeton, NJ: Princeton University Press.
Berkhout, J., and D. Lowery. 2008. Counting organized interests in the European Union: a comparison of data sources. *Journal of European Public Policy* 15, no. 4: 489–513.
Berry, J.M. 1977. *Lobbying for the people: the political behavior of public interest groups*. Princeton, NJ: Princeton University Press.
Beyers, J., R. Eising, and W. Mahoney. 2008. Researching interest group politics in Europe and elsewhere: much we study, little we know? *West European Politics* 31, no. 6: 1103–28.
Bouwen, P. 2004. The logic of access to the European Parliament: business lobbying in the committee on economic and monetary affairs. *Journal of Common Market Studies* 42, no. 3: 473–95.
Bouwen, P. 2009. The European Commission. In *Lobbying the European Union: institutions, actors, and issues*, eds. D. Coen and J. Richardson, 19–38. Oxford: Oxford University Press.
Broscheid, A., and D. Coen. 2007. Lobbying activity and fora creation in the EU: empirically exploring the nature of the policy good. *Journal of European Public Policy* 14, no. 3: 346–65.
Burnstein, P., and A. Linton. 2002. The impact of political parties, interest groups, and social movement organizations on public policy: some recent evidence and theoretical concerns. *Social Forces* 81, no. 2: 380–408.
Coen, D. 1997. The evolution of the large firm as a political actor in the European Union. *Journal of Public Policy* 4, no. 1: 91–108.
Coen, D. 1998. The European business interest and the nation state: large-firm lobbying in the European Union and member states. *Journal of Public Policy* 18, no. 1: 75–100.
Coen, D. 2007. Empirical and theoretical studies of EU lobbying. *Journal of European Public Policy* 14, no. 3: 333–45.
Coen, D. 2009. Business lobbying in the European Union. In *Lobbying the European Union: institutions, actors, and issues*, eds. D. Coen and J. Richardson, 145–68. Oxford: Oxford University Press.
Cowles, M.G. 2001. The transatlantic business dialogue and domestic business-government relations. In *Transforming Europe. Europeanization and domestic change*, eds. M.G. Cowles, J.A. Caporaso and T. Risse, 159–79. New York: Cornell University Press.
Crawford, V.P., and J. Sobel. 1982. Strategic information transmission. *Econometrica* 50, no. 6: 1431–51.
Crombez, C. 2002. Information, lobbying and the legislative process in the European Union. *European Union Politics* 3, no. 1: 7–32.
Dahl, R.A. 1957. The concept of power. *Behavioral Science* 2, no. 3: 201–15.
Dür, A. 2008a. Interest groups in the European Union: how powerful are they? *West European Politics* 31, no. 6: 1212–30.
Dür, A. 2008b. Measuring interest group influence. *European Union Politics* 9, no. 4: 559–76.
Dür, A., and D. De Bièvre. 2007a. The question of interest group influence. *Journal of Public Policy* 21, no. 1: 1–2.
Dür, A., and D. De Bièvre. 2007b. Inclusion without influence? NGOs in European trade policy *Journal of Public Policy* 27, no. 1: 79–101.
Eising, R. 2007. Institutional context, organizational resources and strategic choices. *European Union Politics* 8, no. 3: 329–62.
Esterling, K. 2004. *The political economy of expertise. Information and efficiency in American national politics*. Ann Arbor: University of Michigan Press.
European Commission. 2007. Treaty of Lisbon. *Official Journal of the European Union*, 50, http://eur-lex.europa.eu/JOHtml.do?uri=OJ:C:2007:306:SOM:EN:HTML (accessed September 2010).
Grant, W. 1989. *Pressure groups, politics and democracy in Britain*. London: Philip Allan.
Greenwood, J. 2007. *Interest representation in the European Union*. New York: Palgrave Macmillan.

Hall, R.A., and A.V. Deardorff. 2006. Lobbying as legislative subsidy. *American Political Science Review* 100, no. 1: 69–84.

Hayes-Renshaw, F. 2009. Least accessible but not inaccessible: lobbying the council and the European Council. In *Lobbying the European Union: institutions, actors, and issues*, eds. D. Coen and J. Richardson, 70–88. Oxford: Oxford University Press.

Heinz, John P., E. Laumann, R. Nelson, and R. Salisbury. 1993. *The hollow core: private interests in national policy making*. Cambridge: Harvard University Press.

Hueglin, T. 1999. Government, governance, governmentality: understanding the EU as a project of universalism. In *The transformation of governance in the European Union*, eds. B. Kohler-Koch and R. Eising, 249–66. London: Routledge.

Hojnacki, M., and D.C. Kimball. 1999. The who and how of organizations' lobbying strategies in committee. *The Journal of Politics* 61, no. 4: 999–1024.

Hooghe, L., and M. Keating. 1994. The politics of European Union regional policy. *Journal of European Public Policy* 1, no. 3: 367–93.

Klüver, H. 2009. Measuring interest group influence using quantitative text analysis. *European Union Politics* 10, no. 4: 535–49.

Lahusen, C. 2002. Commercial consultancies in the European Union: the shape and structure of professional interest intermediation. *Journal of European Public Policy* 9, no. 5: 695–714.

Lahusen, C. 2003. Moving into the European orbit. *European Union Politics* 4, no. 2: 191–218.

Landmarks. 2008. *The European public affairs directory*. Brussels: Landmarks Publishing.

Lazarsfeld, P.F., B. Berelson, H. Gaudet. 1948. *The people's choice: how the voter makes up his mind in a presidential campaign*. New York: Columbia University Press.

Lehmann, W. 2009. The European Parliament. In *Lobbying the European Union: institutions, actors, and issues*, eds. D. Coen and J. Richardson, 39–69. Oxford: Oxford University Press.

Lindblom, C. 1965. *The intelligence of democracy: decision making through mutual adjustment*. New York: Free Press.

Lowery, D. 2007. Why do organized interests lobby? A multi-goal, multi-context theory of lobbying *Polity* 39, no. 1: 29–54.

Lowi, T.J. 1969. *The end of liberalism*. New York: Knopf.

Mahoney, C. 2007. Lobbying success in the United States and the European Union. *Journal of Public Policy* 27, no. 1: 35–56.

Mahoney, C. 2008. *Brussels versus the Beltway. Advocacy in the United States and the European Union*. Washington: Georgetown University Press.

March, J.G. 1955. An introduction to the theory and measurement of influence. *The American Political Science Review* 49, no. 2: 431–51.

Marks, G. 1993. Structural policy and multilevel governance. In *The state of the European Community. Volume 2. The Maastricht debates and beyond*, eds. A. Cafruny and G. Rosenthal, 391–410. Boulder: Longman.

Mazey, S., and J. Richardson. 1997. Policy framing: interest groups and the lead up to the 1996 intergovernmental conference. *West European Politics* 20, no. 3: 111–33.

Michalowitz, I. 2007. What determines influence? Assessing conditions for decision-making influence of interest groups in the EU. *Journal of European Public Policy* 14, no. 1: 132–51.

Moore, C. 2008. A Europe of the regions vs. regions in Europe: reflections on regional engagement in Brussels. *Regional and Federal Studies* 18, no. 5: 517–35.

Olson, M. 1982. *The rise and decline of nations: economic growth, stagflation, and social rigidities*. New Haven: Yale University Press.

Olson, M. 2000. *Power and prosperity. Outgrowing communist and capitalist dictatorships*. New York: Basic Books.

Potters, J., and F. van Winden. 1990. Modelling political pressure as transmission of information. *European Journal of Political Economy* 6, 61–88.

Potters, J., and F. van Winden. 1992. Lobbying and asymmetric information. *Public Choice* 74, 269–92.

Princen, S. 2007. Advocacy coalitions and the internationalization of public health policies. *Journal of Public Policy* 27, no. 1: 13–33.

Schattschneider, E.E. 1960. *The semi-sovereign people. A realist's view of democracy in America*. New York: Holt, Rinehart and Winston.

Woll, C. 2007. Leading the dance? Power and political resources of business lobbyists. *Journal of Public Policy* 27, no. 1: 57–78.

The Impact of National Business Cultures on Large Firm Lobbying in the European Union: Evidence from a Large-Scale Survey of Government Affairs Managers

ANDREW BARRON

Department of Management, Strathclyde Business School, University of Strathclyde, Glasgow, UK

ABSTRACT This paper reports research into cross-national differences in corporate lobbying in the European Union (EU). Original data collected through an online survey, conducted between April and June 2010, of 132 government affairs managers in large firms are analysed to ascertain the extent their political activities are influenced by the national business cultures in which they were socialised. Findings indicate significant relationships between (1) respondents' culturally-grounded attitudes towards time and their level of engagement with policy-makers, and (2) their culturally-conditioned attitudes towards power and hierarchy and their choice of political tactics when seeking to promote their political interests. Contrary to expectations, no significant relationship was found between respondents' cultural preferences for acting autonomously or within a group, and their level of participation in the policy-making process. The research makes important contributions to the literature on Europeanization as well as to research into the internationalisation of corporate political strategising.

Introduction

The European Union (EU) and its decision-making processes have been a source of interest for academic scholars across many disciplines. In political science, early studies focused on the creation of supranational institutions at the EU level. These studies treated the EU as an entity 'above' the member states, created from 'bottom up' processes stemming from the objectives and actions of national governments. Over time, studies began to explore the 'top-down' effects of European integration on the domestic arenas of the member states. Against this background of perceived increasing Europeanisation, scholars have investigated whether the EU and its institutions have modified the policies, practices and preferences of political, economic and social actors in the member states (e.g., Kassim and Menon 1996; Schmidt 1996; Bulmer and Burch 1998; Lehmkuhl 2000; Cole and Drake 2000; Cowles, Caporaso, and Risse 2001; Ladrech 2001; Héritier et al. 2001; Fairbrass and Jordan 2002).

Within the Europeanisation debate, some researchers have specifically investigated the effects of European integration on interest representation. Some have argued that we are witnessing a convergence of national lobbying traditions towards a European model of interest representation (e.g., Mazey and Richardson 1993). Others contend that national differences in lobbying practices persist and can be clearly observed on the European political stage (e.g., Waarden 1993; Lanzalaco 1992). This paper builds on this ongoing debate by testing in the EU context a cross-cultural model of corporate political action that, to date, has been subjected to only limited empirical scrutiny (Barron 2010). A more rigorous testing of this model, using original data collected via a large-scale survey of politically active managers socialised in a wide range of culturally diverse countries, makes three primary contributions to the existing literature on interest representation in the EU context.

First, whereas the prior research into interest representation has focused on the somewhat vague notion of national traditions, this paper actively engages with national business cultures, broadly understood as the socially transmitted behaviour patterns, norms, beliefs and values of a given community (Salacuse 1998) which are shared by members of a given society, lie at the core of behaviour, differ between nations, but are stable within them (Hofstede 2001; Schein 1985). This focus on business culture is important since management scholars have demonstrated that national culture impacts on many different individual level outcomes, including perceptions, beliefs and behaviours (e.g., Leung et al. 2005).

This focus on individuals represents the second contribution of the research. Crucially, whilst much of the existing research into interest representation in the EU context has focused attention on the firm level, industry level and institutional level antecedents of interest representation, the emphasis of this contribution is placed firmly on individual managers, and specifically on the national cultural milieus in which they are socialised. Such a focus is important since it allows strategic interest representation behaviours to be unpacked and examined at a deeper, more complex, human level. It also makes sense insofar as firms' political strategies are ultimately formulated by managers, including government affairs staff and politically active chief executive officers.

Third, the paper seeks to connect the literatures of political science and strategic management by innovatively applying to the EU political context of interest representation some theoretical insights drawn from existing research in the field of corporate political activity and the broad literature on international and cross-cultural management to test hypotheses about political actions pursued by government affairs managers in the EU context. The hypotheses generated specifically focus on (1) the extent to which politically active managers engage with EU policy-makers, (2) their preferred forms of political action and (3) their choices of political tactics when entering the European political arena.

Following on from this introduction, this paper first summarises a conceptual model and sets of hypotheses developed to emphasise how culturally-grounded management techniques and preferences can determine managers' political behaviours. Next, it describes an online survey of government affairs managers that was used to test these hypotheses. The methods of data analysis and results of the survey are presented in the fourth section. The paper closes off with a discussion of the results, and proposes future avenues of enquiry.

Conceptual Model and Hypotheses

Corporate political activity (CPA), defined by Getz (1997, 32) 'as any deliberate action taken by firms to influence governmental policy or process', has attracted considerable scholarly attention (for meta reviews of the prior literature, see Getz, 1997 and 2001 and Hillman *et al.* 2004). However, as in the lion's share of research into international business and management, mainstream researchers of international CPA have adopted what Child (2000) has referred to as a 'low context' research perspective. In other words, researchers have tended to be insensitive towards national business cultures as analytically significant contexts, choosing instead to explain differences in corporate political activity using conceptual models (based, for example, on interest group theory, resource dependency theory, institutional theory, agency theory, the behavioural theory of the firm, collective action theory, transaction cost theory, and public choice theory) that were developed by North American scholars specifically for the North American political context.

However, drawing on an ever-growing body of academic work showing that managers socialised in different national cultures approach strategic decision-making in different ways (e.g., Harris and Ghauri 2000; Schneider 1989; House *et al.* 2004), some initial attempts have been undertaken to develop and test more culturally sensitive conceptual models for understanding the effects of national culture on corporate political actions. One such model is developed by Barron (2010). A simplified version of this model is presented in schematic form in Figure 1.

The model is underpinned by three key assumptions. First, it assumes that managers face specific strategic choices when they enter the political arena: They must choose (a) their general approach to political action, (b) their level of participation in the policy-making process, and (c) the

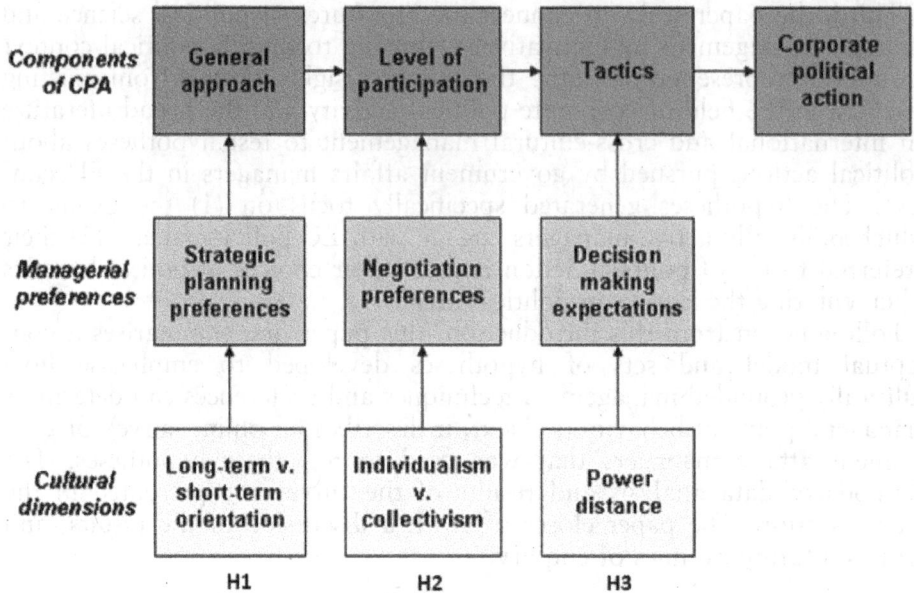

Figure 1. A cross-cultural model of corporate political activity (adapted from Barron 2010)

specific tactics to use when seeking to influence policy-makers. Second, it assumes that how managers respond to each of these choices is respectively driven by their preferences and expectations concerning strategic planning horizons, negotiation, and decision-making processes. These managerial preferences and expectations underpinning corporate political strategizing are finally assumed to be affected by national business cultures. Below, the different components of the model are unpacked to develop hypotheses that more clearly illustrate how the different components of corporate political activity are affected by national culture.

National Cultures' Impact on Managers' General Approach to Political Action

The model draws on the work of Hillman and Hitt (1999) in assuming that managers face a number of strategic choices in the political arena. The first such choice involves deciding upon a general approach to corporate political strategising. Essentially, managers decide whether to engage transactionally or relationally with policy-makers: Transactional engagement involves waiting for specific public policy issues to develop before entering into short-term relationships with policy-makers to influence their decisions; relational engagement involves fostering more longer-term relationships with policy-makers and have in place the necessary contacts and resources whenever policy issues arise.

These different general approaches imply that political strategising involves long-term strategic planning (relational) and short-term strategic planning (transactional). The literatures of international and cross-cultural management point to cross-country preferences in such strategic planning horizons. For example, using the long-term versus short-term cultural dimension developed by Hofstede and Bond (1988) to measure the importance attached by members of a national culture to attaining results immediately or over the long run, Carr and Harris (2004) found that managers socialised in the long-term orientated cultures of Germany and Japan focused on long-term strategic success over a period of 15 years. By contrast, managers socialised in short-term orientated cultures of the UK and the US framed their strategic objectives in two- or three-year terms.

Assuming that managers' choices of general approach to political action (transactional versus relational) are driven by their strategic planning preferences, which are in turn influenced by culturally-conditioned attitudes towards time, it is first hypothesised that:

- *H1: Managers socialised in short-term orientated national cultures will be more likely to engage transactionally with policy-makers, whilst managers socialised in long-term orientated national cultures will be more likely to engage relationally with policy-makers.*

National Cultures' Impact on Managers' Participation Level in Policy-Making

A second choice facing managers in the political arena is their level of participation in the policy-making arena (Hillman and Hitt 1999). This involves deciding whether to pursue political actions alone or with the political representatives of other firms. The model presented in Figure 1 specifically assumes that negotiation preferences play a key role in determining managers' preferred level of participation: Rather than blindly complying with proposed legislation, it is assumed that managers bargain for special consideration from policy-makers whenever they consider conformity with legislation problematic (e.g., Oliver 1991; Boddewyn and Brewer 1994). The model specifically assumes that managers can choose to negotiate such concessions with policy-makers independently, or they can choose to negotiate collaboratively by joining forces with managers from other firms.

Scholars of cross-cultural management have identified cross-country variations in negotiation behaviour using Hofstede's dimension of individualism versus collectivism, which measures the extent to which the members of a given culture prefer acting autonomously or in groups. Specifically, studies (e.g., Drake 2001; Cai, Wilson, and Drake 2006) have shown that managers socialised in individualistic countries tend to view negotiation in competitive terms, and negotiate alone for individual benefit. By contrast, managers socialised in more collectivist cultures generally view negotiation in collaborative terms, and negotiate collaboratively for common benefits.

Of course, research has empirically demonstrated that managers from individualistic cultures such as the United States engage in collective political action (e.g., Getz 1993; Schuler and Rehbein 1997), and that managers from collectivist countries such China engage in individual political action (e.g., Kennedy 2008). However, much in the same way that citizens from countries reflecting average individualistic tendencies generally consider negotiation as a competitive exercise, the model suggests that managers socialised in such countries will have a cultural disposition for individual action. Similarly, managers socialised in collectivist national cultures will, on average, have a cultural preference for collective action.

Thus, assuming that managers' choices of participation level in the policy-making process (individual action versus collective action) are informed by preferred negotiation behaviours, and assuming that such behaviours are shaped by culturally informed preferences for achieving individual or collective objectives, it is hypothesised that:

- H2: *Managers socialised in individualistic national cultures will be more likely to engage in individual political action, whilst managers socialised in collectivist national cultures will be more likely to engage in collective political action.*

National Cultures' Impact on Managers' Choice of Political Tactics

In accordance with Hillman and Hitt (1999), the model assumes that managers face a third strategic choice, namely the specific tactics to deploy for influencing policy-makers' decisions. Two tactics identified by Hillman and Hitt (1999) are the information strategy and the constituency-building strategy. Information strategies involve issuing position papers and technical briefs or making contributions to public consultations in order to communicate their policy preferences and concerns directly to specific policy-makers. Constituency-building strategies involve designing wider-reaching public relations campaigns that generate grassroots support for their concerns amongst voters, who in turn express their policy concerns and preferences to political decision-makers.

In her review of existing CPA literature, Getz (1997) stated that managers, when developing their political strategies, will choose tactics that are aimed at those people whom they believe have the power to make policy decisions that help resolve the specific issues they face. Accordingly, the model supposes that direct information strategies targeted specifically at policy-makers will be preferred by managers who consider that the power to make political decisions resides solely with policy-makers. By contrast, the more indirect constituency-building strategies aimed at wider publics will be favoured by managers who consider decision-making power to be more widely spread across society.

The literature on cross-cultural and international management highlights cross-country differences regarding who is involved in decision-making and who ultimately has decision-making power. These variations have been explained using Hofstede's cultural dimension of power distance, which describes the extent to which the members of a given culture accept power hierarchy and inequality to be legitimate. A number of studies (e.g., Harris *et al.* 2006; Erez 1994; Triandis 1994; Sagie and Koslowsky 2000) have found that decision-making responsibility is widely spread in power–distance rejecting national cultures and concentrated in the hands of a limited number of individuals in power–distance accepting national cultures.

Other studies (e.g., Kohler-Koch 1997; Schmidt 1999; Eising 2003) suggest that high power distance scores are associated with statist countries (e.g., France, Greece). Although pressure from the public might lead in these countries to changes in decisions taken by political elites, statist systems continue, despite international, European and domestic pressures, to be marked by a rather authoritative role of the state (Wright 1997). Thus, political decisions tend to be made by ruling elites of likeminded politicians, civil servants and businessmen who attended the same prestigious education establishments. The same studies suggest that lower power distance scores are associated with more corporatist (e.g., Austria, Germany) or pluralist countries (e.g., UK, USA) where, compared to statist countries, political decisions tend to be made by policy-makers in consultation with other social and economic actors, including firms, trade unions and representatives of civil society.

Whilst acknowledging that the use of one particular political tactic does not necessarily preclude another (Hillman and Hitt 1999), the model assumes that managers' use of information or constituency-building strategies depends on their expectations regarding who has the authority to influence political decisions, and assumes that these expectations are themselves affected by culturally-conditioned attitudes towards power and hierarchy. As result, the final hypothesis is:

- *H3a: Managers socialised in power–distance accepting national cultures will be more likely to use information strategies managers socialised in power–distance rejecting national cultures will be more likely to use constituency-building strategies.*

In summary, the model first suggests that managers' choices of general approach to political action (i.e., relational versus transactional approaches) are affected by their strategic planning preferences, which themselves are influenced by culturally bound time orientations (H1). Second, the model states that managers' level of participation in the policy-making process (individual versus collective action) is influenced by negotiation behaviours, which are determined by culturally-conditioned attitudes towards achieving individual or collective objectives (H2). Finally, it suggests that managers' decisions to deploy information and constituency-building strategies are informed by their culturally-conditioned expectations regarding who has the authority to influence political decisions, (H3).

Methodology

These hypotheses were tested using data collected from a survey of European Government Affairs Mangers conducted in April–June 2010. Potential respondents were identified using the European Public Affairs Directory, the European Commission's register of interest representatives, the list of lobbyists accredited by the European Parliament, and the Permanent Representations of individual member states. Additional contacts were also made through the European Affairs Network and International

Government Relations and Public Affairs groups on LinkedIn, the professional networking site.

The survey was distributed via e-mail to a total of 1358 managers. Spam filters and incorrect email addresses made it necessary to exclude 179 addresses. The survey was sent out for the first time at the end of April 2010, followed by four reminders sent out at two-week intervals. Guarantees of confidentiality were made to encourage respondents to participate in the research. Notwithstanding these guarantees, the survey rendered 132 eligible responses, representing a final response rate of 11.19% (1358–178/100). Table 1 summarizes information about the nationalities of respondents.

A combination of factors can potentially explain the low response rate. First of all, the survey was administered during the economic and financial crisis of 2007–2010 when government affairs managers were focusing their priorities on tackling the difficult economic and financial climate in which they were operating. In this regard, some managers contacted us, stating that they did not have time to participate in such a research project. Moreover, the potentially sensitive nature of some of the survey questions may also have dissuaded potential respondents from participating. Indeed, one French and one German manager phoned to explain that it was company policy not to share such strategic information with outsiders. These incidents echo the work of other researchers (Wilson 1988; Bunel 1995; Stevens 2003) in demonstrating that lobbyists, particularly in a European context, are reticent to release into the public domain any information on their political strategies for fear of weakening their positions vis-à-vis the government or rivals.

Results

Development of Measurements and Descriptive Data

In a first step, it was necessary to identify variations in respondents' cultural backgrounds. Respondents were identified as belonging to (1) long-term or short-term-orientated cultures, (2) collectivist or individualist cultures, and (3) low or high power distances in accordance with the country scores reported by Hofstede (2001). For all cultural dimensions, a dichotomous, categorical variable was created, using as the measure of central tendency (and thus the cut-off point) the mid-point of respondents' country scores. For example, to determine whether respondents belonged to a long-term or a short-term-orientated national culture, a variable called *Time orientation* was created using the scores calculated by Hofstede for respondents' home countries along the cultural dimension of long-term versus short-term orientation. Based on the data collected during the survey, respondents' scores ranged from 24 (for Irish respondents) to 83 (for German respondents). Taking 59 to be the measure of central tendency, respondents were subsequently split into two groups. The first group gathered respondents from countries with a relatively short-term cultural orientation (with scores ranging from 24 to 58). The second group assembled those respondents from countries with a comparatively longer-term

Table 1. Survey respondents by country and national culture of origin (country scores based on Hofstede 2001)

Time orientation	Short-term orientated cultures (24–58)		Long-term orientated cultures (59–83)	
	Country	Respondents	Country	Respondents
	Ireland	3	Austria	4
	United States	3	Estonia	1
	Denmark	7	Italy	8
	Norway	1	France	16
	Canada	2	Netherlands	8
	Finland	8	Bulgaria	1
	Greece	1	Czech Republic	1
	Spain	6	Switzerland	2
	Great Britain	18	Belgium	10
	Romania	2	Germany	11
	Sweden	16		
	Croatia	2		
	Hungary	1		
	Total: 70		Total: 62	

Individualism	Collectivist cultures (30–61)		Individualistic cultures (62–91)	
	Country	Respondents	Country	Respondents
	Bulgaria	1	Norway	1
	Croatia	2	Denmark	7
	Greece	1	Belgium	10
	Spain	6	Italy	8
	Austria	4	Netherlands	8
	Czech Republic	1	Canada	2
	Estonia	1	Great Britain	18
	Hungary	1	United States	3
	Romania	2		
	Finland	8		

(Continued)

Table 1. (*Continued*)

	Short-term orientated cultures (24–58)		Long-term orientated cultures (59–83)	
Time orientation	Country	Respondents	Country	Respondents
	Germany	11		
	Switzerland	2		
	Ireland	3		
	Sweden	16		
	France	16		
	Total: 75		Total: 57	

	Power-distance rejecting cultures (11–37)		Power-distance accepting cultures (38–90)	
Power distance	Country	Respondents	Country	Respondents
	Austria	4	Netherlands	8
	Denmark	7	Canada	2
	Ireland	3	Estonia	1
	Norway	1	Hungary	1
	Sweden	16	Czech Republic	1
	Finland	8	United States	3
	Switzerland	2	Italy	8
	Great Britain	18	Spain	6
	Germany	11	Greece	1
			Belgium	10
			France	16
			Bulgaria	1
			Croatia	2
			Romania	2
	Total: 70		Total: 62	

cultural orientation (with scores ranging from 59 to 83). Table 1 reports the dichotomisation and corresponding cut-off points for the other cultural dimensions. Such dichotomisation may suggest that the research relies on aggregated and simplified variables. However, as per Hofstede (2001), such approximations of underlying cultural characteristics are appropriate for cross-cultural analysis. Furthermore, given the low response rate, categorizing respondents into more than two cultural groups (e.g., extremely collectivist, somewhat collectivist, somewhat individualistic, extremely individualistic) would have led to situation whereby cultural groupings contained insufficient members for meaningful data analysis.

The variable used to measure respondents' general approach to political action was created from questions asking respondents to describe their relationships with representatives of (a) their national governments/parliaments, (b) other national governments/parliaments, (c) their own country's permanent EU representation, (d) other countries' permanent EU representations, (e) the European Commission, (f) the Council of Ministers, and (g) the European Parliament. Specifically, respondents were asked to describe their relationships using a five-point Likert scale (ranging from mostly as ad-hoc relationships covering specific policy issues to mostly as long-term relationships covering multiple policy issues). The data collected were subsequently aggregated to create a dichotomous, categorical variable measuring respondents' average engagement with policy-makers (whereby zero represented mostly short-term, issue-specific relationships (points one, two, and three on the Likert scale) and one represented mostly long-term, issue-spanning relationships (points four and five on the Likert scale).

Respondents' preferred level of participation in the policy-making process was measured using a survey question asking them to indicate on a five-point scale (ranging from never to frequently) how often they (a) represented their political interests alone, (b) joined coalitions of interests, (c) participated in national level business associations, and (d) joined European level business association. Given that they are invariably temporary in character and frequently involve arms-length co-operation, coalitions of interests were considered for the purposes of this research more as a form of individual than collective political action. The average frequencies with which managers engaged in each of these different forms of political action were subsequently used to create a variable measuring their average level of participation in the policy-making process (whereby zero represented mostly individual political action (options a and b of the survey question), and one represented mostly collective political action (options c and d of the survey question).

Finally, the variable used to measure respondents' political tactics was created from survey questions inviting respondents to indicate on a five-point scale (ranging from never to frequently) how often they used different types of tactics. The possible options included (a) participating in face-to-face meetings with policy-makers, (b) contributing to public consultations, (c) issuing position papers and technical briefs, (d) participating in EU level working groups, (e) conducting media campaigns in support of

Table 2. Time orientation versus engagement with policy-makers

Time orientation		Engagement with policy-makers		
		Transactional	Relational	Total
Short-term orientated culture	Count	26	44	70
	% within engagement	76.5%	44.9%	53.0%
Long-term orientated culture	Count	8	54	62
	% within engagement	23.5%	55.1%	47.0%
Total	Count	34	98	132
	% of total	25.8%	74.2%	100.0%

their policy concerns, and (f) organising/sponsoring events to draw attention to their policy issues. The average frequencies with which managers engaged in each of these different forms of political action were subsequently used to create a variable measuring their average level of participation in the policy-making process (whereby one represented mostly information strategies; options a, b, c and d of the survey question — and one represented mostly constituency-building strategies; options e and f of the survey question).

Hypothesis Testing

The relationships between the different variables were examined using cross tabulations. The cross tabulations generated from analysing the relationship between respondents' culturally-grounded time orientations and their general approach to political action are reported in Table 2.

On first glance, the data show that most of the respondents claimed to form long-term, issue-spanning relationships with policy-makers. Indeed, of the 132 survey respondents, 98 (or 74.2%) tended to engage relationally with policy-makers whilst only 34 (25.8%) tended to engage transactionally with policy-makers. However, of the 34 respondents who tended to engage transactionally with policy-makers, 26 (or 76.5%) were — as predicted — from short-term-orientated national cultures and only 8 (or 23.5%) were from long-term-orientated national cultures. Similarly, of the 98 respondents who tended to engage relationally with policy-makers, 54 (or 55.1%) were — as expected — from long-term orientated cultures and 44 (or 44.9%) were from short-term-orientated cultures.

A Chi-square test for independence (with Yates Continuity Correction) indicated a significant association between the time orientation and the general approach variables, $\chi^2(1, N = 132) = 8.87$, $p = .003$, phi = $-.227$). It was therefore concluded that there was support for the first hypothesis.

The cross tabulations created from analysing the relationship between respondents' culturally-conditioned preferences for acting autonomously or in groups and their level of participation in the policy-making processes are reported in Table 3.

An initial reading of the data shows that most of the survey respondents claimed to engage in individual political action. Crucially, the table shows

Table 3. Individualism versus level of participation in policy-making

Individualism		Participation level		Total
		Collective action	Individual action	
Collectivist culture	Count	25	50	75
	% within participation level	67.6%	52.6%	56.8%
Individualistic culture	Count	12	45	57
	% within participation level	32.4%	47.4%	43.2%
Total	Count	37	95	132
	% of total	28.0%	72.0%	100.0%

that, of the 132 respondents, 95 (or 72.0%) of the respondents' favoured individual political action whilst 37 (or 28%) tended to engage in collective political action. Of the 95 respondents who tended to engage individual political action, 50 (or 52.6%) were — contrary to expectations — from collectivist national cultures and 45 (or 47.4%) were from individualist national cultures. Of the 37 respondents who tended to engage in collective action, 25 (or 67.6%) were — as predicted — from collectivist national cultures and 12 (or 32.4%) were from individualistic national cultures. However, a Chi-square test for independence (with Yates Continuity Correction) indicated no significant association between the individualism and the participation variables, $\chi^2(1, N = 132) = 1.85$, $p = .174$, phi = .135). Thus, the survey did not provide any significant evidence in support of the second hypothesis.

Finally, the data used to analyse the relationship between respondents' culturally-conditioned attitudes power hierarchy and inequality and their use of political tactics is reported in Table 4.

On first glance, the data show that the majority of respondents use information strategies to influence policy-makers. Indeed, of the 132 survey respondents, 105 (79.5%) tended to use information strategies whilst only 27 (or 20.5%) tended to use constituency-building strategies. A more detailed analysis of the data exposed evidence in support of the third

Table 4. Power-distance versus political tactics used

Power distance		Tactics used		Total
		Constituency building	Information strategies	
Power-distance rejecting culture	Count	20	50	70
	% within tactics used	74.1%	47.6%	53.0%
Power-distance accepting culture	Count	7	55	62
	% within tactics used	25.9%	52.4%	47.0%
Total	Count	27	105	132
	% of total	20.5%	79.5%	100.0%

groups of hypothesises. Crucially, of the 105 respondents whose use of political tactics tends towards information strategies, 55 (or 52.4%) are — as hypothesised — from power–distance accepting national cultures whilst 50 (or 47.6%) are from power–distance rejecting national cultures. Likewise, of the 27 survey respondents who tend to use constituency-building strategies, the vast majority (n = 20, or 74.1%) are from power–distance rejecting cultures. Only 7 (or 25.9%) of respondents who tend to use constituency-building strategies are from power–distance accepting cultures.

A Chi-square test for independence (with Yates Continuity Correction) indicated a significant association between respondents' power distance scores and their preferred choice of political tactics, $\chi^2(1, N = 132) = 5.019$, $p = .0.25$, phi = .214). Thus, it was concluded that there is support for the third hypothesis.

Findings and Discussion

These findings contribute to ongoing debates regarding whether the processes of European integration are leading to common interest representation behaviours in Brussels. By applying Hillman and Hitt's taxonomy of corporate political action to the political context of the European Union, the research exposes a specific area where culturally-grounded traditions in interest representation appear to be converging towards a common European model. Essentially, it was found that survey respondents had a stronger preference for individual action, irrespective of whether they were socialised in individualistic or collectivist national cultures. This finding points to some degree of convergence in managers' level of participation in the EU policy-making process, and adds weight to the thesis advanced amongst others by Kohler-Koch and Buth (2009) that we might be witnessing in Brussels the professionalization of a special elite of lobbyists which has learned the specific rules of interest representation on the European political stage.

However, whereas these two authors focus on the case of NGOs and find that they follow the same strategy of collective action, the research reported here trains its attention on the government affairs managers of large firms and suggests that they, for the most part, consider individual political action to be a more natural channel for representing their firms' interests in Brussels. This finding challenges a commonly-held view, as discussed by Coen (1998), (2007) and Eising (2007), that large firms, when lobbying in Brussels, Brussels tend to follow a common strategy of *collective* action because this is what representatives in the EU and its institutions expect.

Specifically, the finding demonstrates that there are some congruencies and similarities in EU lobbying strategies, but that the nature of these congruencies differs between different sets of lobbying actors, chiefly government affairs managers, firms and associations. Companies as collective entities and EU level business associations, as analysed by Eising (2007), and NGOs in Brussels, as studied by Kohler-Koch and Buth (2009), have been shown to follow a double route of both collective action and individual action. The research reported here, however, suggests that the government affairs managers located in Brussels have learned to adopt a different vision of their surroundings compared to their firms: They appear to consider it their raison d'Âtre to pursue individual political action as a supplement to their employers' need to also follow collective political action. Being part of the Brussels elite, government affairs managers will usually be oriented towards long-term, issue-spanning relationships with policy-makers, trustworthiness often obtained through many years of professional relations being one of the prime prerequisites of successful lobbying.

Any convergence towards a European model of interest representation should not be overestimated given that the findings of the research also highlight specific areas where culturally-grounded traditions in lobbying persist. Essentially, there were found to be significant relationships between (1) respondents' culturally-grounded attitudes towards time and their level of engagement with policy-makers, and (2) their culturally-conditioned attitudes towards power and hierarchy and their choice of political tactics when seeking to promote their political interests. These findings are in line with other scholars (e.g., Kohler-Koch and Quittkat. 1999; Wilts 2002; Quittkat 2006; Kluever 2010) who claim that, in the EU context, lobbying is marked by some degree of convergence, but also by continued divergence based on national traditions.

By connecting the literatures of political science and strategic management, the research findings also engage with research conducted in other disciplines. The results are interesting for scholars of CPA insofar as they suggest that existing theoretical accounts of CPA provides only an incomplete picture of the factors determining managers' political objectives and strategies. For example, the link identified between (1) managers' preferences for short-term and long-term strategic planning, and (2) their choice of relational or transactional approach to CPA challenges the work of Hillman (2003), who argues that that such choices are determined by firms' dependence on governments, the political system in which they operate, or the diversification of their product offerings.

Moreover, the finding that managers' choices of political tactics are linked to their culturally-embedded expectations regarding decision-making processes challenges existing research suggesting that managers pursue information strategies because they wish to convey factual information to key decision-makers (e.g., Getz 1993), or because government officials depend on their information and expertise (e.g., Mahoney 2007). It also enriches research arguing that managers engage in constituency building to create credibility with individual policy-makers (e.g., Coen 1999) or to generate additional support for their concerns (e.g., Keim and Zeithaml 1986).

The research findings are specifically relevant for scholars engaged with the cultural dimensions of corporate political action in international contexts. Essentially, the relationships found between (1) managers' culturally-grounded attitudes towards time and their level of engagement with policy-makers, and (2) their culturally-conditioned attitudes towards power and hierarchy and their choice of political tactics when seeking to promote their political interests, add weight to the conceptual model developed by Barron (2010) suggesting links between Hofstede's cultural dimensions and the different components of corporate political action.

Conclusions

The aim of the research reported here was to investigate whether there are significant cultural differences in the objectives and practices of government affairs managers, and whether these differences can be explained in terms of national culture.

This objective was achieved insofar as survey data collected from the political representatives of large firms working in Brussels, and interrogated using Hofstede's cultural dimensions, revealed possible relationships between national culture and different components of corporate political activity. Specifically, there appears to be linkages between (1) managers' culturally-grounded attitudes towards time and their level of engagement with policy-makers, and (2) their culturally-conditioned attitudes towards power and hierarchy and their choice of political tactics when seeking to promote their political interests. Contrary to expectations, however, no significant relationship was found between respondents' cultural preferences for acting autonomously or within a group, and their level of participation in the policy-making process.

Two specific limitations of the research are openly acknowledged. First, the survey rendered a low response rate, meaning that the significance of these findings should not be overstated. Given that potential informants were reluctant to participate in our research, possibly as explained above because the economic and financial climate within which they were operating gave them little time to do so, any future surveys would benefit from being conducted once economic and financial stability has been re-established. In addition, the conceptual model underpinning the research draws exclusively on the cultural dimensions identified by Hofstede (2001). Scholars, however, have charged these dimensions with reducing the complexities of national culture to simplistic and overly generalised conceptualisations and for magnifying national stereotypes (e.g., Shenkar 2001; Holden 2002; McSweeney 2002; Kirkman, Lowe, and Gibson 2006; Taras, Rowney, and Steel 2009). Consequently, future research could incorporate theoretical insights from other, richer cultural categorisation studies (e.g., Schwartz 1992). That being said, incorporating a wider range of cultural dimensions could potentially lead to the situation, as highlighted by Taras, Rowney, and Steel 2009, whereby cross-cultural research frameworks become unworkably bulky.

It is also possible that the impact of national culture on managers' strategic decision-making in the political arena may be tempered by other factors that were not covered in the survey. For example, managers' political strategies may also be influenced by their firms' corporate cultures, by the degree of autonomy that they enjoy to devise and implement their firms' political strategies, and by their education and training pathways. Thus, future research could be undertaken to assess the respective weight of these different factors on managers' political strategies.

References

Barron, A. 2010. Unlocking the mindsets of government affairs managers: cultural dimensions of corporate political activity. *Cross Cultural Management — An International Journal* 17, no. 2: 101–17.

Boddewyn, J., and T. Brewer. 1994. International business political behavior: new theoretical directions. *Academy of Management Review* 19, no. 1: 119–44.

Bulmer, S., and M. Burch. 1998. Organising for Europe: Whitehall, the British State and the European Union. *Public Administration* 76, no. 4: 601–28.

Bunel, J. 1995. *La transformation de la représentation patronale en France: CNPF et CGPME* Paris: Commissariat général du plan.

Cai, A., R. Wilson, and E. Drake. 2006. Culture in the context of intercultural negotiation: individualism–collectivism and paths to integrative agreements. *Human Communication Research* 26, no. 4: 591–617.

Carr, C., and S. Harris. 2004. The impact of diverse national values on strategic investment decisions in the context of globalization. *International Journal of Cross Cultural Management* 4, no. 1: 77–99.

Child, J. 2000. Theorising about organisation cross-nationally. *Advances in Comparative International Management* 13, no. 1: 27–77.

Coen, D. 1998. The European business interest and the nation state: large-firm lobbying in the European Union and member states. *Journal of Public Policy* 18, no. 1: 75–100.

Coen, D. 1999. The impact of US lobbying practice on the European business-government relationship. *California Management Review* 41, no. 4: 27–44.

Coen, D. 2007. Empirical and theoretical studies in EU lobbying. *Journal of European Public Policy* 14, no. 3: 333–45.

Cole, A., and H. Drake. 2000. The Europeanization of French polity: continuity, change, and adaptation. *Journal European Public Policy* 7, no. 1: 26–43.

Cowles, M.G., J. Caporaso, and T. Risse. 2001. *Transforming Europe*. Ithaca, NY: Cornell University Press, 138–59.

DiMaggio, P.J., and W.W. Powell. 1983. The iron cage revisited: institutional isomorphism and collective rationality in organizational fields. *American Sociological Review* 48, 147–60.

Drake, L.E. 2001. The culture-negotiation link — integrative and distributive bargaining through an intercultural communication lens. *Human Communication Research* 27, no. 3: 317–49.

Eising, R. 2003. Policy learning in embedded negotiations — explaining EU electricity liberalisation. *International Organization* 56, no. 1: 85–120.

Eising, R. 2007. The access of business interests to EU institutions: towards élite pluralism? *Journal of European Public Policy* 14, no. 3: 384–403.

Erez, M. 1994. Toward a model of cross-cultural industrial and organisational psychology. In *Handbook of industrial and organisational psychology*, ed. H.C. Triandis, M.D. Dunnette, and L.M. Hough, 569–607. Palo Alto, CA: Consulting Psychologists Press.

Fairbrass, J., and A. Jordan. 2002. Interest representation and Europeanization: the case of UK environment policy. In *Integrating interests in the European Union: the new politics of persuasion, advocacy and influence*, ed. A. Warleigh and J. Fairbrass. London: Europa.

Getz, K.A. 1993. Corporate political tactics in a principal–agent context — an investigation in ozone protection policy. In *Research in corporate social performance and policy*, ed. J.E. Post, 19–55. Greenwich, CT: JAI.

Getz, K.A. 1997. Research in corporate political action — integration and assessment. *Business and Society* 36, no. 1: 32–72.

Getz, K.A. 2001. Public affairs and political strategy: theoretical foundations. *Journal of Public Affairs* 2, no. 1: 305–29.

Harris, S., and P.N. Ghauri. 2000. Strategy formation by business leaders — exploring the influence of national values. *European Journal of Marketing* 34, no. 1/2: 126–41.

Harris, P.R., R.T. Moran, and S.V. Moran. 2006. *Managing cultural differences — global leadership strategies for the twenty-first century*. Oxford: Butterworth-Heinemann.

Heritier, A., D. Kerwer, C. Knill, D. Lehmkuhl, M. Teutsch, and A.C. Douillet. 2001. *Differential Europe: the European Union impact on national policy-making.* Lanham MD: Rowman and Littlefield.

Hillman, A. 2003. Determinants of political strategies in US multinationals. *Business and Society* 42, no. 4: 455–84.

Hillman, A.J., and M.A. Hitt. 1999. Corporate political strategy formulation — a model of approach, participation and strategy decisions. *Academy of Management Review* 24, no. 4: 825–42.

Hillman, A.J., G.D. Keim, and D. Schuler. 2004. Corporate political activity — a review and research agenda. *Journal of Management* 30, no. 6: 837–57.

Hofstede, G. 2001. *Culture's consequences — international differences in work-related values.* Thousand Oaks, CA: Sage Publications.

Hofstede, G., and M.H. Bond. 1988. The Confucius connection — from cultural roots to economic growth. *Organizational Dynamics* 16, no. 4: 4–21.

Holden, N. 2002. *Cross-cultural management — a knowledge management perspective.* Harlow: Prentice Hall.

House, R.J., P.J. Hanges, M. Javidan, P.W. Dorfman, and V. Gupta. 2004. *Culture, leadership and organisations — the GLOBE study of 62 societies.* Thousand Oaks, CA: Sage Publications.

Kassim, H., and A. Menon. 1996. *The European Union and national industrial policy.* London: Routledge.

Keim, G.D., and C.P. Zeithaml. 1986. Corporate political strategy and legislative decision making — a review and contingency approach. *Academy of Management Review* 11, no. 4: 828–43.

Kennedy, S. 2008. *The business of lobbying in China.* Boston, MA: Harvard Business School Press.

Kirkman, B.L., K.B. Lowe, and C.B. Gibson. 2006. A quarter century of culture's consequences: a review of empirical research incorporating Hofstede's cultural values framework. *Journal of International Business Studies* 37, no. 3: 285–320.

Kluever, H. 2010. Europeanization of lobbying activities: when national interest groups spill over to the European level. *Journal of European Integration* 32, no. 2: 175–91.

Kohler-Koch, B. 1997. The evolution of organized interests in the EC — driving forces, co-evolution or new type of governance. In *Participation and policy making in the European Union,* ed. H. Wallace and A. Young, 42–68. Oxford: Oxford University Press.

Kohler-Koch, B., and V. Buth. 2009. *Civil society in EU governance — lobby groups like any other?* Bremen: University of Bremen.

Kohler-Koch, B., and C. Quittkat. 1999. *Intermediation of interests in the European Union.* Working Paper, Mannheimer Zentrum für Europäische Sozialforschung, Nr. 9/99.

Ladrech, R. 2001. Europeanization and French social democracy. *Journal of Southern Europe and the Balkans* 3, no. 1: 37–48.

Lanzalaco, L. 1992. Coping with heterogeneity: peak associations of business within and across western European nations. In *Organized interests and the European Community,* ed. J. Greenwood, J. Grote and K. Ronit, 172–205. London: Sage Publications.

Lehmkuhl, D. 2000. Under stress: Europeanization and trade associations in the member states. *EIOP* 4, no. 14.

Leung, K., B. Rabi, N. Buchan, M. Erez, and C. Gibson. 2005. Culture and international business: recent advances and their implications for future research. *Journal of International Business Studies* 36, no. 4: 357–78.

Mahoney, C. 2007. Networking versus allying: the decision of interest groups to join coalitions in the US and the EU. *Journal of European Public Policy* 14, no. 3: 366–83.

Mazey, S., and J. Richardson. 1993. Introduction: transference of power, decision rules, and the rules of the game. In *Lobbying in the European Community,* ed. S. Mazey and J. Richardson, 3–26. Oxford: Oxford University Press.

McSweeney, B. 2002. Hofstede's model of national cultural differences and their consequences: a triumph of faith – a failure of analysis. *Human Relations* 55, no. 10: 89–118.

Oliver, C. 1991. Strategic responses to institutional processes. *Academy of Management Review* 16, no. 1: 145–79.

Quittkat, C. 2006. *Europäisierung der Interessenvermittlung: Französische Wirtschaftsverbände zwischen Beständigkeit und Wandel.* Wiesbaden: VS Verlag für Sozialwissenschaften.

Sagie, A., and M. Koslowsky. 2000. *Participation and empowerment in organizations — modelling, effectiveness and applications.* Thousand Oaks, CA: Sage Publications.

Salacuse, J.W. 1998. Ten ways that culture affects negotiating style — some survey results. *Negotiation Journal* 14, no. 3: 221–40.

Schein, E.H. 1985. *Organizational culture and leadership*. San Francisco, CA: Jossey Bass.

Schmidt, V.A. 1996. Loosening the ties that bind: the impact of European integration on French government and its relationship to business. *Journal of Common Market Studies* 34, no. 2: 223–54.

Schmidt, V. 1999. National patterns of governance under siege — the impact of European integration. In *The transformation of governance in the European Union*, ed. B. Kohler-Koch and R. Eising, 155–72. London: Routledge.

Schneider, S.C. 1989. Strategy formulation — the impact of national culture. *Organization Studies* 10, no. 2: 148–68.

Schuler, D.A., and K. Rehbein. 1997. The filtering role of the firm in corporate political involvement. *Business and Society* 36, no. 2: 116–39.

Schwartz, S.H. 1992. Universals in the content and structure of values: theoretical advances and empirical tests in 20 countries. *Advances in Experimental Social Psychology* 25, 1–65.

Selznick, P. 1957. *Leadership in administration — a sociological interpretation*. Berkeley, CA: University of California Press.

Shenkar, O. 2001. Cultural distance revisited — towards a more rigorous conceptualization and measurement of cultural differences. *Journal of International Business Studies* 32, no. 3: 519–36.

Stevens, A. 2003. *The government and politics of France*. London: St Martin's Press.

Taras, V., J. Rowney, and P. Steel. 2009. Half a century of measuring culture — review of approaches, challenges, and limitations based on the analysis of 121 instruments for quantifying culture. *Journal of International Management* 15, no. 4: 357–73.

Triandis, H.C. 1994. Cross-cultural industrial and organisational psychology. In *Handbook of industrial and organisational psychology*, ed. H.C. Triandis, M.D. Dunnette and L.M. Hough, 103–72. Palo Alto, CA: Consulting Psychologists Press.

Trompenaars, F., and C. Hampden-Turner. 1997. *Riding the waves of culture*. London: McGraw-Hill.

Waarden, F. 1993. Über die Beständigkeit nationaler Politikstile und Politknetzwerke. Eine Studie über die Genese ihrer institutionellen Verankerung. In *Verhandlungsdemokratie, Interessenvermittlung, Regierbarkeit. Festschrift für Gerhard Lehmbruch*, ed. R. Czada and M.G. Schmidt, 191–212. Opladen: Westdeutscher Verlag.

Wilson, F.L. 1988. *Interest group politics in France*. Cambridge: Cambridge University Press.

Wilts, A. 2002. Strategies of business interest associations in the Netherlands and Germany: European priorities or domestic concerns? *Politique européenne* 7, 96–115.

Wright, V. 1997. Introduction – la fin du dirigisme? *Modern and Contemporary France* 5, no. 2: 151–53.

Weakness as Precondition of Smooth Integration? Representation Strategies of Functional Interest Groups from New Member States at the EU Level

HEIKO PLEINES

Research Centre for East European Studies, University of Bremen, Bremen, Germany

ABSTRACT Based on an empirical study of business associations, trade unions and value-based NGOs from new EU member states this contribution argues that interest groups from the new Central and East European member states could smoothly be integrated into the EU system of interest representation with the help of European umbrella organisations. European umbrella organisations offer immediate access to the EU level, provide a role model of engagement at the EU level and also increase information flows from the EU level to national interest groups and with that into national debates and national policy-making processes. Accordingly, theories of horizontal integration should not only look at the limited impact of interest groups on the implementation of the EU *acquis communautaire*, but also at the effects the smooth integration of new interest groups at the EU level has on the Europeanization of new and prospective member states.

Introduction

'While the "lobby system in Brussels" is no longer in its nascent stage of development, the EU system of interest representation remains less stable and less consolidated than some national associational systems', as, e.g., Beyers *et al.* (2010, 11) argue. As a result the integration of a large group of newcomers is clearly a challenge to consolidation and might give an impetus towards further change. A better understanding of the integration of interest groups from acceding countries into the EU system of interest representation is, therefore, an important building stone for a theory of horizontal integration. The following analysis focuses on functional interest groups with different backgrounds, namely business associations, trade unions and value based NGOs.

Research on horizontal EU integration had originally put high hopes on functional interest groups in the context of Eastern enlargement:

> Accession countries face great difficulties in restructuring their economic and political institutions in order to meet the conditions for EU membership. The systematic involvement of non-state actors in the adoption of and adaptation to EU requirements was thought to be a remedy for the problems of European Enlargement towards 'weak' transition countries. Companies and civil society organizations could provide the governments of the accession countries with important resources (money, information, expertise and support) that are necessary to make EU policies work. (Börzel and Buzogany 2010, 158)

However, the weakness of interest groups in the new Central East European member states has largely dashed that hope. Accordingly Börzel (2009) now talks of a 'double weakness' of transition countries which lack governance capacity in the state as well as in the non-state sector.

This contribution argues that whereas the weakness of interest groups in the accession states is seen as a hindrance to EU integration in the implementation-focused view, the same weakness has greatly supported the smooth integration of interest groups from the new member states into the EU system of interest representation.

This argument is backed up through an analysis of the strategies of functional interest groups from the new member states to adapt to and represent their interests at the EU level.[1] After a brief description of the empirical data compiled for this analysis, the strategies of representation employed by interest groups from the new member states are categorized with a focus on direct vs. indirect representation, addressees of interest representation and the degree of network building. In a next step the causes of the smooth integration of new interest groups into the existing system of interest representation will be elaborated. This, finally, allows for an assessment of the role of interest groups from new member states in the EU system of interest representation.

Data

There already is an abundance of literature on interest groups in Central and Eastern Europe. The results of these studies unequivocally expose the structural weaknesses of interest representation in this region. However, there are still very few substantial empirical studies on the integration of interest groups from the new Central and East European member states into EU governance. An investigation of their strategies of interest representation at the EU level is largely missing.[2] Accordingly, the following analysis is based first of all on original empirical research.

In order to get a broad picture of functional interest representation, the following analysis covers business associations, trade unions and classical value-based NGOs from the new Central and East European member states. In order to get first hand information about strategies of interest representation as well as about underlying perceptions, 86 full face-to-face interviews have been conducted with representatives of trade unions, business associations and environmental NGOs from the Czech Republic, Poland and Slovakia in autumn 2007.[3] With that the study covers three of the biggest states which joined the EU during the first wave of Eastern enlargement.

For each respondent the survey comprises a questionnaire with 43 questions as well as a semi-structured interview. For the interviews leading members of the interest groups were selected whose area of responsibility included their organisation's relations with the EU (department heads or board members). To obtain a representative statement on the organisations' position, at least two representatives were interviewed per organisation where possible. This measure was meant to ensure that the testimony was not influenced by the personal preferences of a dissenter within the organisation. Detailed case studies on the interest representation of Polish women's NGOs as well as Polish and Czech agricultural lobbies in EU governance have been added on the basis of related research projects (see Fuchs and Payer 2007; Pleines 2007; Yakova 2007). An overview of the interest groups included in the following analysis is given in the table in the appendix.

In addition to the interview-based analysis of the strategies of individual interest groups, the overall representation of interest groups from the new member states in major European umbrella organisations has been subjected to a quantitative assessment. As common EU-wide membership databases are not reliable (see Berkhout and Lowery 2008), membership information has been obtained directly from the individual umbrella organisations.[4] The analysis of quantitative participation at the EU level covers the umbrella organisations for the policy fields of environment (Green 10), social policy in the broadest sense (Social Platform), development aid (Concord) and human rights (HDRN), which taken together comprise the core topics of value-based NGOs.

Although there are strong differences between the interest groups from the new member states concerning their position in their respective national political arena, their representation strategies at the EU level do not systematically differ along national lines. Accordingly, the following analysis differentiates between types of interest groups (business associations, agricultural lobbies, trade unions and value-based NGOs) and does not focus on country-specific variations. The latter would only make sense if old EU member states were included in the comparison.

As the focus is on lobbying strategies at the EU level, the sample analysed here includes only interest groups which are (at least indirectly) represented at the EU level. With that it obviously ignores large parts of the interest group population in the new member states. This is especially true for NGOs, which on average tend to have fewer resources and capacities than other interest groups. As JoAnn Carmin argues on the basis of an analysis of 632 environmental NGOs in four Central and East European countries:

> ... two clusters of organizations have emerged. The first cluster consists of a small cadre of highly professionalized and internationalized organizations that engage in policy-making in the international and national arenas. The second cluster of NGOs tends to sponsor activities and take action on behalf of their members and provide environmental and government support services at the local level. While the former cluster is comprised of well-capacitated organizations, NGOs in the latter group often are overlooked by agencies, governments, and foundations, even though they make important contributions to environmental governance. (Carmin 2010, 183)

Strategies of Interest Representation

With reference to the criteria laid out in the introduction to this special issue, the interest representation at the EU level, as employed by functional interest groups from the new member states, has been grouped into distinctive strategies based on three characteristics: Direct vs. indirect representation, addressees of interest representation and degree of network building. With that the focus is on channels of representation, as they are the prime indicator of integration into a governance system.

The choice of direct vs. indirect representation describes a trade-off between agenda setting capabilities and increased influence through coalition building (or coalition joining). Direct interest representation (i.e., individual representation or representation with a small group of close partners) allows a high degree of control over which interests are presented in what way. It also helps to avoid collective action problems. At the same time, interest representation by a small group is less likely to impress policy-makers. Coalition joining (i.e., membership in a European umbrella organisation), on the contrary, increases the impact on policy-making, but reduces control over the actual process of collective interest representation. It can be assumed that indirect representation is related to a higher pressure of convergence, as individual interest groups have less power to change the established rules and procedures.[5]

The addressees of interest representation indicate the actual channel of interest representation, but not necessarily the preferred channel (implied by the strategy of the respective interest group) as influential addressees may simply be out of reach. With that they show the degree of integration of the respective interest group into the decision-making process. The addressees of interest representation also indicate whether lobbying efforts are aimed at genuine EU policy-makers, mostly located in Brussels, or national policy-makers, mostly in their capacity as members of the European Council.[6] It can be assumed that the Brussels route implies a higher pressure of convergence towards European lobbying practices, as it exposes interest groups to new actors while the national route can easily be based on a continuation of already existing domestic lobbying strategies.

The degree of network building describes how far interest groups have been integrated into their respective interest community at the supranational level. It is a good indicator of the availability of alternative channels of interest representation. It might also show how likely specific interest groups are to mobilize broader coalitions at the EU level. In summary a broader network is likely to offer additional opportunities of interest representation and it is also likely to increase peer pressure towards a common strategy and position.

Direct vs. Indirect Representation

For most interest groups from the new member states the focus of their EU strategy is clearly on indirect representation through European umbrella organisations. As many NGOs from Central and Eastern Europe joined their respective European umbrella organisation well before their country joined the EU, NGOs from the new member states were in quantitative terms already strongly represented in 2008. At that time the Social Platform had 428 national member organizations from the 10 Central and East European member states which joined in 2004 and 2007, Concord had 234, the Green 10 had 100 and the HRDN had 97. As a result, 15% to 24% of the member organisations of the four biggest European umbrella organisations were from the new member states (for full data see Pleines 2010).

In our case study of Czech environmental NGOs, which are a typical example of the most active civil society organisations from the new member states, cooperation with the European umbrella organisations was generally evaluated positively with only one Czech NGO representative reporting a mixed balance and none giving a negative assessment. At the same time none claimed to often act independently at the EU level.

The picture for trade unions from the new member states is similar. Those trade unions which are active at the EU level are all members of European umbrella organisations (most notably the European Trade Union Confederation — ETUC) and two thirds of those covered in our survey claimed that they represent their interest at the EU level first and foremost through ETUC. The same two thirds evaluated their cooperation with ETUC positively, while only one respondent from a trade union made an explicitly negative assessment (and was contradicted by another respondent from his union).

However, for business associations from the new member states the situation is clearly different. Though they, too, are all members of European umbrella organisations, only a third claims to represent interests at the EU level first of all through these umbrella organisations, while the majority engages in direct representation, most commonly in cooperation with one or two partners. At the same time no business association gave a negative assessment of the cooperation with a European umbrella organisation.

Agricultural lobby organisations from Central and East European EU member states have also joined their respective European umbrella organisations, namely the Committee of Professional Agricultural Organisations (COPA). But as in the case of the business associations COPA is not the preferred way of interest representation in EU governance. As has been shown in case studies of the Polish and the Czech agricultural lobbies, they first of all opt for the national route, i.e., they lobby their own national government to represent their interests at the EU level (see Pleines 2007 and Yakova 2007 respectively).

In summary, it can be stated that non-business interest groups from the new member states focus on indirect representation if they get active at the EU level, while a majority of business associations also engage in direct representation. This difference and the dominance of the umbrella organisations are central features of the representation strategies of interest groups from the new member states, which largely determine their addressees and networks at the EU level.

Addressees of Interest Representation

Our interviews show that even the strongest interest groups from Central and Eastern Europe find it hard to get independent access to EU decision-making bodies. Neither trade unions nor NGOs from the new member states have an office in Brussels — a fact which makes contacts much harder — whereas several of the business associations do (Krech 2008, 58). As a result only a handful of functional interest groups from the new member states have contacts with the European Commission or the European Parliament, mainly through personal acquaintance with an EU bureaucrat or an MEP. Of the thirteen most influential trade unions from the new member states covered in our survey five have access to an MEP, only three engage in direct consultations with their national representatives in the Council of Ministers, and just two claim a direct link to the European Commission.

Moreover, most contacts seem to be based on available options, not on a consistent strategy of effective interest representation. For example, the fact that trade unions from the new member states have a link first of all to the European Parliament, does not indicate that the Parliament is the best addressee of trade union lobbying, but is explained simply by the high number of MEPs from the new member states (namely from Poland) with a strong trade union background (Krech 2008).

Again the situation is different for the most influential business associations. Of the eight most influential business associations from the new member states covered in our survey, six claim a direct link to the European Commission, seven to the European Parliament and five a connection to national representatives in the Council of Ministers.

However, with the exception of one trade union and two business associations, no interest group from the new member states covered in our interviews claims to be able to represent interests at the EU level on its own. Accordingly, they do not decide independently on the addressees of lobbying efforts. Asked about the role of the EU for the work of his trade union, the representative of a Polish trade union tellingly answered:

> I have to define the concept 'European Union'. For me as a trade union official, this concept refers to our presence in our umbrella organisation [i.e., ETUC], which represents us vis-à-vis various European institutions.

Degree of Network Building

As virtually no NGO or trade union from the Central and East European member states has a permanent representative in Brussels, their networking opportunities at the EU level are limited. This organisational weakness, especially of NGOs, has been illustrated in our interviews. Miroslav Suta from the Czech Society of Sustainable Living, for example, who was a member of the Executive Committee of the European Environmental Bureau (EEB, part of the Green 10), stated that he could deal with EU matters only on the weekends. Ondrej Rut, the EU coordinator of the Czech Green Circle, elaborated:

> Employees are not paid well [by environmental NGOs] but are expected to be highly professional and perform as well as those working in private business. As a result, there is a high fluctuation of employees who take the know-how with them when they leave the organisation. This hinders the organisation from further improvement including its ability to engage at the EU level.

As a result, for most NGOs and trade unions from the new member states contacts at the EU level are by and large restricted to membership in (and rarely active participation in the leadership of) European umbrella organisations.

An exception to this general picture is provided by Polish women's NGOs, which have had very mixed experiences with the European Women's Lobby (EWL). The EWL, the major European umbrella organisation for women's NGOs, had apparently not been interested in cooperation with women's NGOs from Central and Eastern Europe until 2003. The Polish Women's Lobby, which was formed to join EWL, soon fell apart over internal controversies. As a result some of Poland's more conservative women's NGOs are now part of the EWL, while other women's NGOs have formed alternative networks, namely the Karat Coalition, and try to get independent access to the EU level (Fuchs and Payer 2007). However:

> ... the EWL completely occupies the opportunity space created by the European Commission, both in terms of political access and

financial resources... Today the Karat Coalition has experienced a clear decline in its activities. (Cisar and Vrablikova 2010, 216)

Next to European umbrella organisations a second entrance into networks at the EU level is offered to some NGOs and trade unions by Members of the European Parliament. Of the seven Czech environmental NGOs active at the EU level, for example, three claimed a link to the European Parliament, while one named a MEP as major cooperation partner. The strongest link to MEPs is given in the case of the Polish trade unions, as 12 deputies from Poland in the European Parliament (2004–2009) had a trade union background and were in the interviews named as major cooperation partners.[7] This is due to the fact that throughout the 1990s Polish trade unions had close links to national political parties in the left as well as the conservative camp. More recently this link has declined in relevance and the number of Polish MEPs with a trade union background has been reduced to five after the elections in 2009. But MEPs with a respective organizational or ideological background are still the major access point to the European Parliament for representatives of interest groups from the new member states. Although, there is not much networking at the EU level, some NGOs and trade unions have developed co-operations within the EU system of multi-level governance, in most cases cooperation with similar interest groups in neighbouring countries. Slovak trade unions, for example, name Austrian and Hungarian trade unions as majors partners. Trade unions in the border region of Poland, the Czech Republic and Germany have united in a formalized network. The three major alternative networks of the Polish women's organisations (Astra, Karat and the Network of East–West Women) are also regional networks bringing together first of all women's NGOs from Central Eastern Europe. In addition national umbrella organisations can also help to integrate into EU governance, as, e.g., some of the Czech environmental NGOs claim to use their national umbrella organisation, the Green Circle, to represent interests at the EU level.

In a similar pattern business associations from the new member states name other national umbrella organisations (mainly from their own country) as major partners next to the European umbrella organisation Businesseurope (formerly UNICE).

However, agricultural lobbies from the new member states do not actively engage in network building at the EU level at all. 'At the EU level Czech actors focus more on information gathering and learning than on coalition building and policy-making' (Yakova 2007, 194), while:

> ... in the multinational agricultural interest association at the EU level, the Polish agricultural lobby is not only marginal but also rather isolated, as most interest groups from the old member states see Poland as a main rival for EU subsidies. (Pleines 2007, 207)

In summary, the interest groups from the new member states have not built major networks in EU governance. They first of all rely on European umbrella organisations. In some cases they also cooperate with MEPs. In addition some have created or joined regional networks with actors from neighbouring countries.

Actor-Specific Strategies

For trade unions and most NGOs from the new member states indirect representation through the Brussels route, i.e., through membership in a European umbrella organisation, is the major strategy of engagement at the EU level. In many cases this strategy is complemented by membership in national umbrella organisations and by cooperation with similar interest groups from neighbouring countries. In some cases there also is a direct contact in the European Parliament or the bureaucracy of the European Commission. But this leads more to an increased information flow than to direct lobbying efforts.

Business associations from the new member states are more likely to represent their interests directly at the EU level. They either act alone or team up with a small number of similar interest groups, but they do not form extensive networks. Their interest representation is, rather, equally targeted at the three main decision-making bodies at the EU level, i.e., Commission, Parliament and Council.

The major example for a strategy based foremost on the national route is the agricultural lobby. In this case interest representation at the national level is indirect as it is based on national umbrella organisations and it is complemented by membership in the respective European umbrella organisation. But it does not imply network building at the EU level. This is mainly due to the fact that agricultural associations are active in a policy field where individual member states still hold veto powers and where redistributive issues make interest groups from different member states potential rivals.

In summary, European umbrella organisations have established themselves as a must for all interest groups and a starting point for most interest groups from new member states. But this does not imply that umbrella organisations are the most important way of interest representation. On the contrary, as all interest groups have joined European umbrella organisations, the more successful interest groups are distinguished by their additional lobbying activities at the EU level, namely through direct access to the European Commission, the Council of Ministers and the European Parliament.

In this sense the large majority of interest groups from the new member states is weakly represented at the EU level as they rely first of all on indirect representation through umbrella organisations and have not developed larger networks at the EU level. This, in turn, makes the European umbrella organisations the most important integration tool for interest groups from the new member states.

At the same time, most interest groups from the new member states covered in our survey see access to information as the main aim of their membership in EU umbrella organisations. This information is first of all used to improve the own position in domestic politics with the help of competent references to EU standards and up-to-date information on policy initiatives at the EU level. Accordingly, membership in umbrella organisations is actually not so much about interest representation but more about information gathering.

Weakness as Precondition of Smooth Integration

In an EU-wide comparison one central characteristic of functional interest groups from the Central and East European member states is their weakness measured by financial resources as well as number and expertise of personnel (see, e.g., Lane 2007 for an explicit comparison). Most interest groups from the new member states lack the money to finance a representative office in Brussels. In addition, they have fewer trained staff. In our survey of interest group representatives responsible for relations with the EU only a quarter claimed to speak English fluently. Among trade unionists Russian was still the most common language. This weakness obviously works strongly in favour of indirect interest representation through European umbrella organisations.

The weakness of interest groups in the prospective member countries has caused the EU to provide specific support measures. This pre-accession support by the European Commission has strongly promoted the integration of interest groups from the new member states into European umbrella organisations. For example, in the case of environmental NGOs the DG Environment of the European Commission already in 1999 initiated an EU–NGO dialogue which regularly brought together 40 environmental NGOs from candidate countries with EU representatives and major European umbrella organisations. In addition, the EU Commission provided training courses, in which in the Czech Republic alone members of 200 interest groups took part. Moreover, in the case of Czech environmental NGOs EU funding provided on average 7% of their budget (Pleines and Bušková 2007, 40–42). The overwhelming majority of trade unions interviewed also reported having received support from the EU Commission in preparation for participation in EU governance. They cited the provision of information, training seminars and support in international networking as important measures.

Most of the bigger business associations engaged in bilateral 'twinning' partnerships with peer organisations from the old member states. This, too, promoted their integration into European umbrella organisations. At the same time most European umbrella organisations started already in the 1990s to recruit suitable member organisations from the future member states in order to guarantee the validity of their claim to representativeness after Eastern enlargement.

This means, while most interest groups from the new member states are simply too weak to transfer their own lobbying strategy from the national arena to the EU level, actors of the EU level have supported their integration into European umbrella organisations. Accordingly, virtually all major interest groups from the new member states have joined European umbrella organisations. Those who have chosen not to join, like the women's organisations forming the Karat Coalition, have not been able to get lasting access to the EU level.

There are only two exceptions to the dominant role of European umbrella organisations in the representation of functional interest groups from the new member states. The very few interest groups with bigger financial capacities, namely business associations, have been able to employ a more proactive strategy at the EU level. And the agricultural lobbies have preferred the national route over interest representation through a European umbrella organisation.

However, another important explaining factor for the smooth integration of interest groups from the new member states into the EU system of interest representation is their satisfaction with EU policies. All environmental NGOs included in the sample evaluate the influence of the EU on their organisation positively and most of them desire an increased influence of the EU on the national level. All respondents claim that their organisation uses the EU 'often' as an argument in domestic politics. As recent examples of a positive influence of the EU on national Czech environmental policy the creation of nature reserves (NATURA 2000), climate policy (emissions trade), transportation policy and new guidelines for chemicals (REACH) are cited.

In a similar assessment, altogether 89% of the respondents from trade unions and 70% of those from business associations see the influence of the EU on their organisation positively and about half of them (61% and 44% respectively) desire an increased influence of the EU on the national level. Even more claim that their organisation uses the EU 'often' as an argument in domestic politics, the others do so 'sometimes'. Representatives of the Czech trade unions, for example, mentioned a broad spectrum of legislative debates from wage issues to job security and from telework to pension reform, in which they explicitly used the relationship to the EU to fuel their argumentation in the national debate.

A representative of a national Polish trade union elaborated:

When the Polish government wanted to change the European directive on weekly working hours without consulting us, we found out about it thanks to our participation in the European Trade Union Confederation and we had a chance to present our own opinion. The result was that the government's action without consulting the public could be hindered. Membership in the European Federation of Trade Unions thus represents an additional information source. It enables one to learn not only about European opportunities, but also about national ones.

Another one explained:

We used arguments of ETUC in order to underline the importance of finding a solution for the implementation of the directive on information and consultation rights. In the end, it became a law on European Works' Councils. In this case it was important that trade unions had the last word in the formulation of the law. I mean the Directive No. 14 of the year 2002.

It is important to note that, as a result of selected references, conflicting interests like trade unions and business associations can both get a positive view of EU regulation. General satisfaction with the state of affairs at the EU level then reduces the need to actively engage in lobbying and increases the demand for information in order to profit from positive regulation. This also increases the role of European umbrella organisations, as they are, especially for smaller interest groups, first of all providers of information and to a much lesser degree an effective channel for the representation of individual interests. Membership in European umbrella organisations thus serves to compensate for organizational and programmatic weaknesses in national policy.

This has implications for the system of interest representation at the EU level, as it indicates that the functional interest groups from the new member states are mostly acting as agents of Europeanization (and with that, one might argue, of the European Commission) in their respective national arenas and only to a much lesser degree as representatives of specific interests of their national constituency at the EU level. At the same time, the dominance of European umbrella organisations *de facto* excludes interest groups with dissenting views from effective access to the EU level.

Conclusion

After Eastern enlargement the European umbrella organisations look like a very effective tool for the integration of a large number of new interest groups into EU governance. They offer immediate access to the EU level and provide a role model of engagement at the EU level for interest groups from the new member states. The European umbrella organisations also increase information flows from the EU level to national interest groups and through them into national debates and national policy-making processes. This holds true for all different functional interest groups analysed here, i.e., for business associations, trade unions and value based NGOs alike.

However, pressure towards convergence is strongest for the weakest. That means, a study of interest groups from the new Central and East European member states clearly overstates the role of the European umbrella organisations.[8] This is confirmed by the fact that the stronger interest groups from the new member states, namely business associations, as well as bigger West European peers of the new interest groups pursue a much more proactive and independent strategy at the EU level, as studies on West European business associations (Eising 2007), agricultural lobbies (Klüver 2010) or environmental NGOs (Roose 2003) demonstrate.

Our study, thus, indicates that weak interest groups from new member states which see the adoption of selected parts of EU regulation as positive, can smoothly be integrated at the EU level with the help of European umbrella organisations. As interest groups in most candidate countries and further potential EU member states are meeting these criteria, theories of horizontal integration should not only look at the impact the 'double weakness' of recent and future accession countries has on the implementation of the *acquis communautaire*, but also at the effects the smooth integration of new interest groups at the EU level has on national politics from a broader perspective.

In this context two aspects demand further research. First, it seems that the pressure towards convergence does not extend throughout the EU system of multi-level governance, but is by and large restricted to umbrella organisations at the EU level. It does not cover the national or cross-border activities of interest groups nor does it extend to interest groups which represent their interests in EU policy-making by way of the national route. Of course, there are Europeanization effects,[9] but there is so far no indication that these effects are able to transform the ways of interest representation in the national arena. Instead interest groups from the new member states seem to clearly distinguish between the EU and the national arena. Accordingly, it is not clear how far Europeanization is just opportunistic in order to back up one's own position in the national arenas and how far it is driven by genuine values and beliefs.

Second, the fact that most interest groups from the new member states have been smoothly integrated into the European system of interest representation through umbrella organisations, does not imply that nothing has changed at the EU level. As Blavoukos and Pagoulatos (2010) rightly point out on the basis of deductive reasoning, the fact that interest groups from the new member states have adopted the prevailing forms of interest representation does not necessarily imply that they have also readily adopted the agenda of the European umbrella organisations. The increase of the membership base may also have led to increased collective action challenges. However, research on the effect of the influx of up to a quarter of new members on the European umbrella organisations is still missing.

Notes

1. With that the focus is put on strategies of interest representation as such and neither on their success nor on the degree of representation, visibility or influence of these interest groups. The reason for this is that the compatibility of newcomers with the EU system of interest representation depends foremost on the compatibility of their strategies with the established rules of consultation and decision-making within EU governance and only to a much lesser degree on the relative success or fair representation of new interests. For an assessment of the degree of representation and influence of interest groups from the new member states at the EU level, based on the data used in this contribution, see Pleines (2010).
2. A broader overview of the state of research is provided by Pleines (2011).
3. The study on environmental NGOs has been conducted as part of the Integrated Project 'New Modes of Governance' (www.eu-newgov.org), financially supported by the European Union under the 6th Framework programme (Contract No CIT1-CT-2004-506392). Interviews in Prague were conducted by Kristýna Bušková (then Research Centre for East European Studies at the University of Bremen, now Cambridge University) and in Brussels by Brigitte Krech (independent consultant). The study of trade unions and business associations has been funded by the Otto-Brenner-Foundation. Interviews were conducted by the Institute for Sociology of the Czech Academy of Sciences, the Institute for Sociology of the Slovak Academy of Sciences and the Koszalin Institute of Comparative European Studies. Brigitte Krech was responsible for the interviews in Brussels. The interviews with business associations and trade unions have been documented in Kusznir and Pleines (2008).

4. All organizations headquartered in a specific country which are formally members of the respective European umbrella organization have been counted. The respective membership chains from the EU to grass roots level can be rather complex. For an elaboration see Kohler-Koch and Buth (2008).
5. For a fuller discussion of this argument in relation to interest groups at the EU level see Beyers (2010, 98–104). For an empirical test see Mahoney (2007).
6. See Greenwood (2007, 23–48) for a description of the two routes.
7. For details see Krech (2008).
8. A comparison of Eastern enlargement with earlier enlargement waves, though, is only of very limited value, as the challenges during earlier waves were rather different due to the number and nature of the countries involved and, much more importantly, due to the fact that civil society organizations began to play a more important role in EU governance only at the time of the run-up to Eastern enlargement.
9. For a thorough discussion see: Beyers and Kerremans (2007).

References

Berkhout, J., and D. Lowery. 2008. Counting organized interests in the European Union: a comparison of data sources. *Journal of European Public Policy* 15, no. 4: 489–513.

Beyers, J., and B. Kerremans. 2007. Critical resource dependencies and the Europeanization of domestic interest groups. *Journal of European Public Policy* 14, no. 3: 460–81.

Beyers, J., R. Eising, and W.A. Maloney. 2010. Researching interest group politics in Europe and elsewhere: much we study, little we know?. In *Interest group politics in Europe*, eds. J. Beyers, R. Eising and W.A. Maloney, 1–26. London: Routledge.

Beyers, J. 2010. Policy issues, organisational format and the political strategies of interest organisations. In *Interest group politics in Europe*, eds. J. Beyers, R. Eising and W.A. Maloney, 86–109. London: Routledge.

Blavoukos, S., and G. Pagoulatos. 2010. 'Enlargement waves' and interest group participation in the EU policy-making system: establishing a framework of analysis. In *Interest group politics in Europe*, eds. J. Beyers, R. Eising and W.A. Maloney, 45–63. London: Routledge.

Börzel, T. 2009. *Coping with accession to the European Union: new modes of environmental governance*. Basingstoke: Palgrave.

Börzel, T., and A. Buzogany. 2010. Governing EU accession in transition countries: the role of non-state actors. *Acta Politica* 45, no. 1/2: 158–82.

Carmin, J. 2010. NGO capacity and environmental governance in Central and Eastern Europe. *Acta Politica* 45, no. 1/2: 183–202.

Cisar, O., and K. Vrablikova. 2010. The Europeanization of social movements in the Czech Republic: the EU and local women's groups. *Communist and Post-Communist Studies* 43, no. 2: 209–19.

Eising, R. 2007. Institutional context, organizational resources and strategic choices: explaining interest group access in the European Union. *European Union Politics* 8, no. 3: 329–62.

Eising, R. 2010. Clientelism, committees, pluralism and protests in the European Union: matching patterns?. In *Interest group politics in Europe*, eds. J. Beyers, R. Eising and W.A. Maloney, 64–85. London: Routledge.

Fuchs, G., and S. Payer. 2007. Women's NGOs in EU governance: problems of finance and access. In *The capacity of Central and East European interest groups to participate in EU governance*, eds. D. Obradovic and H. Pleines, 163–82. Stuttgart: Ibidem Publishers.

Klüver, H. 2010. Europeanization of lobbying activities. When national interest groups spill over to the European level. *Journal of European Integration* 32, no. 2: 175–91.

Kohler-Koch, B., and V. Buth. 2009. Civil society in EU governance. Lobby groups like any other?, http://www.sfb597.uni-bremen.de/pages/pubApBeschreibung.php?SPRACHE=en&ID=148.

Krech, B. 2008. Presence and visibility of Polish, Czech and Slovak trade unions at the EU level. In *Trade unions from post-socialist member states in EU governance*, eds. J. Kusznir and H. Pleines, 57–68. Stuttgart: Ibidem Publishers.

Kusznir, J., and H. Pleines. 2008. *Trade unions from post-socialist member states in EU governance*. Stuttgart: Ibidem Publishers.

Lane, D. 2007. Civil society formation in the post-socialist EU member states. In *The capacity of Central and East European interest groups to participate in EU governance*, eds. D. Obradovic and H. Pleines, 109–28. Stuttgart: Ibidem Publishers.

Mahoney, C. 2007. Networking vs. allying: the decisions of interest groups to join coalitions in the US and the EU. *Journal of European Public Policy* 14, no. 3: 366–83.

Pleines, H. 2007. Interest representation of the Polish agricultural lobby at the national and the EU level. In *The capacity of Central and East European interest groups to participate in EU governance*, eds. D. Obradovic and H. Pleines, 197–209. Stuttgart: Ibidem Publishers.

Pleines, H. 2010. Is this the way to Brussels? CEE civil society involvement in EU governance. *Acta Politica* 45, no. 1/2: 229–46.
Pleines, H. 2011. Challenges of integration and participation: civil society organizations from new member states in EU governance. In *The new politics of European civil society*, eds. H.-J. Trenz and U. Liebert, 178–94. London: Routledge.
Pleines, H., and K. Bušková. 2007. Czech environmental NGOs: actors or agents in EU multilevel governance? *Contemporary European Studies* 2, no. 1: 37–50.
Roose, J. 2003. *Die Europäisierung von Umweltorganisationen: Die Umweltbewegung auf dem langen Weg nach Brüssel*. Opladen: Westdeutscher Verlag.
Yakova, I. 2007. The Czech agricultural lobby in EU governance. In *The capacity of Central and East European interest groups to participate in EU governance*, eds. D. Obradovic and H. Pleines, 183–96. Stuttgart: Ibidem Publishers.

Appendix

Table 1. Interest groups covered in the analysis

Functional interest	Czech Republic	Poland	Slovakia	EU level
General business associations	Economic Chamber SCMVD SP CR	BCC KPP PKPP Lewiatan	AZZZ RUZ	UNICE (now Businesseurope) CEEP
Agricultural lobbies	AA APF CAC	FBZPR KRIR KZKiOR PFPZ ZMWZK ZZ CNMR ZZR Samoobrona		CEJA CIAA COPA
Trade unions	ASO CMKOS KOVO KUK FZZ OS PHGN	FZZ FZZ Metalowcy OPZZ Solidarnosc ZZG	KOZ SR OZ KOVO OZ PBGN	EFFAT EMF ETUC
Value-based NGOs	Arnika Czech and Slovak Traffic Club Environmental Law Service Green Circle Institute for Environmental Policy Rainbow Movement Society for Sustainable Living	Astra Federa Karat Oska NEWW Polish Women's Lobby		Birdlife CAN CEE Bankwatch Concord EWL Green 10 Greenpeace HDRN Naturfreunde Social Platform

Index

actor: bureaucratic 105; capacities 14–15; institutional 119; political 105; social 140; specific strategies 167–8; territorial 81; types 5
agency problems 101
agricultural lobby 161
AIDS/ HIV 44
ALTER-EU 11, 107
Amsterdam Treaty 114
Andersen, S.: and Burns, T. 26
anti-racism 119; European Network against Racism (ENAR) 106, 116
Assembly of European Regions (AER) 80
Association of Finnish Local and Regional Authorities 99

Baden-Württemberg 15, 79, 97
Balme, R.: and Chabanet, D. 92
Barron, A. 12, 139–57
Baumgartner, F.R.: and Leech, B.L. 131
Bavaria 78
Beyers, J.: and Kerremans, B. 3
Birmingham (UK) 24
Bjerregaard, R. 111
Blavoukos, S.: and Pagoulatos, G. 171
Bond, M.H.: and Hofstede, G. 143
Börzel, T. 160
Bouwen, P. 127
Bouza, L. 15
Brent Spar oil platform 110
Bristol (UK) 24
Brussels: North West (of England) Brussels Office 99; offices of the regions 89–102; territorial offices 93–8
Brussels-Europe Liaison Office 128
budget-maximising 119
bureaucratic actors 105
Burns, T.: and Anderson, S. 26
Businesseurope (formerly UNICE) 166
Buth, V.: and Kohler-Koch, B. 152

Carmin, J. 162
Carr, C.: and Harris, S. 143

Castiglione, D.: and Warren, M. 116
Central East European member states 160
Central Europe 160
Chabanet, D.: and Balme, R. 92
Chalmers, A.W. 123–37
Child, J. 141
China 143
civil society 58, 102
Civil Society Contact Group (CSCG) 111, 114
coalition 110; behaviour 110; joining 162
Coen, D. 152; and Richardson, J. 6
Cohen, J.: and Sabel, C. 74
collective action 152
Committee of Professional Agricultural Organisations (COPA) 164
Committee of the Regions (COR) 33, 59, 89–92
common interest 98–100
communicative involvement 82–3
Concord (development aid) 163
conference speakers 57
conferences 56
constituency-building 144
consultation instruments 55–62; inclusive 63–4
consultation regime 53–70
consultative involvement 78–82
convergence 13–14
Corporate Europe Observatory (CEO) 11
corporate political activity (CPA) 141
corporate social responsibility 62
Council of European Municipalities and Regions (CEMR) 80
Council of Ministers 17, 33, 59
cross-border activities 171
cross-cultural management 143
cross-cultural model 140
Cullen, P. 108
Czech Republic 161
Czech Society of Sustainable Living 165

Dahl, R. 126

INDEX

Deardorff, A.V.: and Hall, R.A. 124, 126
democracy: associational 28; experimentalism 8, 23; representative 90
development aid: Concord 163
direct representation 160
Directorate General Employment 53, 59, 118; Social Affairs and Equal Opportunities 58
Directorate General Environment of the European Commission 168
Directorate General for Health and Consumers (DG SANCO) 8, 37–51, 53–70; Platform for Action on Diet, Physical Activity and Health 45–8
Directorate General Trade Civil Society Dialogue 8, 37–51
directorates general 117
Dutch G-4 97
Duverger, M. 24

Eastern enlargement 160
Eastern Europe 160
Economic and Social Committee (ESC) 25
Eising, R. 152
emissions trade 169
EU-15 66
Europe of the Regions 72
European Affairs Network 145
European Alcohol and Health Forum 45
European Association of Regional and Local Authorities for Lifelong Learning (EARLLL) 99
European Citizens' Conferences 83
European Commission 3–19, 53–70, 168
European Community 81
European Council 33, 163
European Court of Justice 29, 40
European Economic Community (EEC) 1
European Economic and Social Committee (EESC) 77, 82
European Environmental Bureau (EEB) 112, 165
European Governance White Paper (2001) 2, 22, 40, 76
European interest intermediation 71–87
European Local Inclusion and Social Action Network (ELISAN) 99
European multi-level system 78–83
European Network against Racism (ENAR) 106, 116
European Network of Social Authorities (ENSA) 99
European Parliament 17, 131, 166
European Public Affairs Directory 128, 145
European Reference Networks on Rare Diseases 45
European regional policy 6

European Regions Research Innovation Network (ERRIN) 99
European Trade Union Confederation (ETUC) 163
European Transparency Initiative (ETI) 44
European Transparency Register 4, 13, 91
Treaty on European Union clauses on subsidiarity 93–4
European Union (EU): activities 130; decision-making 136; EU-15 66; governance 161; Green Papers 130; lobbying 55–8, 62, 81, 123, 126, 134, 135, 152; member states 161; policy-makers 63; Single European Act 2; White Papers 130, *see also* Brussels
European Women's Lobby (EWL) 13, 115, 165
Europeanisation 15, 140, 159; effects 171

federal countries 98
federal systems 25
Four Motors for Europe 80
Friends of the Earth 10, 112
functional governance 23
functional interest groups 159–71
functional representation 37–51

German federalism: Constitutional reform (1969) 29
German Social Democratic Party 24
Germany 81
Gestalt exercise 27
Getz, K.A. 141, 144
goal specificity 93–8
governance: organic 23
government affairs managers 139–57
Grant, W. 76
Green Ten 111, 112
Greenpeace 10, 106, 110
Greenwood, J. 1–19, 89–102

Hall, R.A.: and Deardorff, A.V. 124, 126
Harris, S.: and Carr, C. 143
Hillman, A.J.: and Hitt, M.A. 142, 152
HIV/AIDS 44
Hofstede, G. 146; and Bond, M.H. 143
Hooghe, L.: and Marks, C. 73
human rights 161
Hungary 93
Huysseune, M.: and Jans, T. 98

information processing 126–8
integration: smooth 168–70
interest groups 41–3, 123–37; strategies 41–3
interest groups influence 125–6; research design 128–31

INDEX

interest representation 7–9, 113–17; strategies 82–3, 162
International Government Relations and Public Affairs group 146
international politics 6
International Union of Local Authorities (ILUA) 80
INTERREG 80; People Project 99

Jacobins 24
Jans, T.: and Huysseune, M. 98
Japan 143
Jarman, H. 37–51

Karat Coalition 13, 165, 169
Kerremans, B.: and Beyers, J. 3; and Princen, S. 11, 74
Klüver, H 170
Knodt, M. 1–19, 71
Koch, B.: and Quittkat, C. 75
Kohler-Koch, B.: and Buth, V. 152
Kollman, K. 76
Kotzian, P.: and Quittkat, C. 53–70

Lahusen, C. 133, 134
Lamy, P. 44
Leech, B.L.: and Baumgartner, F.R. 131
Levi-Faur, D. 77
Lisbon Treaty 2, 83, 90
lobbying 62, 81, 123, 126, 134, 135, 152; instruments 55–8; trade union 164

Maastricht Treaty 82, 83
McAdam, D.: and Marks, G. 109
Madelin, R. 45, 48
Mahoney, C. 153
March, J. 126
Marks, C.: and Hooghe, L. 73
Marks, G.: and McAdam, D. 109
Meier, K.: and Waterman, R. 100, 101
MEPs 50, 118
multi-level governance 5–7, 23, 29–32
multinational companies 81

Nanz, P.: and Steffek, J. 75
national activities 171
national business culture 139–57
network building 165–7
Network of East-West Women 166
New Left 28; democracy 28
new member states 159–71; Central East European 160; interest groups 171
No Global movement 109, 114
non-governmental organisations (NGOs) 41, 64, 72, 125, 159
North West (of England) Brussels Office 99

Olsson, A. 98
online consultations 56
Open Method of Coordination 42, 118

Pagoulatos, G.: and Blavoukos, S. 171
participatory democracy 90
Piattoni, S. 3, 21–36, 84
Pitkin, H. 12, 96, 100, 115
Pleines, H. 159–71
Poland 93, 161
policy fields 117–18
policy-makers 142
policy-making 135; participation 143–4; process 135, 149
Polish Women's Lobby 165
political action 142–3
political actors *see* actors
political tactics 144–5
politics: international 6
power hierarchy 144, 151
Princen, S.: and Kerremans, B. 11, 74
private interest group 136
private interests 105, 134
public authority interest 135
Public Health Programme 45
public interest groups 105–20

Quittkat, C. 1–19; and Koch, B. 75; and Kotzian, P. 53–70

Racial Equality Directive 114
racism *see* anti-racism
regional agenda 93
Register of Interest Representatives 128
representation: indirect 160; permanent 95; territorial 21–36
representational missions 95
representative democracy 90
Richardson, J.: and Coen, D. 6
Rokkan, S. 25
Rome: Treaty of (1957) 82
Roose, J. 170
Rose, R. 77
Rut, O. 165
Ruzza, C. 10, 105–20, 116

Sabel, C.: and Cohen, J. 74; and Zeitlin, J. 27
Santer Commission 40
Saurugger, S. 12, 97
Saward, M. 119
Scharpf, F. 29
Schmitter, P. 75; holder concept 75
seconded national experts (SNE) 78
service bureaus 124
Single European Act 2
Slovakia 161

INDEX

small and medium sized enterprises (SMEs) 94
Smismans, S. 26
social actors 140
Social Inclusion Regional Group (SIRG) 99
social movements 105–20, 119; financial arrangements 112–13
Social Platform 163
sovereign governance 75
Spanish Communidad Autonomas 95
Staatenverbund 6
Steffek, J.: and Nanz, P. 75
strategic planning 142
Sustainability Impact Assessments (SIA) 44
Suta, M. 165

Tatham, M. 94
territorial actors 81
territorial interest 72; intermediation 73–8
territorial representation 21–36
Time orientation 146
trade union 134; lobbying 164

transnationalisation 6
Treaty on European Union clauses on subsidiarity 93–4
Treaty of Rome (1957) 82

US Congress 30

veto power 25, 32
voluntarism 48

Warren, M.: and Castiglione, D. 116
Waterman, R.: and Meier, K. 100, 101
Watts, R. 93
West Europe 170; business associations 170
White Paper on European Governance (2001) 2, 22, 40, 76
World Trade Organisation (WTO) 39

Zeitlin, J.: and Sabel, C. 27